The English
Noble Household
1250–1600

FAMILY, SEXUALITY AND SOCIAL RELATIONS IN PAST TIMES

GENERAL EDITORS:
Peter Laslett, Michael Anderson and Keith Wrightson

Western Sexuality: Practice and Precept in Past and Present Times
Edited by Philippe Ariès and André Béjin
Translated by Anthony Forster

The Explanation of Ideology: Family Structures and Social Systems
Emmanuel Todd
Translated by David Garrioch

The English Noble Household, 1250–1600
Kate Mertes

An Ordered Society: Gender and Class in Early Modern England
Susan Dwyer Amussen

Porneia: On Desire and the Body in Antiquity
Aline Rousselle
Translated by Felicia Pheasant

Medieval Prostitution
Jacques Rossiaud
Translated by Lydia G. Cochrane

FORTHCOMING
Wet Nursing: A History
Valerie Fildes

Illegitimacy and Society in Eighteenth-Century Scotland
Rosalind Mitchison and Leah Leneman

Highley 1550–1880: The Story of a Community
Gwyneth Nair

Mobility and Marriage: The Family and Kinship in Early Modern London
Vivien Brodsky

The Country House Society
Jessica Gerard

The Family and the English Revolution
Christopher Durston

The English
Noble Household
1250–1600

Good Governance and Politic Rule

Kate Mertes

Basil Blackwell

Copyright © Kate Mertes, 1988

First published 1988

Basil Blackwell Ltd
108 Cowley Road, Oxford, OX4 1JF, UK

Basil Blackwell Inc.
432 Park Avenue South, Suite 1503
New York, NY 10016, USA

British Library Cataloguing in Publication Data
Mertes, Kate
The English noble household, 1250–1600 :
good governance and politic rule.
1. England – Nobility – Social aspects
– History
I. Title
305.5'223'0942   HT653.G7

ISBN 0–631–15319–5

Library of Congress Cataloging in Publication Data
Mertes, Kate
The English noble household, 1250–1600 :
good governance and politic rule / by Kate Mertes
p.   cm.
Bibliography: p.
ISBN 0–631–15319–5 : $29.95
1. England – Social life and customs – Medieval period, 1066–1485
2. England – Social life and customs – 16th century.   3. Great
Britain – Nobility – History.   4. Great Britain – History – Medieval period,
1066–1485.   5. Great Britain – History – Tudors, 1485–1603.
6. Households – England – History.   I. Title
DA185.M47   1987
942 – dc19   87–25356

Typeset in 10 on 12 pt Sabon
by Columns of Caversham, Reading, Berks.
Printed in Great Britain

'So far as I can make out, it is nothing more exciting than an Abbey's accounts dating from the second half of the fifteenth century.'

'The Golden Pince-Nez', from *The Return of Sherlock Holmes*

Contents

Acknowledgements

I would like to thank Tony Goodman, my PhD supervisor and friend, for all his help, support and critical acumen; the country record office librarians who made available to me their knowledge of the collections in their charge; all the friends and colleagues, too many to name here, who have patiently listened, read, criticized and discussed; the ladies at Tonedo, why typed the book; my editor, Virginia Murphy; and most important of all, my parents, who educated me.

Abbreviations

BL	British Library
HMC	Historical Manuscripts Commission
L & P HVIII	*Letters and Papers, Foreign and Domestic, of Henry VIII's Reign* (HMSO, London, 1864–1920, 4 vols)
NHB	Thomas Percy, ed., *The Regulations and Establishments of the Household of Henry Algernon Percy, Fifth Earl of Northumberland,* privately printed, 1770, 1827 and 1905; also in Francis Grosse and Thomas Anstle, eds, *The Antiquarian Repetory* (Edward Jefferey, London, 1809, 4 vols), vol. IV, pp. 1–344. The original is at Alnwick Castle.
PRO	Public Record Office
RO	Record Office
Rot. Parl.	*Rotuli Parliamentorum* (HMSO, London, 1767–77, 6 vols)
Soc. Ant.	Society of Antiquaries
SR	*Statutes of the Realm* (HMSO, London, 1810–8, 12 vols)
WAM	Westminster Abbey Muniments

The footnotes are referential rather than substantive. They note information derived from specific secondary sources, in general, though some manuscript references are contained. Information and examples derived from household accounts are referred to in the text by the surname of the master, and the exact manuscript reference and published version if any, as well as related texts, can be located under this surname in appendix A. General references as to the topics discussed in each chapter can be found in the select bibliography.

Introduction
Methods, Materials and
Early History

Page: No, my good lord; it is more pleasing stuff.
Sly: What, household stuff?
Page: It is a kind of history.

The Taming of the Shrew (Induction)

The halcyon days of the great households of England are often located in the Edwardian age, amongst starched aprons, liveried footmen and ranks of gardeners. The political country weekends, the shooting parties over which affairs, of state and otherwise, were arranged before the Great War – these, we think, were made possible by the highest development of the art of householding, of creating a community largely self-sufficient in skills and social life, yet revolving around the needs and wishes of a central individual or family group, a little world through which the world at large might be contained and controlled. Yet the Edwardian household is a sere and yellow leaf compared to the high summer of householding in the later middle ages. No nineteeth- or twentieth-century landowner's establishment can be compared with Edward Stafford, third Duke of Buckingham (d. 1521), and his household of over 500 servants, who were not merely a domestic staff but his political power base, his centre of patronage, his home and also in many ways his social community. For his servants too, and for those who lived under his patronage, the household was not just a place of work or trade, but a field for political, social and economic advancement and also for strong personal identification. Between 1250 and 1600 the household, perhaps almost as much as the family, was for nobles and their dependents an important institution for the filtering and controlling of daily living, taking on many of the roles of extended kin groups, stem families and clan relationships common to European and Scottish life at this time but unusual in England. However, despite the existence of a truly magnificent body of documentary evidence, very little work has been done on the structure and function of English noble householding in the later middle ages.

Many historians, such as R.A. Griffiths, Alan Macfarlane and E.A. Wrigley, have stated the need of administrative, economic and social historians for a full study of royal, ecclesiastical and secular noble households of the middle ages. While T.F. Tout, Christopher Given-Wilson and A.R. Myers, among others, have delved into the organization of the royal household, very little detailed work has been done on the households of nobles. Yet these private, bureaucratic and domestic structures were crucial to the functioning of English noble society, regulating personal lives and participating in the exercise of authority on a local and national level. The admirable data available for the study of the noble household is gutted for other purposes. The domestic establishment is cited as a base for private armies or a network of retainers in peace and war; its function as a status symbol is suggested. However, no scholarly work on the noble household in itself has yet been written; as a result, historians using noble establishments, or their data, have failed to employ fully the material available, or have entertained misconceptioins about the role of the household in noble life. For instance, K. Wood-Legh, in *Perpetual Chantries in Britain*, fails to discuss the use of the household chapel as a chantry, despite the existence of considerable evidence attesting to such a role. G.A. Holmes, in *The Estates of the Higher Nobility in Fourteenth-Century England*, discusses the decline in direct demesne farming, despite evidence of considerable demesne harvests in household documents of the fourteenth and fifteenth centuries. This work is a study of these neglected English institutions: their organization and manner of functioning, their role in the lives of the nobles who established them, and their wider significance in medieval society generally.

Of course, the noble household is not a completely neglected historical topic. In fact, around the turn of this century, in the course of an awakening interest in social history, the subject was a popular one, and numerous household account-rolls were published. Certain aspects of household life, such as education and consumption, were treated by such historians as F.J. Furnivall and John Cordy Jeaffreson; Paul V.B. Jones and C.A. Musgrave addressed themselves more directly and generally to the problem of household structure and function. Indeed, popular histories involving the household continue to be written. However, such works as have been published are not entirely satisfactory. Many have emphasized the more immediately attractive aspects of household study, such as food or hunting, to the detriment of such things as practical purveyance and accounting methods. The documentary evidence is not always best used; ordinances such as the *Northumberland Household Book* and other late Elizabethan descrip-

Plate 1 The riding household of the three Magi, from MS Douce 93, f. 30.
Utrecht, 1460. Courtesy of the Bodleian Library, Oxford.

tions of the household such as that of Braithwait, useful as they are,
have been given precedence generally over actual household documents.
In particular, a heavy reliance on descriptions and documents of the
royal household, under the assumption that noble households invariably sprang from and imitated the king's establishment, biases and
often invalidates much work.

Many of those writing on the medieval noble household have taken a
strictly descriptive and rather compartmentalized approach. Paul V.B.
Jones, for instance, in chapter 1 of *The Household of a Tudor
Nobleman*, attempts to describe household structure; but he does this
merely by reeling off the available servants' titles he has discovered, and
places them in 'departments' after the manner of a royal household
ordinance, without attempting to analyse the relationships between the
various roles, or the actual working method of the 'departments' he
constructs. Finally, most works on the household have not taken
account of the vast body of secondary literature now available for the
study of the family in medieval and early modern times. While the noble
household is not always or primarily based upon a family, in its
community aspects it bears many resemblances to family and clan
relationships as they have been studied in Britain and Europe. In
particular, some of the findings of Alan Macfarlane concerning the
English 'peasantry' before 1600 will be echoed in a survey of the

English noble household. This work will therefore give precedence to the evidence found in actual household documents (although other materials will be considered, particularly as they reflect what contemporaries thought about the position and purpose of the noble household), in order to analyse thoroughly the structure and organization of the households they represent, and to allow the presentation of as clear and accurate a picture as possible of the mechanics of household life, the relationships between its members and its interaction with the wider society. From this solid basis of understanding, the noble household may then be placed in context. As recent historians of the family have related kinship and inheritance systems to forms of food production, ecclesiastical influence and market economy, so this work intends to show how the noble household acted as a framework for the lives of its members and those in proximity to it. To arrive at this point, one has to dismantle the household as if it were a watch long unwound, examining each wheel and cog in turn before reassembling it, and seeing how it works and what it is for.

First, however, the terms 'noble' and 'household' as they are used here must be explained. The definition of 'noble' has, indeed occupied western society for well over 400 years, and this book makes no attempt to settle the question, merely desiring to define the use of the term within this work from the thirteenth to the sixteenth centuries. Joel Rosenthal, in *The Purchase of Paradise* and *Nobles and the Noble Life*, and many other historians, have defined it as the parliamentary peerage; but this is far too narrow a range for our purposes, establishing a rather arbitrary line between knights, gentlemen and peers. These moved in much the same county and national society, with similar ambitions, interests, and occupations. Though hierarchical, economic and social differences undoubtedly distinguished them, the twelfth Earl of Oxford had more in common with Sir Hugh Luttrell of Somerset than the latter had with the urban patriciate, though these were Luttrell's fellow MPs. The owners of Dunster and of Hedingham both obtained power from their landholdings; they sat on similar commissions; both were JPs; they were predominantly rural dwellers; and, especially important for our purposes, their households were constructed along similar lines. The distinction between 'gentles' and 'nobility' is at best a fuzzy one, and controversial; here it is seldom made, and 'noble' and 'aristocratic' are used as general terms to cover the rich landholding classes, those whose wealth came from the land but who did not need to till it themselves. While a study of essentially urban households would also be extremely valuable, a very little analysis of the material available for their study would indicate to the reader their major divergences from primarily country-based households, and the need to treat them separately (although the London bases of the households to be considered will be important to this study).[1] Reigning monarchs and their immediate heirs have also been omitted. As Joel Rosenthal posits, 'close proximity to the throne was . . . apt to affect one's social behaviour.[2] Households of royalty, while deserving their own study, are in many ways intrinsically different in scale and style from other noble households, requiring a separate method of approach; their involvement in Exchequer administration alone is enough to create serious difficulties. In addition, the heavy dependence of earlier works on the royal household and the resultant misconceptions prompts me to treat noble households in isolation.

Ecclesiastical noble households create their own difficulties for the historian. Those of monastic establishments, of abbots and priors, existed for somewhat different purposes and served a quite separate sort of community from the noble layman's household, while the households of secular bishops lacked the patrilineal continuity which is such an important feature of the lay establishment. However, the all too secular aims and interests of many church figures, and the participation of ecclesiastical households in the economy and social and political life of medieval England, means that though structure and function many vary, they have much in common with secular households and should be included in any general study of such noble establishments; therefore this work will deal with both ecclesiastical and secular noble households.

The term 'household' is perhaps more difficult to define. Its very commonness, and the resulting broadness with which is it applied, in both modern and pre-modern times, create a considerable ambiguity. But if we are to study the noble household, we need to establish a working definition to provide a silhouette of the household, as a concept within which we may study the phenomenon. The medieval noble household can be superficially identified as a collection of servants, friends and other retainers, around a noble and possibly his immediate family, all of whom lived together unde the same roof(s) as a single community, for the purpose of creating the mode of life desired by the noble master and providing suitably for needs. I have used advisedly the male terms for heads of households and for servants

[1]See, for instance, Alison Hanham, ed., *The Cely Letters* (Early English Texts Society, Oxford, vol. 273, 1975); and John Angers and Jean Vanes, eds, *The Ledger of John Smythe* (HMSO, London, 1974).

[2]Joel T. Rosenthal, *The Purchase of Paradise* (Routledge and Kegan Paul, London, 1972), p. 7.

throughout. For reasons discussed later in this text the household was very much a male institution and it would be misleading to indicate otherwise.

The adaptability of the noble household to its master's circumstances, and its domestic, familial nature, means that an individual household changed in some ways from year to year, generation to generation; for instance, the household of an elderly noble was bound to differ from that of his aspiring young self, and from that of his heir, mature man or child. Similarly, between one noble family and another, and between different ecclesiastical foundations, considerable differences in household structure and role could occur. To define the household in its medieval, noble context further, one must examine examples of this sort of household, to distil its chief characteristics.

A study of the English medieval noble household must necessarily be drawn from three broad categories of source. First of all, what we may call the 'implicit evidence': what letters survive, chronicles, the various calendered government rolls, charters, etc. These documents are not specifically about the household, nor do they spring from it; but in many cases they mention noble households or relate events taking place within one, or make assumptions about household duties and powers. Such evidence tends to be rather thin on the ground, leaves large gaps in our knowledge, is often ambiguous; but it does tend to reveal medieval intellectual concepts of the noble households. Such 'implicit evidence' is often the catalyst encouraging the historian to look further at the subject.

Probably the commonest, fullest and most easily available evidence on the noble household is that contained in what we call ordinances, royal and noble. Technically, such documents were supposed to have some legal status; but historians tend to use the term much more broadly in relation to households, to describe the type of document by its context, rather than by its legal status. 'Ordinances' for noble households, of course, never had the same force of law as a royal ordinance, though lords did attempt to prosecute servants in the courts for breaking rules contained in such documents, either by connecting such rules with legal offences like debt and trespass, or by attempting to show oath-breaking on the servant's part.[3] On the other hand, the *Liber Niger* of Edward IV is usually called an ordinance, though in fact it is merely a draft for one, and could never have the legal position of an oridance. Thus we use 'household ordinance' to describe a broad set of documents which are conscious and systematic attempts to define the

---

[3] Carol Rawcliffe, *The Staffords, Earls of Stafford and Dukes of Buckingham* (Cambridge Unversity Press, Cambridge, 1979), pp. 164–6.

membership of the household, their duties and privileges, and the general rules of the establishment. Many such documents exist; not only those for the royal household, which are relatively well known, but also those of various nobles. Of the latter, the Household Book of Henry Percy, fifth Earl of Northumberland, is probably the best known.

To be classed with ordinances are what one might call descriptions of households, compiled not as official or semiofficial documents but as informative guides to householding among the nobility, often written by foreign visitors, former servants, instructors of clerks at the universities, or early historians. Ordinances or descriptions are very useful documents, as they are wholly and directly concerned with the household; they are exceptionally detailed, leaving few gaps in our information about the household which cannot be filled by reconstruction. Moreover, ordinances give a very clear view of how a contemporary interpreted the makeup and role of the household and household members. But one must always remember that they are conscious descriptions, not of the household as it was, but as its masters and observers wanted it to be. Ordinances are essentially reforming documents; they give us an ideal, not a real, picture of household structure and life. In particular, they tend to create an impression of a rigidly compartmentalized system of duties and a clear householding hierarchy which probably did not exist. The essentially fluid and adaptable nature of householding is largely lost in such documents. In addition, the temptation to use the particularly full royal ordinances to describe and analyse noble households, on the assumption that the latter grew out of or were heavily influenced by the former, is a dangerous trap.

By far the best and richest evidence on the noble household is that of accounts. To keep track of finances and to check stealing, most households kept a set of books recording all transactions and including tallies, bills, indentures, etc. relevant to these. While the evidence in such documents is sometimes ambiguous and disjointed, and is heavily weighted towards the economic side of household interests, it is contemporary material directly concerning and, indeed, coming out of the household itself. Household accounts, or, as they are sometimes called, rolls, were of numerous sorts: daily, weekly, yearly, departmental, personal and household-wide. In some households they were fuller than in others, with detailed descriptions of each purchase; in others, only lists of prices or lump sums survive. In order to study the English medieval households of nobles, one must needs consider as many accounts as possible, in order to distil from their specific idiosyncracies the general characteristics of the noble household.

Luckily, large numbers of household accounts of various kinds have survived, including those of about ten different families, for many of whom the accounts stretch over several generations. Fewer ecclesiastical accounts survive, but they are generally more stringently kept and fuller than their lay counterparts. With the help of ordinances, descriptions and contemporary references, the material can reveal to us the workings of noble households, as structures and also as part of the medieval mental landscape.

This work is primarily concerned with the form and matter of the noble household in the later middle ages, from approximately 1250 to 1600 (material ranging from c.1230 to 1594 is employed in actuality but about 80 per cent of the information available is concentrated between 1380 and 1545), the size and scope of the topic demanding some kind of time-break. While the dearth of studies on the noble household might immediately suggest a concentration on the earlier period, in fact good reasons exist for examining the later middle ages and early modern period. Most importantly, perhaps, many more documents survive from the later centuries; they are generally more plentiful and more complete in themselves; there are more series of accounts, and more varied kinds of account, for a larger number of identifiable individuals. Good documents vastly improve the ease and accuracy of any secondary historical work; and when one is attempting to establish a system for studying a phenomenon, the best and fullest material best permits the creation of a useful paradigm. From the household historian's point of view, the later medieval household presents a more fruitful study.

Moreover, a study of the later medieval household ties up nicely with several excellent works by early modernists involving Elizabethan and Jacobean householding, in particular those by M.E. James. Recent work on the history of the family in the late medieval and early modern periods both enriches and is enriched by any study of the family environment. The plethora of studies concerned with other aspects of the later medieval nobility, by such as Joel T. Rosenthal, G.A. Holmes, N. Denholm-Young, T.B. Pugh and K.B. McFarlane, makes a study of noble households in this same period particularly useful and appropriate. The income crises of the fifteenth-century English nobility, their changes in estate administration, their ways of seeking power at this time, are subjects that can all be added to by a study of their households.

In terms of the development of the household itself, the period 1250–1600 divides naturally into three sections. From 1250 to the last quarter of the fourteenth century households were often relatively small, simply organized and characterized by constant movement. But the households of this period form the basis for the larger, more complex and dynamic community structures which began to appear at the end of the fourteenth century, and it is salutory to observe and analyse the changes in household patterns that took place. Again, after the 1530s the English reformation and the shifts in political power saw many alterations in noble householding, so that by around 1600 many of the distinctive features and functions of the later medieval household had vanished forever. Thus, the period 1250–1600, though it saw many developments, nevertheless shows a cohesion of purpose in household-ing which makes it expedient to consider this period as a whole. However, no study of the later medieval noble household in England should be attempted without at least a survey of the earlier household, to c.1250, in order to place the later establishments within the context of their origins, and to prevent the creation of false 'developments' around later householding practice which in actuality are trends common to early households.

Our knowledge of the earliest baronial households in England is extremely limited because of the paucity of sources. We know that nobles had entourages from the inception of their own existence, but so accepted and widespread was the idea of the noble household that few contemporaries troubled to examine and explain its makeup. In addition, no distinction can be made, so far, between the noble and royal household forms. Historians dealing with the households have often assumed that those of the aristocracy were developed from the imitation of the king's own domestic establishment. Whether this was indeed the case, however, is by no means sure. Certainly we have more evidence of royal household-structure before the eleventh century; but what we do have that tells us of noble establishments does not contradict the information on royal households, until the eighth and ninth centuries, when the earliest concrete evidence of noble households apear.[4] After all, kings merely began as the more powerful and less scrupulous members of an aristocracy, as far as we can tell; royal grew out of noble, not vice versa. The households of royalty and nobles were bound to have common origins, and a common structure and method as long as their masters' needs and interests were similar. With the development of strong regional monarchies around the seventh century, however, royal needs concerning the household must have changed, deviating from the essential requirements of the noble classes.

[4]Laurence Marcellus Lawson, *The King's Houshold in England Before The Norman Conquest* (University of Wisconsin Press, Madison, Wisconsin, 1904), pp. 120–3.

Perhaps the first available description of a northern European noble or royal household occurs in Tacitus' *Germania*.[5] Tribal chiefs or kings and their most powerful peers are pictured within their *comitatus*, a band of warriors and some domestics bound to serve and protect their master in war and peace, tied to him by love, obligation, reverence, and reward. The terminology used by Tacitus suggests mutual friendship and respect, a charismatic leadership, in preference to servitude; the *comitatus* derived its strength from the bonds of companionship. Within the early Germanic kingdoms, in particular those of the Saxons and Franks, where the old nomadic, primarily hunter-gatherer lifestyle described by Tacitus was replaced by a settled and more stable existence, domestic service seems to have gradually taken over the primary role in households; this is typified in the changing terminology of the ninth-century Anglo-Saxon royal and noble households, where *gesith* or war-companion is eventually replaced as a name for a householder by *thegn*, meaning child or servant. In the ninth and tenth centuries in England, additional titles, describing household-servant duties in the king's own establishment, first begin to appear: *beor-scealc* (butler), *hragel-weard* (wardrober), *bur-thegn* (chamberlain), and *bur-cniht* (chamber-menial). The Danes left to England a further legacy of household-servant titles, used by the royal household: *disc thegn* (steward), *staller* (a kind of household constable), *marscall* (stablehand), and *hus-carle* (bodyguard). From a band of what were primarily warriors, the royal household at least had become a group of domestic servants bound to serve their lord at table and in chamber, and to maintain and guard his person and goods.

These early establishments seem to have been relatively small; the ninth-century wills of Kings Eadred and Alfred indicate a household of around twenty persons.[6] By the eleventh century, we can begin to see more clearly the real differences between noble and royal households which must have emerged earlier, and which continued to grow under the rule of the Normans. By the time *Constitutio Domus Regis*, the earliest surviving royal household ordinance, was composed, around 1231, the royal household – in its record-keeping facilities, staff-size, organizational complexity and varied duties – had long since developed into something qualitatively as well as quantitatively different from its origins, and from contemporary noble households.

I have uncovered evidence on only five households in existence before

---

[5]Publius Cornelius Tacitus, *On Britain and Germany*, trans. H. Mattingley (Penguin, Harmondsworth, 1948), pp. 111–13.

[6]Lawson, *The King's Household*, p. 125.

c.1250, none of it really satisfactory; whether due to a real lack of account systems for households at this date, the accidents of document survival, or contemporary destruction, we cannot really be sure, though the last explanation is probably the most sound. Accounting records of any kind are generally only in active use for a short period of time. Once that time – say a year – passes, and the account is checked, finalized and closed, it becomes purely a matter of record, with small practical use. A large establishment like the king's household, with detailed records, might create an archive; but few nobles had the need or inclination to do so. Thus the few surviving partial household accounts from this earlier period have largely been preserved by accident: by being used to strengthen a bookbinding, or because a charter was written on the clean back of one membrane. Of the surviving records, one is anonymous, the fragment of a day-roll, *tempus* Henry II or Richard I. A partial account of Robert of Reading, Abbot of Ramsey (Huntingdsonshire) from 1202 to 1206, is also in existence. Day-rolls of Hugh de Neville, *tempus* John or Henry III, and John de Pusey for 1171, survive, as well as day-rolls for the sixth Earl and Countess of Surrey, William and Isabel de Warrenne, for 1230, and for the seventh earl as well, though *tempus* Edward I. All are but partially preserved parchment rolls, listing, by the day, the household's expenses, usually under various headings (in the de Warrenne accounts, as many as eight; in the others, three – *panis/carnibus/cervisia* or *panis et cervisia/coquina/marshalcia* – but in several, none). The left-hand margin is typically devoted to dates and visitors' names, the right to cash totals. No mention of any other subsidiary or private accounts are made; evidence of careful auditing may indicate that no yearly summaries were made, and that daily rolls may have been the sole method of account. Certainly nothing but daily rolls have survived.

These early accounts also tell us something about household membership and the roles of individuals. Household size, when it may be determined, varies from about thirty-five under the Earls of Surrey, to perhaps no more than eight under John de Pusey. Most of these household members have no titles and can be found performing a wide variety of services. Those specialized services which are mentioned in the accounts are those of cooks, laundresses, stablehands – work which by its nature requires skills and attention. Some of the accounts were kept by a 'clerk of the household', but the term *seneschallus* or steward does not occur in any of these early documents.

These households are all typified by one phenomenon: movement. Travel occurred as often as every two weeks, though on average about once a month, at all times of the year, around a lord's territories or in the wake of the king, stopping at abbeys, manor houses, and inns. These mobile households probably had to be relatively small, unspecialized, and their finances simply accounted, in order to cope with the confusion, transport problems and inconvenience of almost constant travel, each member ready, as Peter of Blois sourly noted of Henry II's household, to do anything or go anywhere at a moment's notice.[7] Rigid administrative structures or elaborate book-keeping systems would have been quickly shattered, and unnecessary servants and hangers-on found to be a hindrance. Even monastic establishments saw a surprising amount of movement; while the entire household did not move, individual monks often travelled between their own house and mother and sister monasteries, and provision for such journeys is a main feature of the later (from 1303) accounts of Finchale Priory (County Durham). Robert of Reading, Abbot of Reading in the early years of the thirteenth century, has recorded in his account the frequent perambulations of himself and his entourage.

In support of this nomadic form of existence, noble households acted as a combination of storm troop, bodyguard, moving van, and, one is inclined to surmise, instant community. Household members, from a strictly practical point of view, were required to ride ahead of the main body to ensure that a place to stay and an adequate food supply were awaiting their noble employers. Other servants were required to organize the actual physical movement of goods and persons (early medieval nobles, like modern nomads, did not travel light), and the caravan with its valuables needed guarding. The available evidence is far too fragmentary to reveal much about the social life of the household, but it is nevertheless difficult not to believe that household members relied upon each other for a sense of community. Livery allowances recorded in John de Pusey's day-roll for 1171 certainly suggest a common household celebration of Easter, for instance; and the frequent small sums passed between the anonymous master and his head servant in the day-roll *tempus* Henry II or Richard I hint at a close association. After *c*.1250, the surviving accounts and other records reveal the continuation of some of these early features, but also major changes as the role of the household shifted.

Various sorts of records are known for about twenty-four households existing in the later thirteenth and fourteenth centuries, most of which are of much better quality than the five earlier accounts just mentioned; in a number of cases entire rather than fragmentary rolls have survived,

---

[7]Grace Stretton, 'The Travelling Household in the Later Middle Ages', *Transactions of the British Archaeological Association*, 90 (1935), pp. 94–5.

Plate 2 A travelling household: the carriage transporting the ladies. Courtesy of The British Library.

some of which are remarkably detailed. Most of these show signs of 'new' characteristics in four areas: household accounting method, organization, stability, and size. One must be wary of calling the appearance of new phenomena 'changes' or 'developments'; one would be arguing from silence. Our knowledge of the earlier noble households is too limited for us to say, in most cases, whether the characteristics did or did not exist previously. Nevertheless, it is during the period *c.*1250 to *c.*1370 that these characteristics first come to light, some of which, we may tentatively posit, were newly instituted, and reflect changes in the purpose of the household and in noble life.

It is in accounting systems that the most numerous new characteristics emerge. While most surviving accounts are still general records of daily expense, one finds the first year-roll and counter-roll (of Dame Godsalve, *tempus* Edward III), and the earliest surviving specialized rolls – wardrobe accounts, of Peter, Baron de Mauley (*tempus* Edward III) and Gilbert de Clare, Earl of Hereford and Gloucester (1307–8). Mention of the individual accounts of servants also comes to light in numerous records. The use of a fiscal year-end, a larger number of specifically clerical servants, and a greater use of vernacular language – some accounts are wholly in French, such as the anonymous account of a noble courtier of Edward III's time – also become recognizable trends in these accounts, though they may not necessarily be recent innovations. The most obvious innovation, however, is an almost universal introduction of a weekly reckoning. Days are grouped in weekly paragraphs, or at the least a weekly sum total is introduced after each Saturday entry: something which occurs is no surviving account before 1299. Despite these 'new' appearances, however, the headings used to divide and organize purchases do not change, nor does the tendency to paragraphical rather than linear entries – in other words, despite internal divisions, daily and weekly entries were run together, rather than each division beginning on a new line.

New characteristics in household organization and perphaps in size also appear, beginning with the accounts of Eleanor Montford in 1265. The titles of *seneschallus* or steward, *camerarius* ('chamberlain' or chamberer), and of *marescallus* or marshall, appear now invariably; and one first finds the implementation of servant 'classes': *garcio* or groom, *valettus* or valet, and *generosus* or gentleman. As more christian and surnames come to light, the feature of kinsmen working within the same household as servants becomes apparent. However, few traces of titles tied to specific duties are found, as in earlier centuries. Size remains (and will continue to remain) somewhat of a mystery; but we find that in 1352, Sir Hamon LeStrange of Hunstanton (Norfolk) could support a household of thirty-three persons; and that an obscure Norfolk squire, *Dominus* Roger de Holm of Holm, had approximately eighteen servants. As the household of the Earl of Surrey in 1230 averaged some thirty-five persons as far as we can tell, one might posit that households were tending to increase in size.

Perhaps the most striking development observed, mainly in fourteenth-century household accounts, however, is the steady growth of stability. Between the household of Gilbert de Clare in 1309, which moved on average once every two weeks, and that of Hamon LeStrange from 1341 to 1352, which over these eleven years never shifted, the intervening evidence shows that constant movement was becoming a short-term exception rather than a long-term rule, other than for episcopal households, which remained highly peripatetic. This trend is typified by several developments. Special 'riding households' of only a limited number of servants were designated, and separate 'riding accounts' were maintained for expenses on the road, as the condition of movement became a special provision.[8] The main account's endorsement came to contain not only the master's and the compiler's name, but a single place of compilation. As well, in the endorsements, *domus* comes to be used as a synonym of *hospicium*, indicating that the household could be thought of as a place, as well as a group of people.

While we can never be sure how much these 'developments' are actually first appearances, in the records, of well-established methods of procedure, it does seem that households during the later thirteenth and fourteenth centuries began to increase in size and in complexity of organization (with increases in size of average household jumping sharply in the early fifteenth century). These changes were made possible by the growing stability of the noble establishment, perhaps the same organizational urge which produced thirteenth- and fourteenth-century estate management systems, and probably demanded by increasing standards of noble living and competitive consumption. These characteristics carried on through noble householding practice until the end of the sixteenth century, when again major changes in noble life affected the structure and purpose of households. It is this period, the high summer of the household, which demands investigation into how the household worked and what it was for.

It is also for this period that massive amounts of documentation survive: literally hundreds of accounts plus all manner of ordinances and other materials, some of them forming 'runs' of accounts for a single

---

[8]See especially Norfolk and Norwich RO NH2, Hamon LeStrange, 1341, and PRO DL 29 1/4 m.3, Thomas Earl of Lancaster, 1319–20.

establishment for two or more generations, for nobles grand and obscure, secular and ecclesiastical, covering most of the country. (The area north of the Humber is less well represented than the south, in the surviving documentary evidence, but the households that are represented from this area have left some particularly complete series of records.) Anyone who could call himself a gentleman had a household of some size, so several thousand establishments must have spawned records in their time.

Probably the majority of historical, and also anthropological, examinations of domestic communities tend to be case studies of an individual family, village or tribe. The extreme variety of the domestic situation in numerous important areas makes such single studies particularly valuable, as they analyse in detail the many facets of a community, rather than attempting to discuss generally a group of units, each of which are strongly diversified. However, the drawing of wider conclusions from individual case studies is a difficult if not quite impossible task, opening up to the scholar the temptation of arguing the general from a single idiosyncratic specific. Ideally, it would seem, such communities as primitive tribal groups, French moutain villages, gentle families, and English noble households, would be best presented in individual case studies of all available examples, which are then analysed as a group. However, such a scheme is, for obvious reasons, virtually impossible in this case; there is just too much information. In addition, the wide variety and number of household structures and methods among the English medieval nobility urges a general survey in order to provide a framework for the general understanding of the noble household in medieval society by historians. While changes over time do occur in the household, there is enough uniformity in the period under consideration to proceed by first examining the structure of households and how they were run, in order to have a firm basis from which to consider the purposes of the household: why and how it was able to function as a primary community both for the nobles it served and the servants and dependants who served in it; and why, in the early modern period, its nature necessarily changed.

1
Household Organization

But what need I thus
My well-known body to anatomize
Among my household?

2 Henry IV (Induction)

Many modern corporations publish, in advertisements and descriptive brochures, diagrams which purport to show the structure and the chain of authority within which the company in question functions. These illustrations are indicative of the way in which twentieth-century humans conceive order and structure. But however hard one tries, one cannot draw the same type of diagram for medieval noble households, either in general or in particular. Firstly, we simply do not have enough information about them to construct anything like a complete picture of household organization: significant gaps are bound to appear. For instance, we do not have a complete list of the servants for any one household in any single year. In addition the changes, the amoeba-like splits and the rejoinings, which occurred within a single noble household from year to year, from season to season, would require a large number of coordinated diagrams before a competent picture could be constructed. One would need to consider the part played by people who are perhaps only connected with, but not part of, the household yet occasionally perform household functions, such as tenants, estate servants, and kinsfolk of the master, and how such people would be represented.

Moreover, there seems to have been no clear 'chain of command' within the medieval noble household. The steward was a *major domus* of some kind with household-wide powers; but we do not know the extent of the authority he had over a kitchen clerk, and how much control over the latter the chaplain, as chief cleric, had. Nor do we know whether the kitchen clerk had any control over the chief larderer or pantler or whether they were independent of him. Inability to reconstruct a diagrammatical hierarchy is perhaps ultimately due to the haphazard circumstances which brought the household into existence. It was not, after all, constructed in the conscious manner of a modern company, but grew up over several centuries. Its structure included an infinity of interrelated responsibilities, duties, powers and privileges. All these problems complicate the study of specific households at specific times. Wide variations between different families, generations and time periods further complicate any general discussion of household organization, and make it impossible to present such structures pictorially. These problems however qualify rather than negate the study of noble household organization. The wide ranging and sometimes bewildering variations between households are in themselves significant and explicable; and certain common denominators exist around which the variations can be grouped and discussed.

Size is one factor affecting the structure of the household. Not surprisingly, small households tended towards simple organization. The rather small households of abbots and priors, which depended heavily upon the monastic structure for many jobs requiring hired servants in secular households, only numbered from ten to twenty, and it was easy to keep track of who did what. Small secular households, like that of the Watertons of Mexborough, 1419–20, with about twenty to twenty-five servants, were small enough also to keep track of, and in addition did not serve a lord with complicated political attachments, public duties, or great wealth. Households numbering between thirty and seventy, however, possibly the majority of establishments that have left records, required through sheer size a greater structural integrity. They were also likely to be at the service of a more important noble with consequently more complicated needs for his household. At the top of the scale, in the households of the great barons and bishops, numbering in some cases 500 servants strong, order was called for – though once again, if these lords were minors or very elderly, their once great households might be reduced considerably and, like abbatial households, rely for many things upon a guardian's household. All households, however, of whatever size, required organization and a hierarchy of responsibility.

Organization, structure, hierarchy: what do these terms mean? For our purposes one can best describe the first two terms as applying to the method of dividing labour and specializing functions for the sake of greater efficiency and convenience; and 'hierarchy' as the relative distribution of authority among and between the members of the organized household to coordinate its actions.

This division of labour is achieved in quite different degrees by the households used in this study. The larger and later households show evidence of a high degree of organization, with many specialized departments and servants; many, on the other hand, are relatively small and show little sign of any organization, not just because of a lack of information, but through positive evidence of little formal structure or division of labour. The evidence for the above statements and for later elaborations upon them lies in the titles of various servants, information as to the duties they actually performed, and the use of various departments or 'offices' in accounts and their discernible actions as corporate wholes. Two basic kinds of labour division may be distinguished. Individuals may be given, in whole or in part, a specific set of duties and concerns. This I shall call specialization; it is largely a matter of individual action. Secondly, a more abstract body, called a department or more commonly an office, consisting of various peoples who worked with a common set of duties and responsibilities, seems sometimes to have been formed, and this group acted as a single entity. This cooperative form of labour division can be called department-alization.

Several sorts of evidence for departmentalization exist. That which is most immediately obvious is the use of a department or office as an agent, rather than an individual, in purchases or the receipts of purchases recorded. However, an oversimplified application of this criterion can lead to error, as medieval clerics often fictionalized the functions of existing departments and created entirely nonexistent offices on paper, to facilitate accounting procedure. For instance, in household accounts, 'pantry' is an important accounting division in daily books, under which bread, pastry, and grain expenditures are listed. But 'pantry' also designates a room off the hall or a dresser in the eating chamber where not only bread but all foodstuffs were kept in readiness to be served. Debt lists show us that grain was purchased by caterers – servants whose titles and duties attach them to the kitchens, not the pantry. Pantry servants, on the other hand, were essentially waiters. Stock accounts, moreover, show that grain was baked into bread in the bakehouse, not the pantry, and that some of that grain, when sent to the kitchen, was so sent by the bakehouse. The pantry might serve bread at table, but its members did not buy it or bake it as the accounts imply. So clearly, the way the accountant uses 'pantry' may be an artificial construction; its role as a department in the accounts does not correspond to its role in the actual life of the household.

Individuals were less susceptible to this kind of manipulation; but one must not take the occupational titles given to servants, such as valet of the larder, at face value, without discovering if they have a practical basis in fact. Therefore, numerous other criteria must be used to determine whether departmentalization and specialization actually exist in any given case. One must be able to show that an office or individual has not only a title but special duties and responsibilities which support that title and which are unique to the department or official in question. We cannot, of course, expect anything like an absolute division of responsibilities. The household was not a modern company, but a very fluid organism which continually adapted itself as needed. The most helpful guides in determining labour division within a household are contemporary chequerrolls, or lists of household members which give their position and wage. Chequerrolls provide a title for most servants, which can be compared fruitfully with other data about the house-holder member in question to provide us with the practical meaning of his title, and they may divide servants into groups, which, as a contemporary method of practical division, can be used as a guide to determining departmental organization.

Duties performed by individual servants are a useful guide to practical specialization. If a bakehouse officer was involved in buying wheat, a correlation between title and actual role is obvious; if he bought wheat and also made candles from tallow, one might conclude that he worked in the bakehouse generally but was not restricted to it; he could occasionally work in related fields. If he bought only cattle, one might question his title and wonder if it is another form of accounting fiction. Determining departmentalization is more difficult. One might, for instance, conclude that five servants called 'grooms of the kitchen' constitute a department, especially if they can all be shown performing kitchen duties; but one must remember that a kitchen can be not only an abstract concept, but also a physical place. Five servants with related duties might work in the same room, but may not necessarily have any corporate identity. One must look for evidence of the department itself, not separate people who look like part of an office, performing functions. For example, in the household of Humphrey, first Duke of Buckingham, in 1454–5, and in that of Richard, fifth Earl of Warwick, for 1414–15, we find exchange of goods by tally and bill in the name of the departments. Wheat was sent to the kitchen by the bakery, and these two corporate bodies were capable of making records of that exchange. Not only did the bakery and kitchen function as departments, but they were capable of producing official documents attesting to actions for which they were responsible as an office. As well as tallies, departments could be called upon to produce more extensive corporate records. Many examples of medieval kitchen accounts survive; these are records of the income and expenditure of a single department, compiled by its own clerk. In addition, the existence of a servant who seems by title, duties and wage to be a kind of subhead – a hall marshal or a head cook – may also indicate some kind of corporate staff under him.

The degree of specialization and departmentalization can be a significant gauge of a household's size, status and date, and is the fundamental determinant of its organization. Of course, some form of particularism in households must exist in all circumstances, at all times. Such jobs and offices as baker and bakery, ostler and stable, require skills that not everyone can perform and share. Nor must one suppose that in the absence of specalization servants took over necessary duties on some kind of rota system. But we do not have to look back very far in time to find examples of the 'general servant'; and they are easy enough to locate in the middle ages. The gardener of Sir William Stonor of Stonor (Oxfordshire) made candles in 1478; Reginald Seynesbury, a servant under Hugh Luttrell of Dunster (Somerset) from 1405 to 1423, styled himself a purveyor and indeed bought foodstuffs, but also made candles, sold unused hides and fetched grain from demesne lands. He is far different sort of servant from John Dallyng, servant of John de Vere, twelfth Earl of Oxford, from 1441–3, titled clerk of the household. Dallyng's sole domestic duty was serving as an assistant to the steward. One must also, of course, keep in mind that households and servants had to be versatile, and ready and able to respond to the lord's needs. Seynesbury could be said to have a general area of concentration; and Dallyng was in 1443 assigned temporarily to assist in the annual audit of de Vere lands. But one is clearly a general servant, while the other has, essentially, a specialized role to play. When discussing the organization of the medieval household, the existence of specialization and departmentalization does not need to be studied so much as does the extent of these phenomena, and their development.

To this end, each broad division of duties can be approached separately. These divisions are a way of dealing with different kinds of duties as they were variously fulfilled by medieval servants. Using the simile of a diagram, these divisions work horizontally, as it were, and also vertically. That is, household members were organized both by the kind or nature of their work (horizontal) and by relative status (vertical). Since the latter 'vertical' hierarchy pervades all 'horizontal' labour division, the nature and extent of the vertical should be discussed first. At the topmost level, the lord (and his family) were served by a number of chief servants, with power over, and responsibilties for and throughout, the whole household. But if we conceive of the medieval noble household as a neat pyramid of related duties and responsibilities, a some writers have done, we will be sure to be frustrated in any attempt to describe this pyramid in detail. If we look, for instance, for a 'mayor of the palace' figure standing at the top of that hypothetical pyramid, we might find not one chief servant but as many as seven or more, each of whose duties and authority was different from household to household.

The steward or seneschal (both terms are used, even as late as 1500) is perhaps the officer whom we think of as *major domus*; and indeed the title is a ubiquitous one. The role is usually defined as that of one who helps determine, and sees enforced, household policy; he is in charge of discipline and order in the household, seeing that all runs smoothly — a kind of general manager. Documents show this to be roughly true, but in different ways and degrees. In many households, for instance, the roles of steward and treasurer are combined (in some cases such a combination is given the alternative title of clerk of the household). In this case he received, dispensed and recorded all movements and household monies. In control of both wide ranging authority and the wherewithal to wield it, he could easily become a surrogate master; especially in such as the households of Sir Hugh Luttrell, Sir Anthony Brown, and Thomas Wolsey, Cardinal Archbishop of York, where the master was frequently *in absentia*. On the other hand, some stewards served only as general overseers and organizers (while keeping accounts for odd general expenditures for the household with the help of a minor allowance), and had to share their power with several other well paid, authoritative figures whose responsibilities, if less all-encompassing than those of the steward, perhaps had more concrete bases from which authority could be exercised.

The treasurer could be one of these officers. As long as the household was small and/or loosely organized, a single authority figure could handle both tasks, of managing the household and also the books, taking the daily reckoning of all expenditures and drawing up the yearly general accounts. A very large household, especially if its organizational system demanded departmental accounting, seems to have required a full-time treasurer. His chief charge of which we have evidence was the keeping of the daily book of expenses and the yearly household account. In some households he was called clerk of the chamber, particularly in those close to the throne, but this is unusual. Several royal ordinances, including the *Liber Niger* of Edward IV and the Ordinances of Eltham of Henry VIII, explain a system by which all accountable servants had to report daily (sometimes twice daily) to the treasurer, and something similar may have occurred in noble households. The *Northumberland Household Book*, an ordinance compiled for the fifth Earl of Northumberland, *c.*1512, tries to enforce regular reporting. The treasurer's job, however, entailed not only the accounting but also the handling of monies paid out for bills and to servants, either in prest (cash given to servants in anticipation of household expenses, for which they had to account) or in payment for expenses already incurred. Thus the treasurer had control of a stock or several stocks of money. The extent of his responsibility was largely determined by the size of this stock. Some masters, particularly abbots, channelled almost all their resources into the household, and he who acted as treasurer was accordingly in charge of all, not just household, expenses of his master. Most nobles, on the other hand, kept most of their resources in the hands of estate receivers, and many treasurers suffered from a constant lack of ready cash.

The treasurer might not be the only householder with banking responsibilities. Kitchen clerks sometimes had a small independent cash source, as did wardrobe officials, who might control considerable funds. There might also be a comptroller. The name (in Latin, *contrarotulator*) means one who counter-rolls, that is, produces an independent daily and yearly account, which acts as a check on the main account of the treasurer in case of its loss or falsification. In theory it sounds a sensible precaution; in practice we find that, in the few cases where both roll and counter-roll have survived, one is a mere copy of the other, even reproducing mathematical errors. Both Tout and Myers have posited that the office of treasurer of the royal household had become a sinecure by the late fifteenth century, and the comptroller essentially became a deputy treasurer (hence the term's use in modern business for an official with general executive management responsibilities, but particularly as regards the formation of monetary policy and expenditure).[1] One is led to suspect something similar may have occasionally happened in some noble households. At the very least, the comptroller could serve to alleviate some of the pressure on the treasurer by assisting him in his duties.

The offices of chancellor and chamberlain appear in very few noble households; only the Staffords, Dukes of Buckingham, as well as Elizabeth de Burgh, Lady of Clare, and some few bishops use these titles for important household officials. (A bishop's chancellor for the diocese was, even by 1250, seldom a member of the household. Richard de Swinfield, Bishop of Hereford, paid some of the clothing expenses of his

---

[1]T.F. Tout, *Chapters in Medieval Administrative History* (Manchester University Press, Manchester, 1930), vol. IV, pp. 223–7; and A.R. Myers, ed., *The Household of Edward IV* (Manchester University Press, Manchester, 1959), pp. 25–6 and 42–5.

chancellor Gilbert de Swinfield through the household in 1289–90;[2] but Gilbert does not appear to have functioned as a household officer or authority figure, and was involved with Bishop Richard solely on diocesan business.) Such offices often would appear to be, essentially, extra-household (although all households used 'chamberlain' in its simplest sense – that of a chamber servant of no especial dignity). For the Staffords, the chamberlain is first to be found in 1400, in a receivers' account, when he receives credit for acting as a purveyor and paymaster on a small scale;[3] but the office never occurs in household accounts. The names of those who held the office are all those of fairly important men: they had their own affairs to arrange. The fifth Earl of Northumberland in his household book lists a chamberlain as a member of his council attending on his household, but this man does not appear to have any householding duties. He may have been similar to Sir William Knivet, an important ally of the third Duke of Buckingham, who was chamberlain from c.1514. Though listed in the chequerroll of 1517 as part of the riding household, he cannot possibly have spent much time fulfilling any household duties as such. An important landholder in Essex and Kent, he was heavily involved in local and national politics on his own account. Thomas Arundel, Bishop of Ely, however, employed as chamberlain a clerk named Walter Ash, who received the highest wage in the household and who was often entrusted with delicate and responsible tasks, often serving as a witness and commissary for the bishop;[4] he was also very active about household business and is prominent in Arundel's surviving household accounts. The 'chamberlain' of Elizabeth de Burgh, Lady of Clare, was in fact called clerk of the chamber and took the place of treasurer.[5]

Similarly, the office of chancellor, when it appears, seems to be extra-household, applying to a member of the noble council, who might be involved in estate business, and who is often himself a prominent landholder. Chancorial duties in the household were generally undertaken by the steward, or by a secretary.

All the households used here had private chapels and employed chaplains who, whether licensed or not to say masses therein, ordered

---

[2]John Webb, ed., *Household Roll of Bishop Swinfield* (Camden Society, London, vols 59 and 62, 1855), vol. 59, pp. 129–31.

[3]Carol Rawcliffe, *The Staffords, Earls of Stafford and Dukes of Buckingham* (Cambridge University Press, Cambridge, 1979), p. 195.

[4]Margaret Aston, *Thomas Arundel: A Study of Church Life in the Reign of Richard II* (Oxford University Press, Oxford, 1967), pp. 242–3.

[5]Clare A. Musgrave, 'Household Administration in the Fourteenth Century' (unpublished MA thesis, University of London, 1923), fo 140.

the religious life of the household. We may not think of this as a source of any real definable authority; but in an age where the moral organization of life was an important part of its structural integrity, a chaplain could exercise considerable influence over the running of the household; he might indeed have experience in this as well. Chaplains often served as treasurers and stewards, especially in the households of abbots and priors, combining offices or succeeding from one to the other. Moreover, a chaplain was responsible for and had control over such instruments of worship as chalices, gospel books and vestments, all of considerable value; he might also be in charge of alms collected and dispensed. Whatever his actual authority, the chaplain was accorded the same dignity as the other chief servants, being grouped with them on chequerrolls and receiving pay concomitant with theirs if not beneficed.

All these officers were, in a sense, surrogate lords. In the smallest households, masters and mistresses acted as their own stewards; the Ferrers of Baddesley Clinton, for instance, kept the accounts themselves. If one demands a pinnacle to that pyramid, the master for whom the household exists is properly the choice to make. But in the case of households as big as, say, those of the Dukes of Norfolk, or of lords as politically active as Richard Neville, or as much absent as William Wareham, Archbishop of Canterbury, or as devoted to pleasure as the thirteenth Earl of Oxford, the time and effort of running the household was best relegated to one or a combination of others. The chief servants or, as the Stafford Chequerroll of 1517 puts it, the *capitum officii*, who are described above, all had responsibility for the entire household in one way or another; they had to keep the organization running smoothly and efficiently. The workers of whom these executives were in charge had more immediate and limited duties; if the chief servants constituted the hammer of a clock, the lower servants were the cogs on its wheels.

In some households, the chief servants formed the extent of the household hierarchy, and labour division by type of work was not very important. In others, however, different kinds of non-administrative work were partially or wholly distinguished and divided amongst servants. In these households we can often see subheads – servants who were essentially 'middle-management'. They did not usually determine policies or make major decisions, but their jobs, essentially administrative, were to oversee the actual carrying out of household policy decided by the chief servants as it applied to the area of household duties over which they had charge. Because subheads themselves were specialized and because they change from household to household, it is better to reserve detailed discussion of them to the following section on 'horizontal' labour division. Many of their titles are familiar ones: marshal of the stables, kitchen clerk, cook, marshal of the hall, etc.

Beneath these subheads, within each area of duty and indeed even among general servants, further distinctions of rank were made, which occur in most households, and apply to status more than work speciality. They are *generosus* or armigerus, *valettus*, *garcio*, and pagettus/puer; or, to use their English equivalents (which are quite common after *c*.1320), gentleman or squire or knight, valet or yeoman, groom, and page or boy or child. Common enough words; but their very commonness then and now makes them difficult to define in themselves and in relation to each other.

Armigerus occurs in the very earliest households. *Generosus* is used as early as 1300 if not before as well,[6] occurring in most of our households. Some historians have quibbled over the use of the word 'gentleman' before 1485, claiming that it had no context in pre-Tudor Britain;[7] but it is difficult to translate *generosus* in any other way, especially as this is the contemporary translation used, as early as 1423.[8] We may, of course, not use 'gentleman' in the same way as would someone of the fifteenth century; but neither thus do we use 'knight' or even 'noble'. The definition of the term's medieval usage in the household is thus essential. *Generosi* or gentlemen (where a houehold prefers the term *armigerus* it is parallel in pay and duties to *generosus* in others) were the chief servants within any group of workers below the subheads, in terms of rates of pay and in the status implied by their names. They tend to have relatively general titles such as 'gentleman of the kitchen' which do not much define their duties; more than other servants, we find them called upon to be versatile. George Cavendish, for instance – Cardinal Wolsey's gentleman-usher of the chamber, who wrote his master's biography[9] – was called upon not only to monitor the Cardinal's visitors, but to carry messages, purvey food, seek out lodgings, act as an emmissary, and diverse other functions; we see his fellow gentlemen-ushers doing much the same. *Generosus*, then, implies responsibilities specific and general. We must ask three questions of it, which must be asked of all such rankings: what does it say about the holder's personal status? does it infer control

---

[6]In the chequerroll of Gilbert de Clare, Earl of Gloucester and Hereford, PRO E 101/91/10.

[7]Denys Hay, *Europe in the Fourteenth and Fifteenth Centuries* (Longman, London, 1975), pp. 62–9.

[8]*The Compact Edition of the Oxford English Dictionary*, 1971, p. 1131.

[9]George Cavendish, *The Life and Death of Cardinal Wolsey*, ed. Richard Sylvester (Early English Texts Society, London, vol. 243, 1959), p. xx.

over lower rankings? and does it reflect any special duties or areas of responsibility?

Generosus as a social rank usually implied, at the least, that its bearer or his father was a landowner who was not also an agricultural labourer, and who had tenants of his own. But 'gentleman' had no legal definition in the way that 'knight' or 'duke' did; its conveyance upon a given person was largely a matter of custom and of social acceptance. Therefore the term was applied to any number of kinds of people, and we must not assume that a householder called 'gentleman' was from an accepted landowning family or was a social success personally. The nobles and knights who conveyed that acceptance, however, extended it to those serving their own kind in a presentable fashion. Of course, some gentleman servants were gentlemen in the inheritable sense of the word – George Cavendish, for example, or Ambrose Skelton, the third Duke of Buckingham's gentleman-usher.[10] But unknown men are as common; and *generosi* also appear in less celebrated households whom we may legitimately doubt to be gently born. Just as a lawyer or bishop of peasant origins was accepted as socially gentle, so some kinds of household service seem to have conferred gentility. But what sort of service was it that made a householder a *generosus*?

It is tempting to suggest that the *generosus* forms a link in the chain of command between subheads and valets, but this is unlikely to be the case. For all his versatility and dependability one cannot call the *generosus* an administrator. None of the duties we have seen him perform involve management. He is a worker, albeit the top rank, probably with little actual ability to command those in lower ranks. One may compare the situation to that of a modern university department. A senior lecturer may receive higher pay and greater benefits than a mere lecturer. He may even be asked to sit on more committees. His seniority gives him a psychological superiority over a lecturer, but he would be unable to tell that lecturer what or how to teach. A *generosus* of the hall in fifteenth-century England might have had some kind of theoretical superiority over a *valettus* of the hall, and received better clothing and more food, according to any ordinance, but both he and the valet would have taken their orders from the hall marshal. Therefore the gentleman's higher status must relate to a sphere of duties which are worth more pay than those of a *valettus*. I have already mentioned that the gentleman was expected to be a versatile and dependable servant, who might be called upon to carry a message which might not be entrusted to a valet. In a few cases his responsibility

[10]BL Royal MS 7f xiv, fos 1–19.

may have been that of direct service to the upper classes, where knowledge of 'gentle' behaviour was required. But does this explain the sole difference between a gentleman of, and a valet of, the kitchen? Might a more concrete difference in duties be suggested? While any evidence for such a difference is far too scanty to let one do more than guess, one might propose a hypothesis which, while not proven, is not contradicted by any known evidence. To go back to the analogy of the university department, one might note that senior lecturers may have their pick of tutorial times, while junior lecturers will probably have the one at nine o'clock Monday morning. Similarly, one could suggest that our gentleman of the kitchen might be versatile and not highly specialized, but certain undesirable jobs he would probably never have to do, such as scrubbing floors, or cleaning out the midden; while the valet may not have had a choice. The apparent dichotomy between 'gentleman' and 'kitchens' to modern ears makes it difficult to picture just what this gentleman would do that is connected with his title – Bogo de Clare, treasurer of York Minster, had a squire of the kitchen in 1284 who did a little purveying, but as with other gentlemen we know nothing about his more ordinary duties – but we can form some conception of what he probably would not do; and his duties probably brought him into direct contact with the upper classes he was hired to serve.

Valetti and *garcioni* present many of the same problems as the *generosi*. The rank of *valettus* is by the fourteenth century translated either as valet or yeoman. The medieval word *valettus*, from the Latin *valeo*, to be strong or healthy, is recorded as early as 1201, and is variously translated in Baxter and Johnson's *Medieval Latin World-List* as young man (hence the middle and early modern 'varlet', or youth), esquire, yeoman, groom, or servant. They fail to mention the English word valet (from old French *valet*, itself from Latin *valeo*) because it now has two specific meanings – a servant in personal attendance upon his master, or (militarily) a footman in attendance on a horseman. Usually the medieval Latin *valettus* and its medieval Englished forms, valet and yeoman, are much more general terms. In household documents, however, the valet is clearly distinguished as part of some kind of group, above the groom, and below the squire or gentleman; in chequerrolls the valet had a lower wage scale than the gentleman, but higher than the groom. Beyond this it becomes difficult to define his position. As a householding term, 'valet' does not apply to young men alone – some servants remained valets for twenty years.[11] As we have

[11]See especially the case of John Forster, valet to the first Duke of Buckingham and to his widow, 1443–64, BL Add. MS Egerton rolls 2208 and 2822.

seen, the valet is differentiated from the grooms and esquires. A servant he clearly is, but that is hardly helpful. The modern meaning of valet is clearly inapplicable, as valets occur throughout the household, and as it is a rank rather than a unique job.

The term 'yeoman', however, is more useful, as it has fairly specific legal and social meanings. The word probably derives from the Old English *yongman*, meaning young man (as in valet) or servant; or from *gingra man*, originally younger man but especially a vassal or a follower of a prince. In the twelfth-century *Pseudo-Cnut de Foresta*, section 2, 'youngerman' is a synonym of *laessthegenes* or *mediocres homines*; these ranked between *thegenes* or *liberales homines*, and *tunmen* or *villani*. In the later middle ages, 'yeoman' came to mean a man holding a small landed estate or freehold, especially one who cultivated his own land. The term in the later fifteenth century became romanticized by such men as Sir John Fortesque,[12] and was used to connote sturdiness, loyalty, homeliness, simple honesty and a kind of basic Englishness, aspects which it still holds. 'Yeoman' can also be used appositvely with bread and ale, to signify the secondary grade of quality. Finally, the term has some military uses, referring to a kind of footman in the army or a bodyguard, and was sometimes used instead of 'pawn' in chess,[13] as well as being used extensively to describe members of households. All these diverse definitions carry one point. The yeoman is common, but free.

What we know of the duties of valets, or yeomen, bear out this definition of *medocres homines* – the middle-men, the secondary servants, the sturdy commoners. We find that a valet's or yeoman's title is often more specific (valet-chamberlains, valet-slaughterers, etc., as opposed to gentlemen of the kitchen or of the larder – far more descriptive of the valet's actual job), and that he is less likely than a gentleman in his department to be used for extra-household business. On the other hand, his position usually required both responsibility and skill; we find him in charge of a stable's grain stock directly under the marshal; he waits at secondary tables in hall, changes the lord's bed, slaughters animals for consumption. He probably did not, however, have to scrub down the larder after the kill or wash the dishes after serving them. These more menial, less skilled positions may have been left to the groom.

The Latin *garcio*, and its fifteenth-century English equivalent 'groom',

[12]Sir John Fortesque, *De Laudibus Legum Angliae*, ed. S.B. Chrimes (Cambridge University Press, Cambridge, 1942), p. 69.

[13]Master Fitzherbert, *The Book of Husbandry*, ed. Walter W. Skeat (English Dialect Society, London, 1882), p. 5.

are also difficult to define. In the household, we know they ranked in wages below yeomen, and indeed occupy the lowest position known, with the possible exception of certain child servants. Of course, *garcio* can also mean boy, as well as groom, and servant generally; but most household records distinguish between *garcioni* – some of whom held this position for many years and were married as well[14] – and *pueri* or *pagetti*. The etymology of the English 'groom' is uncertain, through either Old English or Old French. Once again, the earliest meaning seems to have been a male child, but by at least 1330 also meant a lowborn adult male, often used as the antonym of a noble, or adjectivally for 'foolish' or 'lower-class'. Our modern connection of the word with horses primarily, and its gerund, 'grooming', with care for the person, dates only from the seventeenth century; in the middle ages 'groom' and *garcio* had a much more general application. The crucial sense of the word, however, seems to lie in its intimation of low birth and status. The difficulty of tracing most grooms whose names we know may in itself exhibit their social obscurity. We seldom find household grooms assigned responsibilities outside the bounds of their job descriptions. What we do know of their duties confirms our impression of menial status. Stable grooms, for instance, do the actual washing and brushing of the horses, the cleaning of the stalls, the filling of the mangers. About the only servants we might rank lower than the groom are the *pagetti* and *pueri* – the henchmen, pages, and child servants in the household. They received, after all, a wage which ranged from a pittance of 6s 8d per annum to nothing at all apart from their keep. However, one must make clear several distinctions about child servants which show that theirs is a rank apart, parallel to but not really one with the adult structure of the household.

Henchman (Old English *henx-* or *haunch-man*, perhaps originally an attendant on a horse – a groom in the modern sense) generally refers to wellborn children put out to service in an aristocratic family for the sake of their military, social, and academic education, and often also as a sign of a client–master relationship between the child's family and his lord's. Such service might allow a child to create, very early in life, ties with his peers and superiors of several generations which might later prove useful. His duties were mild and often ceremonial, such as holding the washbasin at table; he was often given the same number of personal lackeys as a gentleman servant.[15] True, his wages, if they

---

[14]See especially the case of the thirteenth Earl of Oxford's John Watson, Soc. Ant. MS 77, and of Hecock and Richard Wodward, grooms to the Talbots of Blakemere, Salop RO Bridgewater Collection SR 0212/1–7.

[15]F.J. Furnivall, ed., *The Babees Book* (Early English Texts Society, Oxford, vol. 32, 1868), pp. xiv–xxv.

existed at all, were nominal; but he also received an education, and he was hardly employed or employable in the strict sense of the word. *Pagetti* might have been used the most often to describe these 'noble babes' in Latin texts, but *pueri* is used interchangeably with it.

Pagetti and *pueri*, perhaps the latter more frequently, were also used to describe a quite different sort of child servant. From uninfluential, common and even villein families, household boys, as I shall call them, were primarily in the household to work; and most often their goal was a permanent household position, rather than an aristocratic career. Many of the higher household servants had their own youthful servitors. Children often served with the lady of the household, fetching for her and doing simple tasks; we find them turning the spit in the kitchen and dusting nightly in the pantry. They were perhaps commonest in the kitchen, and also the bakery. But though their wages were low and their tasks menial, they cannot really be called lower than grooms in rank, except in the sense that all children would tend to be less capable of controlling their lives, of performing skilled tasks, of holding responsibility, than any adults. While primarily workers, they also received training in various householding skills. Their wages were low for adults, but as children they had little expenditure or monetary responsibilities in any case. Finally, as adults, they could become gentlemen, valets and grooms of the household. A number of Thomas Arundel's choristers rose to become yeoman servants, and his page John Hervey became, when grown, his chaplain.[16] Clearly the fact of their childhood puts them on a different scale from adult householders; they are properly ranked separately, with and beneath the henchmen.

Finally, and unfortunately to further confuse the issue, one must caution that all these ranks, while constant in themselves, did not fix or define individuals. While we have perhaps noted a *tendency* in some ranks for the holder to come of a related social class, there is no *necessary* connection. Several examples of grooms becoming valets can be found, and of child servants, the sons of valets, becoming household gentlemen or even, in time, *armigeri* in their own right.[17] The household could be a signal way of social and material advancement; the ranks within it were, as we have seen, a matter of relative and rather loosely defined status, but imposed no ultimate restrictions on the servant who was named within them.

The hierarchy of servants was one framework on which a medieval household organized itself. In some cases, it was the sole structure. But in many households some form of labour division also occurred, not by

---

[16]Aston, *Thomas Arundel*, p. 252.
[17]Rawcliffe, *The Staffords*, pp. 71–3.

the status or responsibility of various duties, but by kind or type. Rather than representing a contemporary concept of labour division, the areas of work described here are a way of defining different types of work handled by servants in all medieval households. Since medieval household organization varies considerably, this plan makes it easier to talk about households in general than would any individual medieval scheme; and medieval labour divisions, where they exist, are concomitant with the different work areas used here. For instance, the household of Sir Edward Don of Saunderton (Warwickshire) did not have many firm or obvious divisions; but it did have to fulfil the various types of duty described below; and those of its servants with titles and some of those without probably worked, largely, within the bounds of one of these divisions. The Stafford households do show departmentalization, often in much finer degrees than the divisions shown here, but these departments are ordered one after the other in their chequerrolls in much the same progression used below, and their duties do not cross the broad divisions we shall employ. Medieval householders would have understood our usage, even if these terms were not always the ones they used. Charles C. Johnson follows a similar policy with *Constitutio Domus Regis*, adding subheadings to the text which are his own, but which clearly are operable in the organization of the manuscript.

The part of the household which probably has been described most, and which figures most prominently in popular histories, is what we would call 'below stairs', consisting of those servants who performed duties necessary to the preparation of the various services and entertainments provided for the noble master, his guests and family. They will here be called 'preparatory' servants, departments and duties. These were the stagehands rather than the performers, who ideally were never to be seen – the cooks, cleaners, replenishers of candles, spreaders of rushes, etc. Writers like John Cordy Jeaffreson and F.J. Furnivall have been particularly fascinated by the making of food from strange beasts in unbelievable quantities. However, no author has paid much nonfictional attention to the problem of determining how these elaborate concoctions were turned out in organizational terms, surely almost as amazing and interesting a feat as the fetes themselves. Luckily, household accounts are much concerned with the expenses of such duties – in particular those concerning food – in what was purchased, where, and by whom, and when it was actually used; so that a great deal of information can be gleaned about the method of their performance. The different 'departments' named in household accounts in connection with preparatory services – kitchen, cellar, scullery, etc. –

Servants preparing and serving a meal. *Luttrell Psalter*, Add. Ms. 42130, f. 207v. English, c. 1335–1340. Courtesy of The British Library.

are for the most part the names of actual rooms in the service quarters of a great household's physical base. Of these, the kitchen is the central chamber and the central department from which these services all emanated; it is common to all households. As posited previously, the cook was in all likelihood one of the first specialized servants, due to the skills required for the job. He, too, appears in all households. Apart from him, however, infinite variety reigns, from household to household, year to year, season to season.

One major guideline that can be discerned in an attempt to classify how households handled preparatory duties is the presence or absence of a kitchen clerk. He was in charge of accounting for all buyings of foodstuffs and sometimes of spices in the household; he sometimes had an independent, if small, treasury upon which to draw for these expenses. We must be careful, however, not to attribute to him authority beyond his position. One tends to think that the control of cash means power; but this is not necessarily always the case. It is unlikely that the kitchen clerk determined purveying policy – the cook and the steward are more likely to have done so – and though he may have been able to affect it somewhat by his hold on the funds, his function is mainly that of book-keeper, not executive. If we are to look for an authoritative head of preparatory activies below the steward, we must look elsewhere. Nevertheless, the presence of the kitchen clerk does indicate some form of departmentalization and organizational autonomy. Not surprisingly, he appears most frequently in households of a complex nature, in which the burden of organizing numerous duties and individuals had necessarily to be distributed more widely.

In many households the cook alone stands out. The Luttrells of Dunster Castle (Somerset) employed a cook, and four household boys *de coquine* (of the kitchen); also one *puer* for the bakehouse. Probably some of the undifferentiated servants also had preparatory duties. William and Margaret Cromwell of Tattershall (Lincolnshire) employed a cook, a combined baker and butler, a baker's servant, and several kitchen pages. Of the two former men, the cook received the greater wages (26s 8d per annum, as against 20s per annum). One perhaps might also include among the Cromwellian preparatory servants some of their agricultural workers, especially those who worked on the demesne as shepherds and pig-watchers. They were sometimes paid household as well as agricultural wages, and at least some of the animals they cared for were probably household stock – a larder on the hoof. By the fifteenth century, however, most households with members numbering over thirty – over half our sample – employed kitchen clerks; and we find with them a larger and better defined kitchen staff, as well as other preparatory 'departments'. They generally employed a large number of cooks and bakers, perhaps ruled over by the chief cook, who again received a higher wage than the chief baker; and as well as boys of the kitchen and bakery, there were adult servants, valets, in these rooms. A wine-cellarer might also be employed, and several cators or purveyors who did the actual buying of foodstuffs. The kitchen clerk accounted for all, except perhaps the wine-cellarer, who often kept his own account. (Few of these wine-cellarers' accounts have survived, but numerous references to cellarage and brewing accounts in year rolls indicate his independence in both purveyance and accounting.)

Preparatory departmentalization in the largest households was more complex. The de Vere Earls of Oxford in 1284 employed only a cook, that we know of, in their small riding household; but living permanently at Castle Hedingham and other homes were bakers, cellarers, brewers, slaughterers, servants *de coquine* and herdsmen. By 1431 at the latest, the twelfth Earl of Oxford employed a kitchen clerk who accounted for the various cooks, purveyors and bakers who accounted and purveyed separately, the slaughterer, the numerous adults and boys *de coquine*. Ale and wine were accounted separately. After his return to England and power in 1485, the thirteenth Earl re-established a household along the lines of his father's, but of greater size and complexity. His accounts, and his will of 1513 speak of the offices of larder and maltery.[18] The larder continued to account with the kitchen, and one of its known members received wages on a scale commensurate with the kitchen clerk or head cook. We could perhaps call it a sub-department, as a room which had a specific group of servants working regularly in it, but the evidence suggests that their organizational thrust and corporate identity was not independent of the kitchen; slaughterers, for instance, continued to be identified as kitchen servants. However, the Earl had a great deal of ale and beer brewed, for household consumption, which is not accounted with the kitchen; the maltery perhaps had some autonomy, or was a sub-department of the cellars. Unique in providing a picture of departmental development over several centuries, the evidence of the de Vere household nevertheless corresponds to that of other households at relevant time periods.

Preparatory staff on paper appear to be even more rigidly organized, especially in episcopal accounts, where 'departments' such as the scullery, saucery, slaughterhouse and *pastillaria*, or pastry-making department, appear. However, none can be shown to act truly as a

[18]Sir William St John Hope, ed., 'The Last Testament and Inventory of John de Vere, Earl of Oxford', *Archaeologia* 66 (1915), pp. 275–348.

department. They may have had some identity as a room or part of a room, but they were in fact accounted for by the kitchen (and the *pastillaria* with the bakehouse), and servants 'assigned' to them by a title are few and usually can be found also acting in the kitchen department. So these 'departments' appear to be accounting fictions on the part of the clerk of the kitchen or the composer of the household-wide account, as a way of organizing his material; this is backed up by the discovery that these departments might be used on a daily roll for days of heavy purchasing or use, but not on other days.[19]

Kitchen departments in abbots' and priors' households are rather different. While an abbot or prior might have his own cook, he generally depended upon the catering and purveyance systems of the monastic establishment itself, and this was usually organized along the lines of the Benedicitine ordering of obedientiaries, which differed in many respects from noble household practice in general. The cook might arrange for the purchase of certain items for the abbatial table, as is clear from the accounts of Durham Priory.[20] In general, however, he got his supplies from the monastic purveyor, and accounting was done by the monastic cellarer, or the bursar if the house was a small one like Finchale, a daughter house of Durham for which many accounts have survived.

Aside from food preparation, we may ask about other backstage tasks necessary to the smooth running of a household. Who spread the rushes, disposed of garbage, scrubbed floors, cleaned the great hall? One must imagine that those 'general servants' with no titles, and probably the grooms in their various areas of the house, were employed in these jobs, as no servants with these kinds of job descriptions have left records. In the accounts of Richard de Swinfield, Bishop of Hereford (1289–90), 'house-cleaning' is a task for which outside staff are employed. However, there were other less menial chores of a preparatory nature, like making torches and candles, preparing the hides of slaughtered animals, clarifying fat for household lamps, and buying, making and repairing pans, pots and dishes; and much of this can be found being done in the kitchen and its related departments. Cooks and valets and grooms of the kitchen, for instance, made candles from the fat and dishes from the hides of animals slaughtered for household consumption. In some rather small households, however, these kinds of jobs were distributed more widely; hence in 1478, the Stonors' gardener also making candles.

[19]Staffs. RO D 1721/1/5.
[20]For details see C.H. Lawrence, *Medieval Monasticism* (Longman, London, 1984), pp. 106–9.

Since the different preparatory departments, when they actually existed, performed duties which were often closely connected, they probably required some coordination of effort. In smaller households, where there were merely the kitchen servants, probably under the steward directly, such coordination could not have been a great difficulty; but in larger households where some degree of departmentalization had taken place, especially when it went beyond the separation of the kitchen as an office, correlation had to be achieved. Departmentalization may have distributed the work load and assigned it more definitely, but could create its own problems such as lack of communication and coordination. Several factors may have helped to relieve this problem.

Firstly, the cook, in many cases the linchpin of preparations in the household, usually can be found to have received the highest wages, bar the clerk, in this area of the household; and he may have had authority to match. As probable determiner of food policy, he would have had a natural right to oversea all food-preparing departments. We know too that the clerk of the kitchen coordinated the accounts for many departments, even some of those with their own corporate identity such as bakehouse, avenery (grainstore) and cellar; and he could have served as a liaison officer. Records of tallies also show us that departments had ways of exchanging goods among themselves. Finally, we must be careful not to nail down servants by their titles. These 'departments' were often all rooms or even parts of one room, all in close physical proximity to each other; and it is highly likely that menials – titled or untitled – and even higher servants could help out in departments other than their own, at least within a general area of work. A kitchen valet might be specialized in various kitchen work, but he need not have been totally restricted to its environs.

In some ways all servants perform preparatory duties. But in the kitchens, scullery, etc. these duties are pararmount, while in other labour divisions presentation is the main type of service provided. Waiting service is the most visible of presentation duties. Waiting service may be defined as those duties involving public attendance on the lord and his guests; primarily this entails the service of food, but it also includes holding the washbasin, incidental fetching and carrying, public entertainment, and whatever else was demanded by the master when in his hall. The rooms chiefly involved in waiting service were the great hall and other dining or living chambers; the pantry; and the buttery. The pantry and buttery were usually small chambers near the main hall; the former was the room in which bread and foodstuffs were laid out, ready to be served for meals, and probably where such things as bread baskets, serving bowls, and linens were kept. The buttery performed the same function for the service of ale and wine. A classic layout of these chambers can be seen at Haddon Hall, near Bakewell (Derbyshire), the original home of the Vernons.[21] Pantry and buttery are small rooms flanking a corridor off the lower end of the old hall, which leads in turn to the kitchen, larder and other preparatory rooms. The old solar, which by the fifteenth century served as the private dining chamber, opened off the upper end of the same hall (which, incidentally, also includes a musician's gallery over the lower end).

Numerous accounts use *aula et camera* (hall and chamber), *panetria* (pantry), and *buttelaria* (buttery) as departments; but in an obviously fictional manner. The use of the pantry in this way has been discussed earlier; much the same could be repeated for the buttery. Under 'hall and chamber' one consistently finds only entries for coal, wood and other fuels. The joining of these two rooms as one department seems unusual and does not fit with our knowledge of the household; this was not the only 'department' which used the fuel purchased; not does it appear to have bought or accounted for fuel. Unfortunately, the waiting services were not such as to require the purchase of a great deal of stuff, or regularly, so that accounts tell us less about them than the preparatory services; nappery, tableware, etc. were usually purchased by the wardrobe or kitchen. Nevertheless, chequerrolls and wage lists add to the accounts, and give us some idea of how these services were organized.

Waiting service required little in the way of special ability. Some people are better, of course, at carving capons than others; but the serving of meals is not really a skilled job. In our society few restaurants require much training; in medieval England children frequently performed it, though not necessarily very well. Therefore, though in a lord's eyes a necessity, it was not considered a specialized function, unlike cooking, which always required labour division. Indeed, waiting service lent itself admirably to the use of generalized servants, if the whole household ate together; each could take his turn while the others ate, a system described in the *Northumberland Household Book*, section 10. Other waiting duties such as fetching, and holding the washbasin, clearly needed little skill. Thus in many households' chequerrolls and accounts, we can detect no trace of servants who specialized in waiting service. Others, however, especially ecclesiastical households, had at least some specialization within this labour division, and also perhaps departmentalization.

[21]Diagrams in Margaret Wood, *The English Medieval House* (Phoenix, London, 1965), pp. 248–51.

Plate 4 Serving and eating a meal – Sir Geoffrey Luttrell at table.
Luttrell Psalter, Add. Ms. 42130, f. 208. English, c. 1335–1340.

Just as the kitchen clerk can serve by his presence or absence as an indicator of the complexity of the preparatory staff, so does the marshal of the hall for the waiting services. We are used to thinking of a marshal as a stable servant, and indeed this is its original meaning, which continued simultaneously with the use of the 'marshal' for a hall servant. The transference of titles probably occurred because of the stable marshal's quasi-military role, especially in its disciplinarian rights. The marshal of the hall was in charge of discipline kept and order observed in the hall, from the prevention of fist fights to the proper seating of guests by rank, as well as the overseeing of waiting service. In smaller households the steward probably took care of this; in large households he would have required a deputy – hence the hall marshal. He appears in the royal household from 1318, in the Ordinance of York. Hall marshals do not appear in noble chequerrolls, however, until the fifteenth century, and are generally to be found only in the largest household, such as those of the Dukes of Buckingham (from 1451), and the Earls of Northumberland (from 1512). Many households, however, had a chief gentlemen-usher with a high rate of pay who may have acted as a hall marshal. An usher, as the name implies, made sure that the seating arrangements were followed, that order was preserved (they could on occasion serve as bouncers) and that all were given their meal. They may also have served as waiters.

The increasingly large number fed daily and the many banquets given in households of size and importance throughout the fifteenth century would have required, not only more waiters, but more deputies of the marshal to make sure all went smoothly. Ecclesiastical households throughout the fourteenth, fifteenth and sixteenth centuries invariably had large numbers of ushers of the hall, gentlemen, yeomen and grooms. The waiting servants of the Prior of Durham in the early fifteenth century numbered almost as many as the rest of his household, and the numbers of hall and chamber ushers in Cardinal Wolsey's household, as recounted by his gentleman-usher George Cavendish in the latter's life of Wolsey, are legendary. Other hall servants besides these overseers performed the actual tasks required in the hall. Pantry and buttery servants (including butlers) worked in their respective chambers, placing the foods in their proper serving dishes, uncorking the bottles, plugging kegs; they also acted as waiters. Larger households from the early fifteenth century also had servants *del ewery*. The ewery was not a place but a thing: a basin or ewer filled with water which was carried around, with towels, to the lord and his guests, for them to wash their hands during and after the meal. The term 'ewery' was applied at times to the dresser whereon these basins were kept. In the halls of many noble households, this ewery – probably a kind of dry sink – and the dresser or sideboard for serving dishes were probably one and the same. Hence John Russell in his *Boke of Nurture* speaking of the servants of the ewery as if they were waiters.[22] This use of the term also occurs in the royal household, which may account for the proliferation of servants *del ewery* in the fifteenth century.

The chequerroll of the third Duke of Buckingham for 1517 provides us with the titles and names of more waiters, some of whom specialized further within this role. It lists three cupbearers, three carvers, three sewers, and three sewers for the body. 'Sewer' is a middle English term for waiter; sewers for the body were thus the duke's and duchess's personal waiters. One general cupbearer was charged solely with the service of wine and ale; the other two waited upon the lord and lady alone. The same was true of the carvers. As has been suggested, carving was the one aspect of waiting service which might require special skills. In the middle ages it was something of an art, with a set of procedures for each animal complete with an expert's jargon, and involved enough time and training to require specialization. One might call to mind the carving skills of Tristan in the Tristan and Isolde legends. Several textbooks on carving from this period survive, including one within John Russell's *Boke of Nurture*.[23] Similar arrangements are found in the *Northumberland Household Book* and the greater episcopal sees, and in the Prior of Durham's accounts of the 1530s.

---

[22]Furnivall, *The Babees Book*, p. 1195.
[23]Ibid., p. 2012.

Though perhaps not attendants in the strict sense of the term, entertainers provided publicly performed theatrical and musical services for their master, usually in the hall, and had therefore to be in some sense under the supervision of the hall marshal. Of course, wandering musicians, local singers and independent players were hired to perform on special occasions, but these people were not a part of the household. Oddly enough it is ecclesiastical households which provide us with the earliest instances of regularly maintained entertainers. Bogo de Clare, treasurer of York Minister, kept at least from 1284 to 1286 a harper (*cytharista*), and an early prior of Durham (*c.*1360) employed a Thomas *Fatous*, or fool. Bogo de Clare's accounts, however, mention payments to the minstrels of secular lords, so the employment of entertainers in the household was never a purely ecclesiastical idiosyncrasy. Musicians, rather than fools, are the most common. Henry IV, when he was Earl of Derby, supported a little band of six men, trumpeters, pipers, and a 'nakerer' or kettledrum player;[24] but a single harpist was more the norm, and this only in the larger households (though the Talbots of Blakemere, it may be noted, usually employed several musicians). John de Vere, thirteenth Earl of Oxford, and the third Duke of Buckingham employed respectively a 'disguiser' and a 'pursuivant'; these may have been similar to the royal master of the revels, who advised and supervised more elaborate entertainments. Cardinal Wolsey employed a similar gentleman servant. All three nobles are known for their fondness for spectacle.[25]

Numerous servants were employed in waiting service in large households, working under the aegis of a marshal. Did they form a department or departments? The paucity of accounting information concerning them makes this question difficult; we have little unambiguous evidence of corporate identity. The status of the marshal or chief gentleman-usher is probably the clearest sign of a kind of departmental division. Certainly the marshal, the ushers and such people as the sewers and cupbearers must have acted as a unit if they were to create any orderliness and efficiency in the hall. But the control of the marshal over minstrels, butlers and pantlers is less certain; the two latter might even be said to be attached to the kitchens. It is equally difficult to call pantry and buttery separate departments; their members are few, large households seldom naming more than three in each, and their wages low; nor does any discernible subhead exist within them. In any case

[24]See Lucy Toulmin Smith, ed., *Expeditions to Prussia and the Holy Land by Henry Earl of Derby* (Camden Society, London, vol. 52, 1894), pp. xcvi–xcviii.
[25]Essex RO D/DPR 137; Soc. Ant. MS 77; PRO E 101/518/5; and PRO E 101/518/14.

the entries detailing the purveyance of waiting service goods such as linen napkins, trestles, trays, etc. are never registered in the name of the hall or pantry or buttery departments. If the hall servants formed what looks like an internal sense of identity and order independent of the chief servants, it has left little positive trace, except in the very largest establishments.

As well as public attendance, the nobility demanded of their households personal private service. This could include guarding the chamber, making beds, caring for clothes, what we would call valeting, or simple companionship. Personal servants worked in the private chambers of the household – before 1420, the nursery and solar; as the fifteenth century progressed, a whole complex of rooms housing lord, lady and their children in bedchambers, schoolrooms and living areas.[26] While few of the needs fulfilled by personal service demanded much in the way of skills or training, lords and ladies were likely to be highly selective concerning whom they would allow to perform these chores in such close proximity to their persons. Those admitted to these inner recesses were also called upon more often to carry out extra-household tasks which a master was only willing to trust to someone he knew well. The third Duke of Buckingham, for instance, used his yeoman barber to convey messages.[27] Thus one seldom finds a household without specific chamber servants; but their duties within that realm were rarely defined, actually or by title.

Personal or chamber service tended to be idiosyncratic, subjective, varying more widely than other services from household to household, depending on the lord's personal tastes and requirements. One finds little real correlation with household size, in contrast to other labour divisions. Margaret, wife of William Cromwell of Tattershall, had an average of seven personal servants; William, two; their son, Robert, two – this is a household which numbered not much more than twenty. The titles given these servants also vary considerably and their duties are hard to interpret. Many are called merely by the Latin *camerarialius*, or *ancille* – 'chamber servant', 'chamberlain', 'chamberer', or 'maid' in English. The titles place them but do not define their duties; 'maid' means only a female servant. Others are entitled *generosa*, *puer*, *puella* – gentlewoman, boy, girl – which tell us little about their duties, whatever we learn of their status. Furthermore, no organizational pattern linking households is discernible. Hall marshall, ushers, sewers and cupbearers appear in many large households in related quantities;

[26]Wood, *The English Medieval House*, pp. 189–207.
[27]PRO E 36/220.

but no similar paradigm appears among personal servants. These served the head of the household, the head's family and his dependants; and many servants of gentleman or valet status had their own personal servant as well, paid on the general chequerroll.

We have already mentioned Margaret Cromwell's bevy of personal servants. Indeed one often finds that women employed more personal servants than men. Margaret Beaufort, in a household of thirty-two, had six gentlewomen.[28] Elizabeth Stonor in 1478–9 had at least two personal boy servants, a gentlewoman and a chambermaid, but none are recorded in this year's day-book for her husband William. Many of these, especially the *generose*, appear to have been as much companions as servants; we know little of any other duties. Mistress Stonor's gentlewoman, however, also served as her amanuensis.[29] Lady Margaret Long of Hengrave Hall, between 1541 and 1564, employed about five maids for herself and her daughters, and two male servants of the chamber. Since the household was very much a male environment, noble women depended more upon their personal servants for companionship than did their menfolk.

Outside of the more august of the parliamentary peerage and the greater episcopacy it is rare to find a noble man with more than one or two personal servants. The first Duke of Buckingham employed only several female chambers and a nursemaid, that we know of; but his great-grandson, the third duke, employed in 1517 forty-six personal attendants – though some of these may have been for the 'exterior chamber' or private dining room. These included three gentlemen-ushers and five valet-ushers, probably employed (like George Cavendish, Cardinal Wolsey's usher, and those described in the *Northumberland Household Book*, section 10) to guard the chamber, admitting, ejecting and controlling visitors thereto; and to act as 'managers' of chamber activity and decorum. They were not so much personal servants as a kind of guard of honour, made up of wellborn young men hoping to advance through the lord's favour, and often indicative of his clientage. There were also fourteen valets and seven grooms of the chamber (one of the valets was a barber); and five henchmen. The duchess had four of her own servants – three gentlewomen and a chamberer. Henry, Lord Stafford, the heir, had a master, schoolmaster, valet, chamberer and groom of robes to himself, and his four sisters in the nursery had a female 'master', two gentlewomen, and a chamberer. The fifth Earl of Northumberland also employed 'rokkers' for his infant children.

[28]WAM 5479**.

[29]Charles Lethbridge Kingsford, ed., *The Stonor Letters and Papers 1290–1483*, (Camden Society, London, vols 29 and 30, 1919), vol. 29, p. xlvii, and no. 170.

Though our knowledge of the Stafford servants is drawn from a fair-copy chequerroll, so that we are bound to have more information about their household than about others, it would still seem that they employed an exceptionally high number of personal servants, when compared with nobles of similar status such as the Earls of Oxford, the first Earl of Rutland and the Earls of Warwick. Indeed, only among the households of Stafford, Percy and some bishops such as Wolsey and Beaufort can we detect some sense of interior order among the main group of chamberers, with their executive staff of ushers.[30] In addition, some of these personal servants have titles which indicate greater specialization: the ushers, barbers, horsemen, schoolmasters and grooms of robes. But once again the majority hold titles which tell us their location and status, rather than much about what they are hired to do; and we actually find them performing many varied tasks.

Two exceptions to the general lack of specialization in chamber service may be mentioned: the secretary, and the wardrober. Even lords of modest status had servants employed specifically as secretaries. Robert Radcliffe of Tattershall had a personal clerk, and Hugh Luttrell of Dunster's 'Lyttelwill' wrote letters and kept private accounts for him. These were employed for both personal and 'business' correspondence, and to deal with the growing bureaucracy of their master's public administrative posts, with charters, indentures and other legal papers. The third Duke of Buckingham also employed a clerk of the signet, perhaps in connection with such secretarial work as required a seal. But we find secretaries doing many other things, from purveying items to riding round the master's estates; versatility was expected of them. We frequently find secretaries acting as accountants for a 'privy purse', for, for instance, the Dukes of Buckingham, the Dukes of Norfolk, Thomas Hillary (1548), Elizabeth de Burgh, Lady of Clare (1326–59), and many others.

As was discussed earlier, nearly all servants must have kept some kind of account of the monies with which they were entrusted. Chamber servants in particular were often in charge of small amounts of cash. Medieval masters did not care to carry cash on their persons overmuch, it seems, and accompanying servants were ordered to pay even the smallest expenses their masters might incur: alms, gambling debts, *regarda* (a tip or gratuity), etc. In some cases, however, a lord might set up a more formal privy purse, a small treasury for his personal use, quite independent of the household's income both

---

[30]Beaufort had a household ranging in estimate from 300 to 500 to 800, many of whom were chamber servants; Aston, *Thomas Arundel*, p. 169.

physically and on paper. In a few households such as that of Elizabeth de Burgh, Lady of Clare, the chamber was in fact the main accounting office, but this is rare. These private coffers provided the lord with ready cash and also gave him more personal control over at least part of his income. Such a treasury could be small or great. Those of William Stonor seldom registered receipts totalling more than £25 a year and were accounted for by himself and another chamber servant;[31] while the privy coffers of the third Duke of Buckingham had two physical treasuries, in Thornbury and in London, serving as administrative centres for the duke's entire finances. They were so busy with his greater wealth that he had a separate 'privy privy purse' for his personal expenses.[32] Secretaries were sometimes called upon to be treasurers for such a private cash box; but the wardrober was the most frequently used privy treasurer, and can be found in many households, large and small.

A 'guarderober' or 'wardrober' was an official in charge of an object similar to that wooden box in the corner of a modern bedroom, or a small closet serving the same purpose – a place in which to store clothes – in the literal and original sense of the title. In the middle ages this apparel might be part of a master's fortune, and a considerable investment. Just as the king turned to his servant, already responsible for much wealth in kind, and made of a closet a great accounting department, so nobles sometimes used their wardrobers as treasurers.

In some cases, however, the wardrobe was separate from the privy purse, as yet a third treasury within the household, which cared only for bulk items of value – not only the lord's personal clothes and jewels, but furniture, plate, bolts of cloth, ornaments, candles, tapestries, spice, paper and other items used in the household. In these cases the wardrobe became a somewhat schizophrenic organization, accounting for wardrobers of beds and robes who were actually the lord's chamber servants, and treasurers and accountants in charge of household, personal and investment goods. Some lords ameliorated the situation somewhat by keeping an extra-household wardrobe, often in London. But in general the clerk of the wardrobe had a difficult job. He might have departmental independence as an accounting agency, with his own small staff, but many others who were connected with his department were chiefly chamber servants rather than wardrobers alone. His funds often came from the receivers of the lord direct, so that he was financially independent of the steward and treasurer; yet he was the

[31]PRO C 47/37/4/35, 36 and 37/5/11.
[32]BL Royal MSS 7f xiv and 14B xxxv; PRO E 36/361/20.

custodian of household goods, too, which made him in some ways accountable to them. In the final analysis the wardrobe can be depicted as only partially an independent department in noble households; in many ways it is still a part of the chamber organization.

The proximity of chamber servants to the master explains many apparent anomalies: the general sameness of their numbers regardless of size of household, specialization by general labour division as personal servants, but seldom beyond that wide category; and the extreme diversity of chamber organizations from household to household. We must remember that these chamber servants, though primarily domestics, were often the most trusted of the lord's servants because of their proximity to him. We frequently find them carrying messages, purveying food and wines, and buying personal items for him as well as making his bed. Thus they were not likely to be highly specialized, nor is a pattern to be seen between noble households' chambers, as the numbers and organization of personal servants were particularly susceptible to the lord's own needs and idiosyncracies. One also must remember that there was only one of him; he could only use so many personal servants. Chambers like the third Duke of Buckingham's are very much the exception.

The usual evidence for departmentalization is absent for the chamber. It is seldom used by accountants except in a fictional sense, as in *aula et camera*, for fuel costs. No separate accounts for it exist unless we count the wardrobe, which accounted for more than the chamber. As we have seen, no single obvious servant subhead is in existence. But in a sense chamber servants were set apart quite definitely from others by their proximity to the master, who himself superseded a servant leader.

The chapel is another part of household organization where we may find quite elaborate arrangements even in relatively small households. One can state almost categorically that every noble and gentle had a chapel and at the least one chaplain. One must not rely on licences to say mass in these chapels as a gauge of private worship; none can be traced or perhaps ever existed for the Luttrells of Dunster, who maintained not one but two chapels. The Stonors celebrated a wedding mass in their chapel eighteen years before a licence was granted them.[33]

Chapels varied considerably in size and shape. Some surviving ones are as large as a medieval parish church, as large as a great hall. Alternatively, there are tiny chapels lodged in a tower of a Norman keep and measuring approximately ten feet square. A surprisingly small Norman chapel can be observed at Castle Riding, in Norfolk, a royal

[33]Kingsford, *Stonor Letters*, vol. 29, p. xii.

castle. Multiple chapels, while less common, are (like twins) not unusual. In the 1490s, the thirteenth Earl of Oxford kept up at least three chapels at Castle Hedingham: a tiny private one in the Earl's 'closet'; one in the old Norman keep; and a later, freestanding church in the inner courtyard. The newest chapel was considerably roomier and was probably constructed to provide more room for an expanding household as well as for grandeur; but the older chapel in the keep was still used, as we find in accounts entries of plate, linen, candles, bread and wine purchased for both.[34]

Considerable variation in the staff which ran the chapel occurs. Though sometimes there is only one chaplain, the Stonors supported in (1349) six, though we do not know if all of these were priests. Of course, many clerics besides the chaplain lived in the household, such as kitchen clerks, secretaries, etc. Ecclesiastical households usually contained a number of clerks, and sometimes stewards and treasurers were in minor orders at least. But unless they were priests these other clerks did not require the use of the chapel more than other servants, or enter into its organization. In some households, however, chaplains were in charge of other staff hired specifically to work in the chapel: priests, minor clergy, singers and sacristans. I already mentioned that the Stonors had six priests in 1349; throughout the fifteenth century we never find them with less than three. The *Northumberland Household book* mentions many priests. Though it may be imagined that they must have had some sort of rota or calendar system as to who would say mass when (at Stonor, however, at least three altars stood), their titles – bare 'chaplain' – indicate no real specialization in this matter, and this was also the case in other households. But then chaplains were expected to be extremely versatile. The Luttrells' John Bacwell doubled as steward and treasurer for a time, and William Cromwell's 'dominus' John de Kyghley purveyed, escorted Cromwell's wife, helped with auditing of estate accounts and transported money between France and his home at Tydd (Lincolnshire).

A chaplain's versatility was less when he was in charge of an actual staff. In the 1500s, the fifth Duke of Northumberland's chaplain presided over a Ladymass priest, two 'yeoman-pistelers' (epistle readers) and a sub-chaplain. Thomas Langley, Bishop of Durham, and Richard de Swinfield, Bishop of Hereford, in 1408 and 1289 respectively, had massive chapel staffs including boy and adult choristers, a common thing in episcopal households. Abbatial establishments, on the other hand, had little more than a private chaplain to the abbot or prior, who

[34]Longleat MS BPA 5949.

often undertook wider household duties such as purveyance as well. One or more sacristans were frequently employed as custodians of the chapel goods, which were valuable items – not only silver and gilt plate and statuary, but fine linens, silk vestments and illuminated books, all of which required both care and guarding. Choirs, however, were generally restricted to the greater baronage, and the episcopacy; for secular nobles, they are rare before 1440. Those of Percy, Stafford and de Vere were in all likelihood the most elaborate of the later fifteenth century, rivalling and probably imitating the king's. They included both gentleman singers and boys (who might also serve as pages: – the third Duke of Buckingham had over twelve of the latter) as well as a singing master to train and conduct them.

Obviously, service of the chapel required particular servants; in some households, as we have seen, priests and clerics might concentrate on certain types of worship or, in the case of the chaplain, administration. These 'specialists' also worked as a department. The presence of an easily recognizable servant head who was needed to correlate the liturgy shows this. We also find chapel servants keeping accounts, preparing inventories and making purchases as a corporate office, and that they are grouped as a body on chequerrolls. The nature of the chapel, its makeup and the special skills of its staff, even when they were all chaplains, its expensive purchases and its particular responsibilities made departmentalization of the chapel necessary and indeed inevitable in almost all households.

Johnson, in his edition of *Constitutio Domus Regis*, refers to those servants who are hunters, horsemen and soldiers as 'outdoors servants'. The term is not a happy one, and appears both arbitrary and of little use in describing these servants. However, those household members it includes were, in both royal and noble households, often grouped together on wages lists and livery assignments; hunting equipment was sometimes bought through the stables; these household members did indeed perform most of their duties outside the domestic buildings; and the term has been picked up by other historians from Johnson; so it is perhaps best to continue the use of the term 'outdoors service' until a more satisfactory term suggests itself.

In the royal household under Henry III, the king's bodyguard was under the control of the marshal, or master of the horse; thus the quasi-military connotation of the title. Interestingly, however, no record of a private standing army, at least one whose members were not otherwise entitled and employed, appears in noble households in our period – only, occasionally, a door-guard. It may be that such men were given non-military positions in the household or were perhaps paid by an outside source (though no mention of a private militia appears in the surviving accounts of any receivers-general). In any case, by the fifteenth century the bulk of the armed might of most lords probably came from the retainers, tenants and clients who did not dwell within the household regularly; though the lack of any specialized bodyguard is surprising. Thus the stable marshal's authority in a noble household was, at least by c.1370, largely restricted to supervising the care of horses, hawks, hounds and their accoutrements, and to directing others retained for that purpose. Though never the important, powerful person the king's master of horse was, he remained a ubiquitous figure in medieval noble households. Of those households used here only a very few fail to record the employment of one, a marshal appearing even in quite small households.

The care of horses, hawks and hounds requires special skills; marshals and stable hands must have always been specialized servants in the 'outdoors division of duties. The marshal (or a clerk for him) drew up separate accounts which perhaps were later included in the day-book, including the wages of the stable hands, who were often paid through the marshal by the week or day, rather than by the quarter year and with the other servants. The stable purveyed most of its own goods as a department and usually had its own grain stockpile; in the Stafford household it exchanged tallies with the bakery over a transfer of oats and bran, in 1454–5 and presumably at other times as well. The number and kind of individual members of the outdoors services varied. This is especially true regarding the hunters, falconers and kennel-keepers whose makeup largely depended on the lord's fondness for hunting. In the later fifteenth century, their numbers are perhaps less than one might expect, considering the traditional importance placed on hunting as a pastime by most historians. None can be traced in as big a household as the thirteenth Earl of Oxford's, though he certainly had at least a few. Finchale Priory in the mid-fourteenth century, on the other hand, kept a number of hounds for the abbot's use, and a man to keep them.

Most outdoors servants in noble households were actually stable-hands, employed to care for horses. In most households the broad specialization of ostling serves to detail their function, and doubtless they performed a variety of related tasks, from grooming to cleaning out stalls to mending harness, with such jobs divided if at all by rank – stables encompassed *pagetti*, *garcioni* and *valetti*. Sumptermen (men who packed, led and cared for sumpter- or packhorses), charioteers and carters, however, specialized in their relatively skilled fields. Bishops often kept vast and elaborate stables, in part at least because of the continual travelling required of them in their duties; Bishop Stratford, of Canterbury, kept over 100 horses in the mid-fourteenth century. Households with many horses tended to departmentalize their grain stocks, or avenery. Usually the avenery had its own staff who accounted separately and who could exchange tallies with other offices in the transference of grain between bakehouse, kitchen and avenery as needed.

Most servants and their duties and responsibilities can be readily seen as part of some labour division. But a few are hard to classify; even in contemporary chequerrolls they are set apart, not seeming to fit easily in any one department, or even within a broader division of service. Almoners, medical servants, and laundresses cross the boundaries of our neat schemes.

Carol Rawcliffe calls the Stafford almoner an assistant to the chancellor;[35] but this is a one-sided look at his many functions. Technically, 'almoner' refers to one who solicits alms, collects and distributes them. Sometimes called the clerk of alms and prayers, he might also have taken charge of the payment for and performance of petitions, remembrances, indulgences, etc. Restricted to larger households, he was usually a cleric, and had some connection, especially in the charge of prayers, with the chapel; but he was sometimes also grouped with the chamber-servants, perhaps because he was supposed to be the household conscience, provoking holy works. Because of his position as a collector of money he sometimes acted as an accountant or banker or as a helper to such accountants – for instance, we find him collecting loans solicited by the chancellor for the third Duke of Buckingham.[36] Almoners are more commonly found in their traditional role in ecclesiastical households.

Physicians and apothecaries appear on the chequerrolls of the greater baronage receiving yearly wages, but we may also find in the same household doctors called in for treatment and paid *per visitum*. They treated not only the lord but his servants throughout the household. It seems likely that they were retained by but did not live in the household. Much the same problem occurs when we consider the laundress. She is difficult to pinpoint, either as a household member or a pieceworker. For some households, we can tell that a laundress got an annual wage; but also that she lived outside the castle, as washing had to be carted to her. On the other hand, laundresses got livery wages in some establishments, such as that of John Brabant (1292), which would seem to indicate that she lived in. It is also difficult to classify

[35]Rawcliffe, *The Staffords*, p. 90.
[36]PRO E 36/220.

laundry work. Laundresses are sometimes called 'of the chamber' and in one case 'of the nursery', yet these also cleaned the clothes of many non-chamber servants, as well as table and chapel linen. All these servants who are difficult to categorize highlight the fundamental versatility and flexible qualities of even the largest, most structured households.

The organization of medieval noble households shows considerable variation from one to another; yet a number of basic similarities do appear which enable us to discuss them as a group. Major household divisions running through establishments of all sizes reflect basic needs common to all nobles – the provision of food, the need for personal service, fulfilment of religious duties, hospitality. Departmentalization and specialization provided both for the smooth and efficient carrying out of these, and for the most effective means of supervising servants and accounting for expenses. Thus the larger the household, the greater the need for elaborate organization, as we have seen. There were few major structural changes in households between 1250 and 1600, though households did tend to grow larger and to travel less, which perhaps slightly increased the tendency towards more complicated structures of command and responsibility. But within that period, basic household structure was subject to variation.

The adaptations made by nobles to their households were affected by various factors. Some were due to the general circumstances of the lord; others to the kind of life he chose to lead. The status of the master in society – his political power, his economic position, his inherited status, his favour with his peers, etc. – exercised a great effect on the kind of household he needed, and the way he chose to live. Other changes were cyclical in nature, and caused differences both between and within households. Generational changes could make for considerable variation over a period of years. Seasonal, and circumstantial, physical movement of the household also caused temporary adjustements in its organization. Households seldom were stable establishments. The factors affecting household organization were numerous, based on the needs each lord expected it to fulfil. These various needs, the various ways they were answered, and how this affected the basic form of a household, are the subjects of the following chapters.

2
Household Members

Pray, think us
Those we profess, peacemakers, friends, and servants.
Henry VIII (III. i)

Households and their organizations consisted of people – individuals, not abstractions, who did not exist in a vacuum, or even solely within a single household. They were born and raised somewhere, by someone, in a wide variety of circumstances, and as adults or children often held working positions outside the household in which we find them, before, after and during their tenure there. Some knowledge of the social status, geographical origins, and biography of the people involved and of their circumstances outside the household is necessary to our full understanding of how the household functioned, and is helpful in examining the role of servants as individuals within the household in terms of their length of tenure, chances of advancement, reasons for placement in a given position, etc.

One needs to clarify two problems, however, which one encounters immediately upon trying to isolate and research individual householders. Firstly, difficulties often arise when one attempts to determine just who is to be included as a household member. The head of the household and his immediate family lay at the core of the establishment, the centre around which it revolved. A great deal has been written about the history and structure of the family in the middle ages in Britain and Europe, and household records contribute some interesting evidence about families to the general discussion, because by recording the expenses of the family and the duties of those surrounding them they tell us who dwelt together, and often under what circumstances and with what sort of interrelations. By and large, household records of lay nobles bear out the evidence of Peter Laslett, Alan Macfarlane and others that English families, at least, were almost always nuclear; where there were family groups actually living under

Plate 5 A gentleman with his retainers. *Book of St. Albans*, Westminster 1496. S. Selden d.17, opp. page 1. Courtesy of the Bodleian Library, Oxford.

the same roof, they usually consisted of a married couple and their dependent children. Variations upon this are significant. The husbands and wives were often not both in their first relationship; in many households one or both had been married before, and the children living with them might include the offspring of the previous marriage of one or both as well as of the present union. If, however, the woman had a child by a previous marriage who was heir to property, that child might not be under the guardianship of its mother (though it frequently was), and might therefore live with a relative, client, patron or friend appointed in the father's will, and only visit its mother's new family.

The age of the children involved is also important to note. Noble children were put out to service in the households of their parents' peers often at a very young age, or boarded with a religious house or a caretaker for purposes of schooling, and teenage children living in the household who are members of the actual family at its centre are relatively rare. Their return to the household at various times in the year is recorded in kitchen accounts which list guests, and clothing and money are sent to them periodically through the wardrobe or the household treasurer. Letters from such absent offspring and the parental replies survive in the Paston, Stonor, Plumpton and Lisle letters. Children over the age of eighteen or so often returned to the parental household for a year or more before marriage, further service or entrance to religious life. But even the male heir seldom lived with his parents after his marriage, being granted a subsidiary house to set up his own establishment.

Widows (but not widowers) are also common as the heads of households. Indeed, their accounts are among the best kept and preserved, and their establishments among the most economical and orderly. Women young enough to have dependent children usually remarried (and sometimes remained, for their treasurers, their comptrollers and stewards at any rate, the heads of the household – note the headings of the accounts of the remarried Margaret Beaufort and of Anne, first Dowager Duchess of Buckingham, which name them as the mistress of the household). Most of the surviving accounts of widows are, then, for older women. Sometimes they retired to a subsidiary home, often on part of their dower lands, but sometimes they continued to live in the same household as the heir, especially if he or she was unmarried; not always with happy results. Joan Stonor and her son William eventually came to litigation, and she moved out of the main house at Stonor when her son remarried. It is very rare to find a household in which a parent resided with an adult married child. One possible example is Lady Margaret Long of Hengrave Hall (Cambridgeshire), whose husband died in 1545; the Elizabeth who lived with them in 1541–5 appears by her expenses to be a likely daughter by a previous marriage, and may be the same Elizabeth Kytson who appears in the accounts for 1563–4, possibly having married Margaret's ward Thomas Kytson. Elizabeth oversaw the latter accounts, so presumably she and Thomas were adults at this time.

Siblings cohabiting is equally unusual. Orphaned siblings (or cousins), of course, might form the sole familial core of a household, particularly among the higher nobility (see, for instance, the accounts of John of Brabant and Thomas and Henry of Lancaster, 1292–3, and the sons of Humphrey de Bohun and Roger Mortimer, 1341–2), and the royal children often lived in their own separate household apart from the court; but it is unusual to find adult siblings living together, unless during the few years between childhood and marriage. Joan and Thomas Arundel are a notable exception. When the latter was Bishop of Ely his older sister Joan, a widow, often lived in his household for long periods of time, and the two were obviously very close.[1] Again, in some families adult siblings visited each other frequently, with more protracted visits at Christmas or Easter. But such familiarity is by no means a rule. Often siblings, by the accounts' telling at least, appear to have nothing to do with one another. One possible exception is, oddly enough, the monastic household. The *generosi* servants of the abbot were often related to one of the monks under him, or to the abbot himself, or to a monk who was a member of his household; and the relationship may have been brotherhood.

Outside monastic households, less immediate family – nephews, nieces, aunts, uncles, cousins of various degrees – living in the household as members of the family or as servants is uncommon. When it does occur, they are almost always children. Adults are found in this situation most frequently in episcopal households; not, for instance, Richard de Swinfield, Bishop of Hereford, whose brother Stephen, with Stephen's juvenile son, another young nephew and on occasion the bishop's nephew Gilbert de Swinfield (who was also his chancellor for the diocese), all dwelt in his household.[2] The obvious lack of immediately family on the part of bishops or abbots may account for their greater tendency to gather around them collateral relatives, a kind of surrogate familial nucleus. Actual servants bearing a kin relationship to the lord are very uncommon, practically nonexistent, and, apart from possible exceptions in some monastic households, are very distant relations, often by marriage. Hugh Luttrell of Dunster's chamberer, for instance, was a cousin of his wife Catherine's first husband. It is possible that the problem of combining both employment and kinship was then, as it is now, at best an uneasy juggling act, and that the very fluidity caused by living together, which may have allowed for no firm divide between family and servants, made the situation even more difficult. Significantly, it is not so hard to find kin, including close kin, serving as estate officials and as members of the lord's council, where day-to-day relationships were not so intimate.

Friends, clients, counsellors, retainers, allies, and estate servants can also be troublesome to define. Many of these spent considerable time in the household; some of them purveyed for it, or carried messages, or even paid servant's wages. The later medieval noble household was a loosely defined organization whose boundaries were never clear.

[1]Margaret Aston, *Thomas Arundel: A Study of Church Life in the Reign of Richard II* (Oxford University Press, Oxford, 1967), pp. 171–4, 181.

[2]John Webb, ed., *Household Roll of Bishop Swinfield* (Camden Society, London, vols 59 and 62, 1855), vol. 62, pp. xxxii, lix.

Nevertheless a receiver-general, a knightly member of the lord's affinity (the nobleman's allies, tied to him by feudal bonds or monetary arrangements) with his own estates, a social equal who sat on commissions with a master of the household – these were perhaps in the household frequently, but they were not always of it; they were not invariably part of its organizational framework. The duties they fulfilled for it were casual; their time spent in it was that of guests served by it, not members working as part of it; they were not accountable to its chief servants. However, it is important to remember that the household was in a sense there for them as well as for the lord. As the most intimate of his tools for patronage, hospitality and the organization of his life, it was the basis of his affinity, of his widest *familia*, and its finances might be closely tied to the estate servants' duties. But for purposes of definition, we shall treat as household members only those who are salaried on a household wage list, who are given household titles or who are held responsible to its masters, though we will at times discover interesting parallels between household members and membership in the lord's wider affinity.

A second complication in determining household members is a rather different problem of identity. Even when we have before us a list of household members, we may not be able to say anything about them as individuals. In some cases we have only christian names, or just titles; but even household members whose surnames survive may present difficulties of identification. Surnames which are occupational in origin, like Hunte and Cook and Gardner and Smith, are in the late fifteenth century still only partially hereditary and not necessarily fixed to their owners.[3] In other words, while most John Huntes were sons of persons named Hunte or Hunt, some still received that surname because they were hunts or huntsmen; and the same Hunte might be called John Hunte or John Thomson, interchangeably. One must always keep in mind these problems of identity, and act cautiously in attempting to place individuals. Most deductions in this endeavour are likely to result in probabilities rather than proofs, unless the internal evidence of the account is particularly strong. Since, however, it has been estimated that one quarter to one half of the population of England in pre-modern times were servants (though not of course solely in noble households) at some point in their lives,[4] any light shed on noble servants illuminates a

---

[3]P.H. Reaney, *A Dictionary of British Surnames* (Routledge and Kegan Paul, London, 1958), pp. xxxviii–xlii.

[4]P. Laslett, *The World We Have Lost – Further Explored* (Methuen, London, 1983), pp. 13–16, 64–5.

significant portion of medieval life. Several thousand names of household servants survive in the remaining records, but only for about a quarter of these can some specific biographical information be provided, and much of it would be very scanty indeed. Here a more general analysis of household servants will therefore be presented, divided into four main areas of concern: the background of the household servant; the connections which led him to take service in the household; the nature of his tenure within the household; and his relations with the household after he left it.

The reader may note here that the household member is assigned the male pronoun. This is less chauvinistic than it may seem, as female household members were practically nonexistent. Those we do find are invariably chamberwomen and companions to the lady of the household and nursery servants, restricted to the private portions of the house (and often married to another servant); or laundresses, who much of the time lived outside the household. The medieval serving wench is a myth created by Hollywood and the extravagances of restoration drama. Not until the seventeenth century did women really come to form a significant part of a great household's staff. The multiple roles of the household as an important political mechanism and economic unit as well as a domestic centre probably helped to exclude women from major offices in the household – though there are a few examples of women serving as clerks and stewards and estate agents, usually in the years following the death·of a husband holding that office and often in the employ of a widow. As long as household service was a job of some prestige it was coveted by parents for their sons, not their daughters. The proliferation of women servants at a later date accompanies the household's decline in more than domestic significance.

The household was also, however, actively hostile to the presence of women. Numerous courtesy and householding handbooks warn against the dangers of women and especially laundresses in the household; King Henry VI allegedly believed that women of all kinds should be kept out of the royal household.[5] Most lords seem to have agreed, clearly preferring to appoint single rather than married men even if the married man's wife lived outside the household. Single men were always more common in any household than married ones – due, of course, in part to the number of those in clerical orders – and it is single men who

[5]'The ABC of Aristotle', 'Bishop Grossetestes's Household Rules' and Hugh Rhodes' 'Boke of Nurture', in F.J. Furnivall, ed., The Babees Book (Early English Texts Society, Oxford, vol. 32, 1868).

most often held the most responsible positions as chief servants and
who achieved the most dramatic changes in status through the
household. The financial drain on the servant required to support a wife
and family, and the dangers to women in a house full of frequently
unoccupied men, may have prompted such strictures. Margery Kemp's
indignant record of her rough greeting at the hands of the servants of
Thomas Arundel supports this.[6] But ordinances and courtesy books
make clear that it is the reputation and honour of the household, not
the women, which is a matter for concern. 'Maids', 'women', 'boyes',
and 'symple servants' are discouraged as camp followers of the
household members, whose attendants were, by the fifteenth century,
laid down by statute; they were supposed to be interviewed and
approved by the chief officers of the household, both noble and royal,
to see that they were honest, and 'of good stature, gesture and
behaviour' so as not to bring discredit upon the household.[7] All statutes
specify male servants. By removing women from the household,
particularly unattached women of lower social status, lords sought to
preserve a private vision of a decorous and orderly following which
would redound to their credit, and within which life would be quiet and
contained, undisturbed by the sexual intrigue which a man's world saw
to be caused by women. It is a vision of life not unlike that of certain
monastic rules.

But the household was never wholly devoid of women. Even abbatial
establishments admitted laundresses (male clothes-washers, except in
the royal household, were not common), who might be associated
closely enough with the household to receive a daily livery of food and
drink, and any lady in the household required personal servants and
companions. Parents sought to place young daughters in the coveted
position of lady-in-waiting to a noble mistress, and competition was
fierce, for such positions were of necessity few in comparison to the sort
of posts in the household available for sons. In most cases 'the ladies of
the lady' were her social equals or nearly so (except for a few humble
individuals who performed the most menial tasks in the lady's private
quarters), and were generally young single women and girls. A few,
however, were widows, and some married couples were appointed to
the household, in tandem as it were, usually he to a fairly important
post, she to the lady's chambers. Widows at the head of a household

[6]Margery Kempe, *The Book of Margery Kempe*, ed. S.B. Meech and H.E. Allen (Early
English Texts Society, Oxford, vol. 212, 1940), pp. 36, 274–5.

[7]See, for instance, the Ordinances of Eltham of Henry VIII and the ordinances for the
household of George Duke of Clarence, Soc. Ant., eds, *A Collection of Ordinances and
Regulations* (John Nichols, London, 1790), pp. 146–9, 94.

tended to a wider complement of female servants, though posts outside personal service were still generally preserved for men. Brew-wives were employed by many households but they were usually local women, who did not live in the household but were merely retained to supply it with ale from their own cottages. So the majority of women in the household were of gentle or well-off yeoman stock.

Household members as a whole covered a wide spectrum of social events. Gentry, and, in some cases, nobility; farming or mercantile families; the urban and rural poor; foreigners, locals and Londoners; all had their place in any household, though in general the bulk of household members were from local, agriculturally employed family groups, peasant or yeoman. Most exceptions to this rule occur at the upper end of the household hierarchy, and more commonly in the bigger and more noble households. The posts of chief servants, heads of departments, and some positions for gentlemen might often, though certainly not always, be filled by those of gentle birth, particularly in the households of the greater baronage. Where men of considerable standing, landholders, active in political life and well known at court, heads of households themselves, might hold household positions, particularly as ushers, esquires or gentlemen of the hall or chamber. The *Northumberland Household Book* throughout implies that such positions were often filled in rotation; that is, the Percys employed large numbers of household gentlemen but only a quarter or so were required to be in attendance at any one time. This stretched the number of men the Percys could legally retain, and allowed men of considerable standing to be part of their household, whilst it was still possible for them to look after their own affairs the rest of the year. For many gentles these positions were probably sinecures which involved them in little actual work and less commitment to the household.

It is also generally the case, however, that these individual servants or their families were part of the lord's affinity or retinue in its most commonly applied sense: that is, they received annual fees or annuities from the lord in question, and in some cases were bound to him by indenture,[8] in the hope that they would provide him with moral, political and, ultimately, armed support and counsel when he required it. The *Northumberland Household Book*, again, allows for the payment of members of the Earl's Council as householders if not feed by patent (in section 5). Gentle servants most often came from families whose members had traditionally been retained by the servants' masters. The livery roll of Edward Courtenay, Earl of Devon, for

[8]See, for instance, PRO C47/37/3/24, Stonor chequerroll, 1468–72.

1384–5 includes such names as Prideaux, Camoys, Malet, Clifford, Ferrers and Champernoun. While in lesser families the names of the upper servants are not so illustrious, peers are retained on a commensurate level. The Cornwallis family of Brome Hall (Suffolk), for instance, employed as their household steward Robert Melton, a well established local landholder of gentle status.[9]

These ties between the household was the wider affinity add to our understanding of how retaining worked. For the lord, such double connections might strengthen the bonds between himself and his gentle retainers, who usually received annuities from more than one magnate; and they might provide him with an effective means of sanction over retained individuals and family groups who withheld support when it was required. Recipients of annuities who also had a connection with the lord's household certainly gained, not merely more income, but also an 'inside ear', as it were, which could both entreat for favours and obtain important information more easily than a retainer outside the householding establishment. In any wise, household members retained by annuity formed a significant part of a lord's feed annuity – about a quarter of the first Duke of Buckingham's retinue[10] and retainers with relatives inside the lord's household are not uncommon.

These same men might have been more involved in the actual life of a gentle household when younger. Those gentles who actually took service were usually either younger sons who needed to make their way in the world and could aid their family by a household connection; young children and teenagers, male and female, serving as henchmen, pages and companions to the lady while completing their education in a grand establishment; or heirs prior to their assumption of the family responsibilities, who were educated in an environment suitable to their station, and also achieved early connections for themselves and their families through their positions. Their length of service might not be very great, but it was often significant for them in its consequence of alliance and patronage; and while they served, they were often deeply committed to the household in terms of time and energy. Finally, some gentlemen did make a career of household service, particularly if they were younger sons or held little land of their own. Cardinal Wolsey's devoted gentlemen-ushers had in some cases served him for twenty years, and many stayed by him after his fall from grace.

However, even in the households of the greatest nobles, many

[9]Accounts of 1499–1508 in Lady Caroline Kerrison and Lucy Toulmin Smith, eds, *A Commonplace Book of the Fifteenth Century* (Trubner, London, 1886).

[10]Carol Rawcliffe, *The Staffords, Earls of Stafford and Dukes of Buckingham* (Cambridge University Press, Cambridge, 1979), appendix D, pp. 232–42.

important servants as well as those in lesser positions were drawn, not from the ranks of the gentry, but from simple yeoman or peasant families. One could cite many examples, such as that of William Wistowe, a Stafford clerk of the *forensica* and *magna hospicium* and later treasurer and steward (1438–70), who came from the yeoman or peasant classes of the village of Wistenstowe, Staffordshire.[11] These yeomen and peasants, with their families, for whom household service could be an important basis of individual or family fortune, form the basis of the background of most household servants. Household service was often for them a lucrative full-time career, and if they were able they could attain the heights of household responsibility. Since they put the household first, most lords probably found people of humbler station preferable in chief posts like steward, treasurer, etc., jobs which required an attention a gentleman might not be able to give.

Geographically as well as socially, the backgrounds of servants can be identified. By far the great majority of householders were 'locals', that is, natives of the general vicinity in which a lord and his household usually dwelt. This holds true for servants of all classes. Of some twenty traceable servants in the Luttrell households from 1405 to 1432, fully twelve have geographically placeable names, all of which are from Devon and Somerset, and most from the hundred of Carhampton, the seat of which was Dunster. More specifically, a comparison of the surnames of this household with those on the manorial records of its home estate show many correlations.[12] Simply in terms of sheer availability, local people were the obvious source for householders; servant and master had greater access to sanctions should the household tenure prove unsatisfactory to either; and of course both local and lord had a vested interest in forming an alliance with each other, whether this was the lord's or gentle family's desire to create a local power bloc, or the peasant's to find a ready buyer for his ale.

Two exceptions can be noted to this tendency to employ as household servants local people of various classes. Firstly, lords with major holdings or business connections in London often hired people from that metropolis to serve in their country households. Families like the Petres, the Stonors and the Pagets, whose business and court connections brought them to London often and who maintained houses there, are examples. The retinues of the higher baronage and episcopacy, similarly, often included Londoners. Their attendance at

[11]Ibid., pp. 71–3.
[12]H.C. Maxwell-Lyte, *Dunster and its Lords, 1066–1881* (privately printed, 1882), pp. 428–43.

court and Parliament meant that they generally maintained a London house, through service in which Londoners often moved to service in the main household. One also finds that in most households a few foreign servants were employed. It is not always easy to tell by surname the origins of a servant, but oddities of English usage or outright statement in a chequerroll about origins in the case of foreign servants show that French people at least are not all that unusual in English households. Families like the Lisles, Sir Anthony Brown, and clerics like Anthony Bek who served overseas, were most likely to employ foreigners.

With a modicum of exceptions, however, the vast majority of servants in any household were likely to be from a yeoman or peasant family which was local to the general area of the employing household. But many people were local to a household without becoming servants within it. We need to examine the kinds of connections between an individual and a household or master which led to the taking of service.

Those gentle families whose members joined a noble household almost always formed part of the master of that household's community of peers, people he probably grew up with and as an adult saw frequently – gentles and nobles who served with him as MPs, sheriffs, members of commissions, JPs, royal administrators of various kinds. These families' members and heads, as we have seen earlier, often sat on the lord's council and received his annuities, or granted annuities to him. They formed with the lord the network of local, and sometimes national, power. Most such families had younger sons who required a position in life; their children when they reached their early teens also had to be found a proper environment. Naturally enough, gentle families turned first to the households of their peers, which were a prime source of profitable, honourable employment, and which had the additional advantage of strengthening ties between the families. In turn, the master of a household would be likely to seek his upper servants by enquiring among his peers.

Unless the employment was unsatisfactory, such a system tended to strengthen the bonds which held together the upper classes, particularly on a local level. For instance, on the Essex peace commission of 1547, the names of those appointed along with the sixteenth Earl of Oxford were Wentworth, Darcy, Waldegrave, Pyrton, Tyrrell, Wiseman, Josselyn, Lucas, Danyell, Tay, Cardinall, and Heigham – all families who had provided servants to the de Veres over the preceding seventy-five years. Of these twelve families, moreover, seven had relations serving the sixteenth earl in 1550–1.[13] William Paston, who served with

13CPR 1461–76, p. 405.

the thirteenth de Vere earl from c.1487 to c.1503, shows us the working of this system of relationships in more detail. In his three surviving letters home and the replies sent to him from his brother John, he reports on the earl's every movement and is plagued for information on his master's state of mind and attitude to the Pastons; the earl and the Pastons use William to convey frequent messages one to the other. This was the same sort of system which operated in the king's household: one need only recall John Paston II's activities on behalf of his family when he was a member of Edward IV's household.[14]

Less exalted households of the gentry also took their higher servants from among the families of their community of peers. Robert Waterton of Mexborough (Yorkshire), for instance, employed members of the Best and Whitwode families in his household who almost certainly came from the local landowning families of that name, and the LeStranges of Hunstanton (Norfolk) regularly had in their household members of the Camoys family. Much in the way that public school men keep hold of their personal and professional ascendancy by using personal connections to forge a network of influence, preference and power, relying on each other to find or fill desirable jobs, the nobles of the realm created a web of relationships which was very hard to break through, so densely was it woven. The employment of each other's family members in the household was one thread of this sytem.

Lesser jobs and menial services required in the household did not, however, generally appeal to gentle relations, however poor; nor were such positions close enough to the master to provide any extra advantages for the lord or the gentle servant. Butlers, cooks, sewers, laundresses, stableboys, etc. were drawn from outside the master's community of peers. But they, too, were not retained through an employment bureau, but tended to come from families that had more humble connections with the household or the master. Most of those lower servants who can be identified came from the area most immediately around the household's main geographical centre; and many of these seem to have been members of families that were tenants of the lord, or with whom his household dealt for supplies. Robert and Thomas Bennett, household members from 1417 to 1420 to William and Margaret Cromwell, were members of a Tydd tenant farming family which also sold grain to the household. Walter Kebbell, steward to Ralph Cromwell 1444–6, was a tenant farmer of his master. John Cobham's *camerarius*, Thomas Gyffard, was almost certainly related to

[14]Norman Davis, ed., *Paston Letters and Papers of the Fifteenth Century* (Clarendon Press, Oxford, 2 vols, 1971 and 1976), vol. I, nos 72, 116, 120, 231, 232, 392, 414; vol. II, nos 748, 848.

the John Gyffard who sold fish to his household in 1408.

The simple availablity of these people who were already connected with the household or the master in some way made them an obvious choice. Household service provided well for some of the landless members of smallholding families and offered a potentially useful connection with a noble whose power over them was an important factor in their lives. For the lord, the employment of tenantry and trading families could help to tie local loyalties to himself. Very similar sources of employment were exploited to fill the ranks of the lord's estate services; and we often find that families and individuals who served as estate ministers also filled household positions.

The family was a political and economic as well as a social unit in the middle ages, so that it is not surprising to find that initially household servants got their positions through various kinds of family connections. But it also becomes apparent that families as a whole, not just individual members, could hold a tradition of household service to a particular noble family, just as some families were traditionally members of certain affinities. A list of household servants in a given year may prove not only to show a predominance of local families but to include many relatives. A comparison of chequerrolls covering several generations of masters and servants usually expresses even more clearly such a tradition of service passing from father to nephew or son to cousin or grandson. Many examples could be given, falling into three classes.

Firstly, one can discover numerous members of a single generation of related servants working for one master. We have already mentioned the frequency of married couples. In 1411–12 Ankaretta, Lady Talbot of Blakemere (Shropshire) had in her service two brothers, Hecock and Richard Wodward. Robert Waterton of Mexborough's two servants (1914–28), Richard and William Best, were either brothers or cousins. Several generations of a family, sometimes father and son, might also serve one lord. John Tamworth and his adolescent son were part of Ralph Cromwell's household, 1445–7; the Stonors employed from 1468 to 1472 a John White the elder and an adult John White the younger, his son; and, in the 1470s, at least seven Blackhalls, including at least one father and son. Furthermore, one frequently finds that such family traditions were so firmly rooted as to carry from one master to his heir. Many of the surnames of servants in the accounts of John Howard, first Duke of Norfolk, in 1462 are found in that of Thomas the second duke of 1525; this phenomenon is indeed common in all household records which cover several generations, including monastic households, and involves both gentle and humble servants. The establishments of bishops, perhaps not surprisingly, show little of this sort of familial continuity between bishops succeeding each other to the same see, though it was not uncommon for a bishop to take on some of the servants of his predecessor, depending on his own previous state.[15] Where it did occur, the continuation of these familial bonds of service over several generations served to strengthen further the ties between a lord's family, his peers and his followers.

Various traditional community ties brought individuals and groups into household service, and in turn affected the nature of their tenure in the household: who tended to fill what positions, for how long and under what circumstances, and what servants in general stood to gain from household service. It has already been mentioned that recruits from the gentry usually entered the upper ranks of the household. This did not, however, rebound on the yeomen and peasant men who entered the household. They too might become stewards, or treasurers, and receive the title of 'gentleman'; especially if they came of a family with a long record of service. William Wistowe, John Heton, the Hextalls, and William Cholmeley, all of obscure origins, rose to the highest positions in the Stafford household,[16] probably the most prestigious princely court (excepting the royal court) in the fifteenth and early sixteenth centuries. 'The commons', however, also filled the lower positions of the household, while no example of a born gentleman taking on a household job of little prestige can be found.

In brief, yeomen and peasants probably had to show merit to obtain profitable household positions, while gentry normally seem to have come to such offices as of right. Besides the positions of chief servants and heads of departments, gentry were especially assigned to chamber service, which by closeness to the lord raised such positions above other household placements in terms of influence, responsibilities and salaries. Though naturally not all chamberers were of gentle birth, lords probably preferred to associate with men near their own social status, and clearly the gentle servitor preferred and expected such a position. It is perhaps significant that most commoners, such as Wistowe and Cholmeley, who rose to key household positions did so through accounting positions and became *majores domi*, rather than rising through or into the chamber. Members of common families with a tradition of service, however, probably obtained prestigious appointments more readily than other commoners. They were also, probably, absolutely as well as individually preferred for household service. The

[15] Aston, *Thomas Arundel*, p. 251.
[16] Rawcliffe, *The Staffords*, p. 166.

Plate 6 Companionship engendered by a common occupation. Egerton Ms. 3307, f. 72v. English, c. 1440. Courtesy of The British Library.

Jegons, for instance, began serving the de Veres as gardeners and stable hands; by 1513 one Jegon entered the fourteenth earl's household as a caterer, a position of considerable responsibility.

Having obtained a placement in the household, the evidence suggests that servants stayed there a long time, making of householding a life's career. Examples of twenty years' tenure are not at all unusual. When we consider that any household account certainly fails to mention all the servants employed in the year accounted, and that long gaps of twenty or more years may intervene between accounts, so that the tenure of any given servant is likely to be longer than the period we can be sure of, the percentage of servants who served in households over ten years is likely to be considerably higher than the 40 per cent continuity common to all households with records covering a long period of time. In the households of lay nobles, continuation of service between a lord and the heir is very much the rule.

The exceptions are significant. Families and individual servants of the Cromwell family can seldom be traced for more than three or four years in their accounts. This may be due to the inheritance pattern in this family. It was indirect – from uncle to nephew to niece; it involved in the first instance a geographical change, from Tydd to Tattershall; and it occurred in the adulthood of the heirs, when they had already formed their own groups of servants around themselves. They were thus more likely to carry their own households with them to their new inheritance rather than take on their predecessor's men. Cromwellian figures are also misleading because gaps of twenty and more years occur between the three sets of accounts, during which time individuals and even families common to several Cromwells could die off. This, added to the problem of accounts seldom tending to register all servants, obviates the apparent lack of continuity among servants of the Cromwells. Episcopal households also generally do not show much continuity between one bishop and his successor, for much the same reasons – most new incumbents already had a following, and the lack of familial ties between succeeding bishops removed one reason for employing the servants of a predecessor. Conversely, monastic servants customarily had very long careers; in 1495 a prior of Durham remarked that 'it is one custom of owr place to discharge none old officer ne seruand of hys office ne service with owte reasonable cause require it.'[17] Servants spanned two or more generations of masters, major reversals of fortune, and sometimes fundamental geographical upheavals. One suspects that

---

[17]Richard Barry Dobson, *Durham Priory, 1400–50* (Cambridge University Press, Cambridge, 1973), p. 120.

positive advantages as well as altruistic loyalties combined to encourage servants to stay on in households.

I have already suggested that household service provided a convenient, honourable living for landless younger sons of the upper ranks of society, and an education for gently born children. It also provided a further contact between the master and his servants' families, gentry yeoman or peasant. More personally, the servant himself, and his descendants, could also gain considerably through household service. Food, clothing, and shelter were provided free, on top of a generous salary. While sleeping conditions could be crowded, upper servants sometimes got their own rooms. The regular grants of livery given to servants, meant to reflect the master's wealth and status, were often much more than adequate. Relatively high living standards were part of a servant's perquisites, and did not encroach upon his salary, which ranged from stable groom and kitchen boy at 6s 8d–13s 4d per annum, to the gentleman or chamber valet at 40s, to the steward at 10 li or over. If they wished, servants could amass a small fortune over years of service, especially as salaries were frequently supplemented by rewards, tips, Christmas and other holiday bonuses, and annuities granted by the master, usually after a long period of service. Bartholomew de Crek, former servant of Eleanor de Mountford, Countess of Leicester, and his wife Margaret were given an annuity, many presents and a holding;[18] and John Russell, Humphrey Duke of Gloucester's marshal, can also be cited as an example of comfortable retirement on proceeds from household service.[19]

A further illustration of servants' living standards and status achieved through household positions can be found in contemporary sumptuary laws, which regulated individuals' conspicuous consumption by their position in society, especially by means of personal costume. Among those types of people specifically mentioned as offenders are merchants; rich peasants; and household members, who are accused of using their positions to wear clothes improper to their station: types of fur, 'dagged' or intricately cut cloth, exceptionally long sleeves and shoe points – all matters of costume technically restricted to the nobility. Nevertheless, due to the gentility conferred upon them by household service, servants (while not a separate classification in sumptuary laws) were allowed privileges in costume denied others born into a similar position in society. A yeoman farmer, for instance, was not allowed to use some of the dyes legally permitted in the livery of a yeoman groom

[18]Margaret Wade LaBarge, *A Baronial Household of the Thirteenth Century* (Eyre and Spottiswoode, 1965), pp. 49–50.
[19]Furnivall, *Babees Book*, pp. xc–cii.

or usher in a great household. Clearly, the advantageous position of household members is shown in these laws. They could legitimately raise their status, and their standards of comfort and elegance, higher than that of their relatives outside the household. Moreover, servants could and did use this householding status, excess funds and their masters' indulgence to adopt the outward signs of a gentility which Parliament was not willing to award them.[20]

Little that is concrete can be said about the actual satisfaction of servants with their masters and vice versa, or the fierceness of competition for favours and advancement within the household; but the long terms of service and low rate of turnover of many household members, as well as the advantages outlined above, suggest a relatively relaxed environment, and show that the maintenance of a household position was not particularly difficult. The *Northumberland Household Book* throughout stresses that servants such as ushers, sewers, etc. should work in shifts, morning and afternoon and evening, rather than all day, and the hours at which even the chief servants are expected to be at work seldom amount to a total of more than four or five per day. All ordinances, including such as 'Bishop Grosseteste's Household Rules', emphasize that lords and stewards should be careful to regulate servants' trips home (presumably to their wives and families if married) so that they are not all gone at once, indicating perhaps that servants were inclined to go off without warning and presumably without much interference.

Some lords were rather hard and exacting masters; the third Duke of Buckingham, the Pastons and John Mowbray, third Duke of Norfolk, had reputations for being irascible and suspicious of servants.[21] And of course, disagreements and tensions occurred among the servants of every household, as in any community, sometimes to the point of affecting their duties. Stonor servants Goddard Oxbridge and David Wryham became embroiled in a series of charges and countercharges, concerning each other's fitness and honesty, that took William Stonor some time to sort out.[22] Again, much of the legislation restricting retaining includes exhortations to masters that part of their responsibilities as lords was to prevent their legally retained servants (that is,

---

[20]N.B. Harte, 'State Control of Dress and Social Change in Pre-Industrial England', in D.C. Coleman and A.H. John, *Trade, Government and Economy in Pre-Industrial England* (Weidenfeld and Nicolson, London, 1976), pp. 132–65.

[21]Rawcliffe, *The Staffords*, pp. 165–6; Davis, *Paston Letters*, vol. 1, nos 72, 73, 75, 117.

[22]Charles Lethbridge Kingsford, ed., *The Stonor Letters and Papers, 1290–1483* (Camden Society, London, vols 29 and 30, 1919), vol. 30, no. 213.

Plate 7 An argument over a game of backgammon – often a reason for gambling. Stowe 17, f. 268v. Flemish, 13th–14th century. Courtesy of The British Library.

household members) from quarrelling and lawless behaviour, both among themselves and with outsiders, especially the servants of other lords.[23] But it was still possible for someone like Reginald Seynesbury, who lost a horse and ruined twelve stones of tallow, and whose surviving personal account is a lesson in poor clerical procedure, to work in the Luttrell household for at least nineteen years, from 1405 to 1424.

Nevertheless, there was a place for ambition and advancement, especially through the establishments of the greater magnates. Within the household, some servants of ability could and did advance to responsible positions, entailing greater salaries, more annuities, some influence, authority within their sphere – a kind of vicarious power, in short, or second-hand greatness. Advancement could occur over a long or relatively short period of time; but in most cases where it can be identified it follows a pattern.

The most spectacular cases of advancement occurred among the accountants of the household, who might rise from obscure origins to positions of great authority. William of Wortham rose from a minor position in the household of Bishop Robert Grosseteste of Lincoln (c.1253) to that of steward of the household and counsellor of Simon de Mountford, Earl of Leicester.[24] In the household of Thomas Arundel, Bishop of Ely, boy choristers rose to yeoman status, yeomen to clerical orders and a clerical post in the household, and from thence to a benefice and a post like chaplain or treasurer or an estate post.[25] Robert Draper, a Luttrell sub-clerk from 1420 to 1422, became steward in 1426. Richard Bell, steward of the Prior of Durham's household 1443–6, became his almoner in 1447, warden of Durham College in 1450, prior in 1464, and Bishop of Carlisle in 1478. These men were, probably, at least minor clerics; they progressed sometimes in less than ten years through lower clerical positions, where they could gain practical experience, before proceeding to the more important offices. One does not find men progressing to responsible accounting positions through the chamber, or via hall or stable service. Laymen who held the other positions of chief servants usually were of gentle blood, and did not progress to such positions through the household, but were appointed to them straightaway, usually with some experience in estates service behind them.

It would perhaps be wise, here, to consider clerical servants in more

[23] A.S. Turberville, 'The Protection of Servants of MPs', *English Historical Review* 42 (1927), pp. 89–106.
[24] LaBarge, *Baronial Household*, p. 63.
[25] Aston, *Thomas Arundel*, pp. 245–6.

detail. Those terms '*dominus*', '*clericus*' or sometimes 'sir' were an important element in the household, and were those who most commonly gained the greatest advancement. By the fifteenth century, the use of *clericus* may refer to a lay accountant as to someone in holy orders; since we cannot trace many ordinations of household *clerici* – even of those who were chaplains and therefore assuredly in orders of some kind – we must be careful not to assume they were all in orders. We may note, however, that the term was by far most commonly applied to those in clerical orders, even as late as 1600, and the use of complimentary terms like '*dominus*' and 'sir' were also often used to distinguish clerks. Many of those servants called *clerici* were of obscure origins rather than of the gentry. Many have no kind of familial connection with the lord as part of his affinity or clientage (though their names may show a locality connection). However, many examples exist of lords, especially bishops, acting as sponsor to a bright but poor scholar who eventually came to his service. The model letters of Thomas Sampson cite numerous such situations.[26]

Such churchmen, unmarried, with no inherited interests, might owe everything to their patrons, and must have seemed especially valuable and loyal servants. They might also be the best educated. The Oxford grammar masters provided business training, much of it specifically directed to teaching the skills needed for running a great household or estate. After these died out in the mid-fifteenth century, scholars may have obtained training at local grammar schools, learning the diplomatic, accounting and legal skills necessary to their positions. Some, of course, probably learned their skills through reading treatises, or by experience and observation. In any case accountants were likely to be the most learned and able men in the household, whether in religious orders or not, and were able to aspire to its highest positions. Episcopal households relied most heavily on those in clerical orders for servants of all kinds, often paid by benefice instead of wages; but all households contained some clerical element.

Though accounting training of some kind was virtually imperative if a servant were to rise to the highest household positions, servants without gentle blood or clerical qualifications could also advance themselves, though less dramatically. William Tylly, a general house-holder earning 13s 4d per annum from Hugh Luttrell in 1405–6, had become household cook by 1420, with a wage increase to 20s per

[26]H.G. Richardson, 'An Oxford Teacher of the Fifteenth Century', *Bulletin of the John Rylands Library* 23 (1939), pp. 436–57; and H.G. Richardson, 'Business Teaching in Medieval Oxford', *American Historical Review* 46 (1940–1), pp. 259–68.

annum. John Kirk, a valet of the guarderobe to the third Duke of Buckingham, rose to become a gentleman-usher of the chamber.[17] Though these may seem minor advances, they represented substantial increases in status and living standards to the servants, often of peasant or yeoman stock, who achieved them. Such promotions could also carry over into life outside the household, and perhaps on to future generations.

Despite the tendency to long tenures, not all servants died, as it were, in harness. Those who left the household did so under varying circumstances, and with different results. Gentry who had their own political careers and financial interests had the shortest tenures, as has been noted, unless their positions were wholly sinecures; but many of these continued to receive annuities from their erstwhile employer, clearly remaining within his affinity. One might also suspect that their time as household members, if satisfactory, strengthened the bonds between them and their lord within the local and national community. This was certainly true of wellborn child servants. Antony Danvers (probably a son or nephew of Sir John Danvers of Dauntsey, Wiltshire), who was a henchman to the thirteenth Earl of Oxford in 1506, received an annuity in the earl's will; Lord Fitzwalter, who before his attainder was reversed was also a child servant to him, remained a member of the earl's retinue as an adult, receiving a yearly fee.[28]

But even those who had made householding a career might leave the service of a lord. Some, of course, left under unhappy circumstances, but most servants seem to have surrendered their positions more happily. Servants changed households on occasion, some even entering royal service. Others became estate servants or turned to farming. But old age seems to have been the most frequent cause of some kind of retirement. John Russell, in the *Boke of Nurture*, speaks of the annuity granted him by Humphrey, Duke of Gloucester, which allowed him a secure and comfortable old age.[29] Pensions, annuities and lump sums were often provided for servants in the wills of their masters, especially for those with a long record of service. At the very least, servants were usually granted their wages for six months or a year beyond their master's death – a form of redundancy pay – and such pensions were as commonly granted in the master's lifetime. Hugh Luttrell's clerk of the

[27]PRO E/101/518/5 and PRO E/36/220.

[28]J. Payne Collier, ed., *Household Books of John Duke of Norfolk and Thomas Earl of Surrey, 1481–90* (Roxburghe Club, London, vol. 61, 1844), pp. 509–20; and Sir William St John Hope, ed., 'The Last Testament and Inventory of John de Vere, Thirteenth Earl of Oxford', *Archaeologia* 66 (1915), pp. 336–7.

[29]Furnivall, *Babees Book*, pp. 511–20.

household, Robert Draper, may also have been of retirement age, or experienced some religious fervour, when he became a monk in 1426. He continued in close relations with the household, being sent presents by Sir Hugh and accompanying Hugh's sister Joan, a nun at Shaftesbury, on her journeys to Dunster in 1428 and 1429.

Satisfactory household servants clearly could expect a comfortable and secure life, perhaps well above that which their personal, social and financial status at birth might have indicated. Whether they were able to raise the position of their families and descendants, and how far, is, however, another question. This problem is complicated by the fact that those servants who made the most dramatic ascents were clerics or unmarried men who had no families to provide for. Similarly, younger sons of families – gentle or peasant – did not necessarily profit from or contribute to their families' status directly. But could such younger sons establish a cadet branch, through a fortune gathered from household service? We may consider George Cavendish, Wolsey's gentleman-usher, who was able to support wife and children in a manor house and leave a comfortable inheritance, which his own inherited wealth could not have afforded.[30] I have not found, however, that many families in which father succeeded son in household service rose significantly in social status either within the household or without it, though their standard of living must have improved. Household members may have become more comfortably established in their social niche, but they did not often climb into a higher one. Such social climbing as did exist was restricted, perhaps consciously, to unmarried men or clerics who would not pass on any meritocratic advances to a second generation. Household service, then, provided comfortable and advantageous positions for individuals and their families, and also aided and participated in systems of loyalties and alliances between peers, lords, clients and peasants as the basis for an extended network of political, social and economic relationships.

[30]George Cavendish, *The Life and Death of Cardinal Wolsey*, ed. Richard Sylvester (Early English Texts Society, London, vol. 243, 1959), pp. 7–10.

3
The Household and the Economy

If I
Had servants true about me, that bare eyes
To see alike mine honour as their profits,
Their own particular thrifts, they would do that
Which should undo more doing.

The Winter's Tale (I. ii)

The medieval noble household existed to create an environment which its master found congenial, and to provide for his needs and comforts. We tend to think of those needs fulfilled by the household as domestic in nature, and indeed they were, primarily. But these homely requirements sometimes had larger consequences for medieval society as a whole, and the household was on many occasions called to wider duties, far-reaching in their implications. When we look at the household from an economist's point of view, we discover not only how a noble's establishment was funded, and how and where it spent money, but also something of its master's estate management system, and his role in national, international and especially local trade. We discover important information about cottage industries, and factors of supply and demand. Our knowledge of the noble household and medieval economics is particularly aided by our source material: accounts are essentially economic records, and tell us most directly about money and its movements. The study of household economics is best divided, as in both modern and contemporary book-keeping, into method of accounting, income and expenditure. While the nature of household activity was directed more towards the spending of money rather than its garnering, the medieval noble household was always involved in the collection, storage and creation of income, both in order to perpetuate itself and to aid its master's wealth.

PART I: The Method of Household Accounting

O my good lord,
At many times I brought in my accounts,
Laid them before you; you would throw them off,
And say you found them in my honesty.

                     Timon of Athens (II.ii)

The chief source of information available for the study of the medieval noble household is, as I have noted, the household account – documents produced in the household, by household members, as records of its financial transactions. As with most documents, accounts both have advantages and create problems.

First of all, the accounts that have come down to us are unbiased. They were not intended, in the way of narratives and chronicles, to present any particular view of the noble household out of which they came. Accounts also show us the household in action. Through them we observe its workings almost at first hand without having to depend on an intermediary's conceptual explanations. Furthermore, accounts were generated by the household itself – they are, as it were, the very lava disgorged from its tumultuous insides. Finally, most accounts contain much detail: they are very rich documents enclosing considerable information in a remarkably concise form.

Problems arise, however, when one attempts to interpret these accounts. One has to be aware of the accountant's use of artificial organization, which may be paper rather than real, and to be alert for accounting creations such as the fictional loan. One must be careful not to impute too much authority to the accountant, who may have been a book-keeper rather than an executive, simply because he seems so important in the documents which have survived. A similar 'misrepresentation by proximity' tends to occur when we try to observe trends in household evolution. These have a disturbing tendency to match the rise of incidence of accounts. Thus we must be cautious about imputing apparent increases in size or greater complexity of accounting systems in the fifteenth century, when we have over twice as many accounts and hence twice as much information for it. As well, the very richness of accounts can be dangerous. They are highly sophisticated documents and we can easily fail to take into account various crucial factors in their structure and vocabulary which are not immediately obvious, such as the nature of the balance, the varied meanings of *forensica* as an accounting term, and the purpose of the stock inventory. Accounts also take for granted much that is strange to us; sometimes we are forced to turn to ordinances and other, narrative descriptions of the household in order to solve the mysteries accounts present, such as the function of arrears. Finally, despite their richness, we must realize that we can never deal with full sets of accounts over a period of several years. No case of the survival of the accounts kept for a single household over one year can be traced; moreover, very few runs of any sorts of account, representing a household over a number of consecutive years, survive. Gaps of a generation are common.

Nevertheless, if we are careful to use accounts imaginatively and with thought, we can find in them not only the framework of the household, but the implications of that structure for its members, its master, and the society for which it was constructed. The purpose of most accounts was not, as in a modern financial document, to arrive at a balance of receipts and expenditures, but to display that he who was in charge of the money was honest. In essence, medieval accounts were arguments, in which the author attempted to overwhelm the various charges of the auditors with his list of costs, backed up with bills, vouchers, and references to other accounts for that year which act as authorities behind his assertions of allowable expense. Thus one finds that expenses listed in an account may considerably overwhelm receipts, which in a modern record of transactions would be impossible. Some historians have taken this to mean that the noble household continually lived above its means, existing on credit. While this did indeed happen on some occasions, we must remember that an accountant usually entered costs under the expenses which it was his responsibility to record; but some of these costs were in fact paid out of the pocket of the caterer who is recorded as doing the actual buying, rather than by the accountant directly, and the caterer may or may not got this cash out of the accountant. Hence money could be spent in the discharge or expense part of the account which was not registered among the receipts.

As well as making clear the liability of the accountant, accounts must also have been useful to servants in charge of buying; who could use them to estimate the amounts of various items likely to be required. Accounts could serve other purposes as well. Though they were not primarily intended as pictures of economic status, lords and their ministers, accustomed to their real purpose, were able to get from them a rough idea of the financial state of the household, and also of the whereabouts of part of their net income. Household accounts were often included in 'views' or 'valors', which were surveys of a lord's entire income and often attempted to give some idea of his expenditure.

Though they estimated a lord's potential rather than actual income, valors could provide a noble with a guide to the reasons behind his economic status, which he could use for the establishment of financial reforms.

To fulfil all these purposes, accounts were usually set forth in some kind of organized manner; but these structures were not rigidly fixed – almost as many forms survive as accounts. Nor are any of these forms really related to modern methods of accounting. We are so accustomed to the double-entry system that we find it difficult to comprehend the existence of other methods. Medieval household accountants sometimes double-entered items, particularly goods received, but not all the time or in any systematic way that has any relation in kind to the modern ledger and journal; and a modern sense of balance was of little importance.

Almost all medieval household accounts are constructed on a tripartite basis encompassing the charge, discharge and stock inventory. The charge lists the receipts of the book-keeper for which he must render account; the discharge recites the items he had legitimately used that cash in purchasing. Auditors compared these charge and discharge totals, and pronounced judgement in what we would call a balance, perhaps best named a remainder. This was the *respondeo* of the accounting argument. If the total income was in excess of the discharge, the accountant was not expected to come up with this sum he owed – unless he was leaving his office – but carried it over to the next year as arrears. If the total expense was in excess this might be carried over to the next year, paid to him or more likely simply ignored, being, as I have suggested previously, often due to some of the expenses being not his monetarily. Appended to the argument could be bills, vouchers, warrants and other items used as proof of the correctness of entries in the charge and discharges; various pertinent additions such as chequerrolls, lists of creditors, etc. actually written on the account-roll; and an *ut supra*, that is, an entry of further charges and discharges incurred after the balance was struck but before a new account was begun. At the end was the stock account, which summarized the flow of wealth in the household in terms of goods rather than money.

However, outside the very general structure of charge, discharge and appendices, accounts varied widely, depending on who and what they represented, the time span they covered, and the method by which incomes and expenditures were organized. Theoretically anyone who received a prest, or forwarding of money for expenses not his own, had to render an account arguing his legitimate use of that sum. Some accounts for individual servants who received such prests, from caterers to minor general servants, survive, and many references to long-lost ones can be found in greater accounts. Most of our lords or their valets also kept records of the master's pocket monies. As well as these personal accounts kept for and by individuals in the household, records were also kept by and for departments, and for the household as a whole. Any department which necessarily had expenses and which had its own small treasury could draw up accounts defending their use of that money. Kitchens, wardrobe and/or chamber, cellars and stables most commonly had such funds, and various accounts survive for all these departments. Finally, the chief servants (or, in the case of small households, the master himself), kept accounts for all household expenditures, both of receipts and expenses not entrusted to other departments or accountants but in their charge directly, and also, through departmental and some personal accounts, of household-wide receipt and expenditure. The form of these economic records varied, depending on for whom or what they accounted.

Individuals and departments often kept several different kinds of account, which covered time spans and organized charge and discharge into different sorts of categories. Firstly, memoranda of day-to-day transactions had to be kept, which usually ranged receipts and expenses in chronological order. These memoranda were used to draw up general summaries of transactions over a long period of time – a year to half year – which tended to group charges and discharges by category rather than chronologically. These different daily and yearly accounts were used in all households in order to keep an accurate record of and a careful check on the flow of valuables in the household.

The daily account was the basis of all household accounting practices. Many contain entries for each day; others organized these accounts by the week, or, if their expenses were not constant (such as in the account of the master or his valet, who might not spend money daily), at more irregular intervals, whenever expenses occurred. The important thing about daily accounts is not the date of entry, but the arrangement by time sequence and the compilation of the account at reasonably short intervals, as a memorandum rather than a summary. When compiled by individual servants, these chronological accounts tend to be roughly drawn up, frequently on a single, oddly sized sheet of paper or parchment: they often omit the charge altogether. Often they are merely a compendium of bills from individual shopping expeditions. These private accounts are seldom organized within themselves, items being simply written one after another as they occur, sometimes without a modifying date.

Personal daily accounts recorded the transactions made by individ-

Plate 8 A day roll belonging to the De Vere family, 1250–1290. ref. D/DPr 136. Courtesy of the Essex County Council.

uals; whether private or for the household, theirs was a restricted scope. They tended to be small, informal documents involving limited amounts of money. Departmental accounts, on the other hand, dealt with larger responsibilities and greater charges, and correspondingly were more complex and more formal. Departmental accounts for the kitchen, cellars, stables, chamber and wardrobe survive, but not all households used departmental accounts for all these departments. Generally the larger the household, the more departmental accounting was utilized. Kitchen accounts – the actual documents and the mention of them – seem to be the most common; the kitchen clerk took some of the pressure of accounting off the steward by dealing with the foodstuffs which passed through his hands (though these might not include all the foodstuffs used by the household). Such departmental accounts were largely based upon the private accounts of servants in charge of buying, who reported to the clerk of the appropriate department. Wardrobe and/or chamber accounts, for instance, recorded purchases and use of clothing, materials, and jewels as well as things like bedding. In large households this might represent considerable wealth.

In addition, some departments were entrusted not only with monies provided from the household treasurer, but with income from lands and rents rendered direct. This is especially true of those households with a wardrobe and/or chamber department, which had high expenses and which might also serve as a privy treasury for the master. It is not surprising that in some households – though admittedly not in very many, and mainly in those close to the royal household – the wardrobe became the central treasury, and the clerk of the wardrobe in effect the treasurer of the household, and sometimes also of the noble's estates. Departmental accounts, or the mention of them, also indicate a real departmental organization as opposed to an accounting fiction, because they show the existence of a clerk with staff reporting to him. Note that 'departments' like the pantry and buttery, indicated as departments in yearly accounts, never submit departmental accounts as far as can be ascertained.

The most elaborate daily accounts were drawn up for the expenses of the household as a whole, of edible and 'foreign' (in the sense of non-food) items alike, compiled by the steward or treasurer. In large households the kitchen clerk was also enlisted and household-wide expenses were separated into two categories, food and non-food, the kitchen clerk accounting for the first category, the steward or treasurer for the second. These food accounts were not departmental kitchen accounts; these would have recorded the buyings by servants of and for the kitchen alone, while household food accounts registered the purchase of all foodstuffs by household members, whether valets of the chamber, stable grooms or caterers. Records of non-food, household-wide daily accounts also survive. Rewards, payments to messengers, wages, the buying of such items as stools, benches and forms, arras cloth for hanging in the great hall, and other items of expense which were either the concern of the household in general or were not immediately applicable to any specific department, were paid for and recorded by the steward or the treasurer of the household. This sort of document generally was compiled in a simple fashion by the steward or treasurer. A page of receipts listed in order of payment headed the document. The body of the account was devoted to expenses. The scribe entered his expenses chronologically, including the date with each entry, and the sum in the right margin; in the left he entered the name of he who paid the expense.

All the accounts we have looked at so far have been relatively simple in form. Daily food accounts for the household, however, had to deal with considerable daily expenditure on a multitude of items, foodstuffs being the household's greatest expense and chief concern. When non-food payments were not accounted separately, these daily 'journals', as they were often called, had even more material to record. Naturally the forms used to organize these records tend to be more complicated than those of personal and departmental accounts. Many have survived to demonstrate that households conceived a plethora of methods for organizing these books, and that they did so thoughtfully, experimenting and making changes and improvements. Daily journals are one aspect of the household in which we can trace, with some certainty, a developmental pattern (though we must be careful not to assume that all households developed at the same rates or at the same time).

A very basic form for the daily food account appeared as early as the reign of Richard I;[1] it is common to almost all household accounts. Numerous early examples of this form could be suggested; the accounts of Eleanor, Countess of Leicester, for 1265; for the Earl and Countess of Warrenne in 1240; for Joan de Valance, Countess of Pembroke, from 1284 to 1286. One is tempted to suggest that this is the aboriginal account form. Simple and flexible, it continued in use right through our period. Such an account would be written on a roll, consisting of several membranes of parchment. In the left margin the date and day of the week is entered, parallel to which is that day's entry of purchases in the body of the roll. Within this paragraph entry, headings may or may not be given, and separate items are not begun on a new line until the late fifteenth and sixteenth centuries, but an order of expenses by type within the entry was always observed. First is listed the bread, then ale, and finally meat, fish and poultry (in accounts with headings, entered under *de carnibus*), each with individual prices, or with the amount used *de stauro*, from stock. The accountant calculated totals for the week, but not for individual days.

Most daily household accounts before 1300 are very similar to this form, differing only in such matters as the use of saints' days rather than a numerical date; sometimes listing purchase categories in a slightly different order; separating all stock use into its own separate category following purchases; and often computing a daily, but no weekly, total. In addition, some accounts also include non-food items, entered within the daily paragraph or on a list at the end of the account, as well as a list of receipts. There are also a few examples of books rather than rolls being used for daily household accounts, but with the same method.

These rolls and books were fairly simple, compact and well-organized accounts, easily comprehended, which arranged for the recording of most of the household costs. When at the end of the year an account

[1]PRO E/101/631/1, anonymous day-roll, *tempus* Henry II or Richard I.

arranged by category rather than chronology of expenses was compiled from them, they would have been relatively easy to use. The transactions of a very large household, however, were in terms of sheer bulk and (usually) in greater diversity of items and sources much more difficult to register in a convenient form. In the rapidly expanding households of the greater lords, during the fifteenth century, the basic form of account had to be modified. One way of doing this, as we have seen, was to delegate accounting responsibility to numerous departments, and, for items not so easily paid for, divide transactions between a food and a general non-food account. In some households it is possible that the kitchen clerk and the clerk of the wardrobe never reported daily to the steward or treasurer, all household expenses only being brought together in the yearly account. This appears often to have been the case in abbots' households, and particularly in those of priors dependent upon a mother house. Finchale Priory, an outpost of Durham, only seems to have made a general household account for the yearly review submitted to Durham. Certain great lords however, kept versions of a *Liber Providenciis* (as the third Duke of Buckingham's book was called). These massive tomes accounted expense not only chronologically but by category.

Such a book might be divided into five sections. It opens with a list of chronological receipts. Then a section is devoted to categories – cattle, sheep, wine, spices, foreign expenses, etc. – under which appropriate costs were listed chronologically, as they occurred. The third section consists of the usual pattern of daily expenses, though cast in a gargantuan mould, allowing one entire page per day (or occasionally, two days). Under each date-heading, purchases and stock usage are marshalled under the divisions of *panetria* (breads), *buttelaria* (ale and wine), and *coquine* (meat, fish, poultry, dairy produce, etc.), with a regular, weekly entry for the *stabularia*. The margins are filled with notes on gifts received, dinner guests and totals at meals, and who in the household purchased what from whom. As well as a daily sum, a total may be drawn up for each month, to which index tabs are sewn for easy reference. After these chronological entries come a categorical page listing gifts received, organized by the month; and on the last page the full costs of all the categories are registered and added up to a total sum. Even the vouchers which served as evidence for various purchases are sewn into the binding of this monstrous sort of volume.

Such books survive for the Stafford Dukes of Buckingham, the Beauchamp Earls of Warwick, and the eleventh Earl of Devon, and are mentioned in the ordinances of George, Duke of Clarence, and the fifth Earl of Northumberland. This double system of entering each item, by day and by type, provided a way of checking on legitimate expenses, and also went a long way towards the compilation of a yearly account by category. However, it must also have taken a considerable amount of time to keep up to date, and the *Liber Providenciis* is still a cumbrous document to handle. Most lords, especially those with large households and those who moved about regularly (and hence particularly bishops, whose households were both large and continually mobile) chose to divide the responsibilities of household-wide accounting. This might, for instance, be done by the division of food and non-food items between two daily accounting books.

One final category of accounts yet to be considered is of those which were intended especially for the foreign household. 'Foreign' is used in household accounts in two ways. It can be intended to mean 'foreign' items, that is, non-food buyings that are not regular purchases. But it can also be used to describe a state of being rather than an object: the state of being in transition. Thus we get a foreign, or travelling, household. The household in motion posed certain accounting problems. The carrying of heavy books was a tiresome burden; they might get lost or damaged in transit. The household was usually smaller and less organized on the road. It could use very little stock provision. Moreover, those servants left behind – the skeleton staff of a normally inhabited castle – also had to account for their own consumption, which was paid for by the household even in its general absence.

Lords and their major servants came up with numerous ways of handling these difficulties, satisfactory and unsatisfactory. Some households moved about so much – this particularly applies to accounts before *c.*1320 – that only one general household roll was kept for both the foreign and great households. This system could work for households which were either continually and wholly on the move, or those which were extremely sedentary. In both cases the household tended to be made up of largely the same members and the same structure whatever its stage of being; and the accounts *in janticulis* and *in situ* were easily combined. However, when the lord moved frequently but not continually, and when his riding household was a smaller, looser and differently proportioned band from his more stable establishment, an arrangement typical of episcopal households especially right up to the reformation, the accounting of both together was less successful, and separate foreign rolls evolved.

In such households, three sets of accounts could have been kept: those for the great, the foreign and the skeleton households. Though there are many mentions in yearly accounts, ordinances, letters, etc. of skeleton staff accounts, only one can actually be traced, that for the servants of Ralph, Lord Cromwell, at Tattershall for 1447. It is a very roughly kept but highly interesting document accounting for about fifteen servants up to and including the Christmas of that year. It was not made by a trained cleric and was probably never intended as a separate accounting system, but was probably later incorporated – as other skeleton staff accounts were – into the great or foreign roll.

Until 1468, Henry, Lord Stafford, and Margaret Beaufort attempted to combine their foreign and great household accounts, but with some curious and confusing outcomes. Their 'fresh achats' book – that is, the account-book for goods purchased for more or less immediate use – for 1467–8 exhibits some of the convolutions required to account for travelling, great and skeletal establishments in a single volume. The time sequence runs first from March 1467 to October 1467, accounting for the great household at Woking and the skeleton household there after August. It then doubles back to August 1467 and runs to November 1467, covering the foreign household at various places; reverts to October 1467, covering the skeletal and then the great household at Woking, continuing until June 1468; and then switches back to April 1468, finishing at May 1468, during which time the foreign household was on the road.

Though ultimately decipherable, the book is highly confusing to use, even when one has untangled the basic idea. The mobile Stafford/Beaufort household seems to have found it so, and after 1468 kept separate accounts for the foreign household, like most mobile nobles. Unlike the highly structured accounts of great households, these are very simple, resembling the basic form of the daily account, with short entries for each day *sans* headings (though the items are ordered, as bread first, then ale, then meats and odd expenses), and with foreign expenses included in each day. Both stock and fresh purchases and expenditure are accounted together. The smallness and loose structure of the riding household, and its lack of dependence on stock foods, made this kind of foreign accounting possible. Almost all daily accounts for riding households reverted to the basic form of registering transactions, which was originally developed out of the early, relatively small households such as are shown in the accounts of Eleanor de Montfort and the Earl and Countess de Warenne – households which travelled with great frequency.

When the time period which the day-account covered was over and the last chronological entry was made, the account became evidence, data, fodder for the annual argument of the accountant and auditor. First of all the day-book itself could be audited, either by a clerk hired for the occasion, another household cleric besides the keeper of the day-account, or in some cases the lord himself. Any wrong sums, illegal expenses (that is, those the auditor did not accept as true expenses of the household) and inaccurate entries were supposed to be revised. Just when the audit took place is hard to ascertain. In some cases it may have been checked daily, as was planned in Edward IV's royal household; certainly many lords and stewards signed nearly every page of the household's day-book. In many cases, especially when the accountant was an outsider, the audit was done at the end of the fiscal year used by the household; but whether before or after the year-account was drawn up it is difficult to say. It seems more likely, however, that the accountant first drew up his yearly record from the day-book, submitting the latter as evidence for the former; and that the auditor checked out the day-book item by item as he traced his way back to the expenses listed from it in the yearly account.

Thus the day-book became primarily the authority used by the accountant in, and also the source of his compilation of, a yearly account. This was a summary of the year's receipts and expenses, containing much or little detail, which related transactions by category rather than chronologically. As a record and as an argument it was generally preferable to a daily journal. It was first of all easier to use and to store than a bulky book, its entries being condensed; as an argument its form was perhaps more obvious and coherent; and as a record of a year's expenses, the next caterer would have found the yearly categories easier to use, when he needed to know how many stock cattle to buy. Many more year-accounts survive more completely than day-books, probably because the latter became extraneous after the audit, while the former remained useful and relatively easy to keep.

The compilation of the year-account from the day-book was no small task, however. As we have seen, most households in the fifteenth century carried out some categorization within the daily accounts which would have made the task easier. The separate lists in *Libri Providenciis* are the most extreme example. In some households, however, records which, like year-accounts, summarize receipts and expenses by category were kept over periods of less than a year. Many lords had compiled half-yearly views, or categorical summaries of the transactions for that period, which were in form and intent like small yearly accounts. Events were fresher in the mind, the vouchers less likely to be lost, the amount to be compiled smaller over a six- than a twelve-month period. Since so many households took Michaelmas as the start and end of their fiscal year, when rents were also due, a six-monthly survey removed some of the pressure and paperwork from the presiding officials at that busy time. The quarter was another major division of the fiscal year. Like the seasons, standing accounts and servants' wages were due every three months. Many households drew up a quarter-roll for a particular category of expenses: servants' costs and wages. These chequerrolls covered the amounts due to servants for their wages, and also what they might be owed in expenses of catering, and what they themselves owed out of prests unspent. Few households, however, use the month, as we do now, as an important fiscal division and time for a view of accounts.

The year-account proper, which by its categorical summary of the fiscal period's transactions superseded all other records of that space of time, assumed like the daily journal a basic form at some very early date. This form remained within it through all the elaborating experimentation of the later fifteenth century. Some early examples survive, for Gilbert de Clare, Earl of Gloucester (1307–8), the Talbots of Blakemere (1394), and Sir John Cobham (1408).

All year-accounts were constructed in three sections: charge, discharge and stock inventory. First, the accountant listed the charge, or the receipts granted to him for which he had to account sufficiently to his master. He consulted his chronological records and categorized the receipts listed therein, usually as either *recept' denar'* (cash receipts, sometimes divided into receipts from lands and receivers, and those from the lord) or *recept' forinsec'* (foreign receipts, that is, being goods received, or money received from the sale of household goods). A more complicated series of divisions was undertaken in some year-accounts.

Also included in the charge was the category of arrears, *arreragia*. From the French *en arrivère*, used absolutely it means simply 'that which is behind'. We usually use it in relation to money, as medieval accountants employed the term; but we tend to think of it as a debt remaining unpaid, and conceive of it as an expense, not a receipt. The arrears, however, consist of those monies from the previous year which the accountant failed to balance with a discharge. Hence he was still charged with this 'debt' as he should still have had that money in hand, since it was not handed over at the end of the previous year's accounting unless the clerk was leaving his master's employ. Even if, the previous year, he had spent over rather than under the sum with which he was charged, the category of arrears was still entered and *nulla* registered as its total. After entering his receipt categories and giving subtotals, for each one, the accountant computed the sum of the whole charge; after which he began the second part of the year-account, the discharge.

The discharge was a categorical register of expenses which the accountant claimed as legitimate expenditures for the use of the cash with which he was charged, and he backed up these expenses with the evidence of his chronological records, vouchers, bills, indentures and other documents. The categories of the discharge vary widely, from account to surviving account. In some, all food purchased was listed in a single huge paragraph; in others, it was broken down by department, such as bread, pastry and grains under *panetria*, or categories were made by food type, such as bread, grain, sheep, cattle, etc., or even more specifically as bread, rye, wheat, barley, lambs, mature sheep, calves, oxen, etc. Though not as common as the *arreragia*, a category called *excessum* sometimes headed the discharge. It is the opposite of arrears. If expenses exceeded receipts in the previous year the amount then technically owed the accountant was either paid him, or simply ignored; probably because in many cases the *excessum* was due to the accountant entering in his discharge sums for items within his jurisdiction but paid not out of his charge but out of the prest of a caterer. But when the accountant remained unpaid he might enter an *excessum* under the discharge, because it was still owed him by the source of his receipts.

Finally, as in the charge, a total for each category was entered, and a final sum for all of the discharge. The charge and discharge were then balanced – or to describe it more properly their totals were compared and analysed – and the arrears or *excessum* for next year computed. Often, additional entries of expense and charge were added, after the balance was done. These were usually of items forgotten by the accountant when making up his document, and occasionally of transactions made after the actual compilation of the year-account but in the interregnum of two weeks or so, when accounts were being audited, before a new daily record was begun. These *ut supra* were computed to modify the *excessum* or *arreragia*.

The charge and discharge were usually registered on the front or verso side of a paper or parchment roll, and formed the accountant's argument, *videtur* and *sed contra* – 'it seems that' and 'but on the other hand'. The inventory or account of stock written on the back of most yearly accounts was based on, but separate from, the charge/discharge. Rather than an argument, it was a record of the flow of goods in the household. It was divided into quite-specific categories, as in the third example of discharge groups given above, under each of which were three sections, microcosms of the charge, discharge and remainder of the verso. These were: the amounts of the item (not its price) received, whether by purchase or receipt, and the total; the amounts expended, and their total; and the amount remaining, if any. This stock inventory was a useful record in determining how much food or how many horseshoes to purchase, because it showed the average rate of expenditure over a year. This gave the caterer an idea of the quantities in which he needed to think, and let him know what to buy and what was not needed. Even more than in modern pantries, it must have been possible to lose quantities of goods stored out of sight in barn or chamber. Today's big shops compile January inventories with much the same aims in mind.

The stock account was probably drawn up from the year and day records as well as a tour of the storage places. As such, though separate from the yearly account, it was also dependent on it. Therefore the stock and year records could act as checks, one upon the other. The charge and discharge register only the receipt or purchase of goods, and not the remains of goods carried over or their actual use, because these cannot easily be rendered in terms of cash receipt and expense, and because if they were so entered, they would be accounted twice. For instance, if a pipe of wine were entered in the discharge for its purchase, and also then for its use, twice its actual value would be registered. The charge/discharge, then, was interested in the flow of cash, as in a daily fresh achats book; the stock inventory recorded the movement of goods, rather like a daily record of provisions.

This was the basic form of every yearly household account: a categorical summary of transactions in cash and in kind. However, variations on this simple structure abounded, though less than for the day-account. Many such differences are connected with the area for which the yearly record accounted: whether personal, departmental, or household-wide. Obviously for each of these sorts of document the categories must differ. Sometimes, however, the nature of the concern accounted for also affected the way the record was put together at a basic level, or encouraged one sort of categorization over another. While several quotations from personal year-rolls exist in household-wide accounts, such as that of the third Duke of Buckingham's secretary,[2] few have actually survived. Few individual servants received prests large enough for them to have paid personally for really massive shopping expeditions, or to necessitate highly organized accounts, especially as these were eventually incorporated into the yearly household-wide records – which is probably why so few are extant.

Much the same could be said of departmental accounts. Kitchen accounts, concerning as they did all or most of the entire household's food supply, are in form quite close to the great household-wide year-accounts and may be discussed with them. Other surviving departmental accounts exhibit some of the greatest variations found in year-

[2]Staffs. RO D 641/1/3/6.

rolls, due to their special requirements. Chequerrolls are a case in point. These consist of a list of servants by position, broken into such categories as *capitum officii*, gentleman-ushers, clerks, etc., arranged lineally (that is, with each position receiving its own line instead of being written into a paragraph), with the name of the holder of the office, his wage and his rights to personal servants and horses. Because of the linear arrangement, positions, names, wages, etc. are lined up in vertical columns, and the total wages cost, number of servants' servants, and horses can be shown almost pictorially. These chequerroll accounts, while they show wage expenses – a kind of discharge – are not argumentative in the way of most accounts. They contain no receipts to balance the expenses, no final balance, and of course no stock account. Compiled by the clerk of the chequerroll for the treasurer, who made the actual payments, the chequerroll represents no separate organization or individual who received a prest, and are therefore more in the nature of information sheets.

Other departmental accounts are not so idiosyncratic, being true to the orthodox accounting form: but they produce some interesting variations. Those by the clerk of the wardrobe generally are constructed along the traditional lines of receipt, expenditure and stock accounts. The great quantities of many different kinds of cloth, as well as armour, harness, paper, wax, etc., and the value of each item mean that the wardrobe's yearly account might cover the major part of household expenses. Indeed, in a few households the wardrobe account had taken over the function of the household-wide yearly reckoning. Kitchen year-rolls were invaluable aids for the treasurer in the making of the great household roll, as they did well over half the groundwork for him. Those which survive show highly detailed categorization, using in the discharge individual types of grain, meat, etc., and in the actual entries considerable information is given, with individual buyings priced and dated. The household-wide accounts compiled with the help of these kitchen year-rolls may also include these detailed categorical titles, but tend to give little or no information beyond the total costs in the actual entries, usually referring the reader to the separate kitchen account for details of purchase.

The majority of surviving household year-accounts follow the pattern of charge, discharge and stock account. The main variations occur in categorization. The groupings used by accounts are never exactly the same, even when we compare two from the same household for succeeding years. Nevertheless, we can note three essential methods of creating categories in more or less detail. The least complicated is also the least common by the fifteenth century. In these the charge is usually only divided into two categories: cash, and stock and sale. The discharge is organized into three: food expenses, foreign or non-food costs, and wages. The stock account, however, is categorized by individual item, as in wheat, rye, cattle, calves, etc., in these and all sorts of year-accounts. Another type of account is organized somewhat differently in the charge/discharge. The charge is broken down into specific sources of receipt: from the privy coffers, from individual receivers, the receiver-general, sales, and stock receipts. The discharge groups expenses into fictional departments – breads, pastry and grain, for example, are listed in the category *panetria*, ale and wine under *buttelaria*. A third type, on the other hand, dispenses with trying to group purchases and enters as headings the bare name of the item – hence wheat, rye, and barley have their own categories, as in the stock account, instead of being inaccurately grouped under *panetria*.

By the mid-fifteenth century, some accountants began also to introduce linearism and diagramming into the stock accounting form. Regardless of the categorical system used, some kind of set order prevailed among the general listing of expenses. Wheat, whether grouped with all other food purchases, under *panetria* or alone, almost always opened the discharge; grains are usually followed by wine and ale, alcohol by meats. In a sense, once one has seen one standard year-roll, one can find one's way about all others. The order used is also very similar to the divisions of the basic daily account. Indeed, one finds that in households in which this typical order of the day-account was somewhat rearranged, the same rearranged order was followed in the year-account.

This section has attempted to explain the methods of account-keeping in medieval and noble households. I have noted the persistence, in this period, of basic forms of book-keeping which are highly conservative, showing little sign of the influence of the double-entry and other revolutions in commercial accounting; as well as trends in the direction of a more systematic and detailed categorization. But this method was a means, a way of expressing and recording the flow of wealth, in cash and kind, into, out of and within the household. We seek to understand accounting systems for themselves, but also in preparation for the examination of the income and expenditure of the medieval noble household.

PART II Income

Forsooth, an inventory, thus imparting
The several parcels of his plate, his treasure,
Rich stuffs, and ornaments of household; which
I find at such proud rate that it outspeaks
Possession of a subject.

Henry VIII (III.ii)

It is a modern platitude of landholding history that by the mid-fifteenth century a significant number of rents originally due in labour or in kind were commuted to cash payments, and that the old demesne farm lands were often rented, rather than cultivated for direct profit by the lord. However, household accounts in many cases show evidence which modifies this picture. In all the households used here, there are examples of demesne farm profits, in particular from the home estate; and of food items, especially grain, obtained from estates held by the master, without payment. Most noble estates were by this time administered by a chain of ministers whose organizations, while changing somewhat from noble to noble, were in the main variations on a common theme. Estate administration has been the subject of eminent historians and we need not deal extensively with it here. If an aristocrat was particularly rich in lands, he often divided them up into (usually geographcial) districts, each with its own general steward, and a receiver who supervised the collection of rents, dues and fines and the audit of the accounts of estates ministers in this area. A receiver-general was charged with the legal and financial administration of all the lord's lands. Receivers and receivers-general, and occasionally other estate ministers, usually also acted as treasurers of land profits, establishing several repositories for their employer's wealth.

This is an admittedly simplistic picture of a complex topic, but it is the essential core of most arrangements and will serve our purposes. As has been mentioned, numerous variations occurred; one of the most common is the dropping of the second stage, when the lord had few or very compact estates, so that the officials of individual manors reported direct to the receiver-general. Several frequent variations involve the household and household members, and it is with these that we are concerned.

In several cases the household contained the central estate administration agency for its master's holdings. This could come about in a number of ways. Firstly, a household officer or department could be this agency. The steward of the household, or the treasurer, might double as the receiver-general. In some households, as we have previously noted, the wardrobe or chamber doubled as the chief treasury and auditing department for the lord's estates income. The income of a monastic house especially was not unusually filtered through a chief household servant of the abbot. This did not give the household direct access to or control over the estates income necessarily, but it did make it easier for the household officers to obtain funds. In the case of lords with small or compact holdings, we find that the master himself might act as his own receiver-general, riding around their holdings to collect monies, audit accounts and generally oversee their lands. On these journeys the lords took household members with them as aides, as rent collectors, as witnesses, and sometimes as auditors (the chaplain of William and Margaret Cromwell, *Dominus* John de Kyghley, served as an auditor in 1419–20). Even in those households where the central estate agency lay outside their bounds, servants were sometimes called upon to perform chores for that agency: most usually the collection of rent in kind, or of rents due from the estate in which the household was dwelling. Therefore, in a minor way, almost all households were involved in estate administration.

In the fifteenth century, lower rents encouraged nobles to search for other sources of profit in order to maintain their income levels, some of which were filtered through the household system. The sale of agricultural produce was a moderately profitable method of making money, and a logical outcome of farming. Lords had long put to profit the resources of the demesne farm and other assets, supplying themselves with wood, coal and other fuels from their holdings, and also selling these at a profit to tenants and local farmers; the Stonors in 1471 sold thirty-seven quarters of grey peas and barley, grown on their demesne lands at Horton Kirkby, to tenants and other local people, using the household as an agent.[3]

Lords obtained income in numerous other ways: through gifts, gambling, borrowing and pawning, or selling personal items. For some lords, notably the 13th Earl of Oxford, Thomas Cromwell and Bogo de Clare, gifts formed enough income to be entered separately as a category on accounts. Giving gifts – usually in the form of food, sometimes of cloth or jewels – was an important social function, sometimes with political implications. Gifts could be a way of currying favour or extending protection. A popular and powerful man was likely to receive much, both from his peers and from his clients, especially

[3]PRO C 47/37/3/37–43.

around Christmas time. Gifts, being objects, were usually handed over
to the warderober or kitchen clerk of most households, to record and
put to use, or to sell. Gambling was a matter of the lord's privy purse
and seldom involved much cash, but all in fifteenth- and sixteenth-
century secular households, ladies and gentlemen alike indulged in it;
and chamber servants were often called upon to pay gambling debts out
of their own pockets. The accounts of Elizabeth of York, Queen to
Henry VII, are full of repayments to her ladies for gambling debts
settled, sometimes using her winnings. The third Duke of Buckingham
used his chamber servants to pawn and also to sell family plate when he
was particularly in need of cash.[4]

Household income – that is, the wealth available to the whole
household through the treasurer to expend on the various costs
necessary to its functioning – was not one and the same with its
master's net income. The bulk of his wealth was likely to be placed with
an estate official, or with a household office such as the privy coffers,
which were not funds over which the treasurer or other *major domus*
had control. Household income was largely a matter of allowances
upon that greater wealth. When documentation allows us to make fairly
reliable calculations, the total household income available for expenses
is found to vary widely, not only from household to household, but
within one household from year to year. These widely varying incomes
were the result of a number of factors: the lord's net income and the
status he wanted to convey through his household; the extent of his
entrustment of income to the household as a treasury; and the nature of
the household's income sources, which themselves might garner a varied
amount of income from year to year.

The household's income came from diverse sources, some of which I
have already touched upon, but I shall now look at them in greater
detail. Most household, as most net noble, income derived from estates
and their various profits. But there were numerous pathways along
which these profits could reach the treasurer, the various forms in
which they appeared. In many cases the household was largely funded
by the receiver-general, out of his conglomerate treasury of estate
profits. However, such households did not receive anything like a
regular allowance from the receiver-general, but were paid in odd sums
at uneven intervals, in anything from five to forty instalments over one
year; nor is the total contributed the same or similar from one year to
another. Some of these sums made over by the receiver-general appear
to have been 'voluntary' in the sense that this chief official, having

[4]BL Royal MS 14B XXXV D.

undertaken to fund his master's household, sent cash without specific orders to do so. But the receiver tended to be a busy man, often with considerable expenses, who sometimes experienced difficulties in obtaining rents, fines, etc. from tenants and local officials, and in many cases cash was got from him by the command of the lord or by the household issuing an approved warrant for a certain sum. Receivers often had problems meeting such demands, and paid the sums in two or more instalments. We also find that in some cases the household received cash from the receiver-general only or largely by the presentation of a bill of goods purchased, for which specific bill the receiver would hand over cash to the household, an arrangement mentioned in a number of ordinances.

Obviously, the above methods of obtaining cash had a distinct disadvantage, which is clearly evident in accounts; many households suffered under a chronic shortage of cash. Unless the receiver or his treasury were readily available, this lack of funds could be highly inconvenient, despite the credit most lords and their households seem to have enjoyed from farmers and merchants. Unable to rely on the receiver-general for cash requirements, some households circumvented him by going direct to the individual estates. Profits of home manors seldom went to the receiver, being absorbed immediately by the household who lived there. Episcopal households often obtained funds from the steward or whatever estates they stayed on.

As well as money, households obtained income in kind, which could be used directly, from the lord's lands and through estate officials. It is a negative sort of income; it did not really add to the household treasury, but did make unnecessary certain expenditures, and provided needed goods without detracting from the cash supply. This kind of income can be further divided into three categories: estates purveyance, rent in kind, and demesne produce. Numerous examples may be uncovered with ease of estate officials paying for goods and services intended for the household, including commodities such as wine and ale, but more commonly livestock. Purveyance by estate servants for the household is most common for the establishments of abbots, and for early households which moved around their estates a good deal. These purveyances were not repaid by the household but came out of the buyer's funds of his office. A few examples of bailiffs doing this kind of buying occur, but it is commonest among receivers and receivers-general. The intention of such purveyance can be sought in the large amounts in which such goods were usually purchased. Instead of sending a warrant to the receiver-general, waiting for the funds to arrive, and then dispatching a servant to the place of purchase for three of four days, it was far easier and far cheaper for the household to pass the entire job on to the receiver-general, who held the cash and who was liklier to be passing near the source of goods in any case.

Earlier we considered the noble's income by rent in kind, and its continuance in the fifteenth century; I indicated that the household was supplied from this sort of income. In fact, the majority of income which appears to be rent in kind did go direct to the household. Receivers were primarily set up, at this date, to handle and store cash; and rent in kind was, in incidence, little enough for the household to dispose of by itself. Most cases of this rent in kind of which records have survived were of small amounts, such as the forty-eight conger eels from Minehead tenants of the Luttrells in 1405; a welcome enough recipt of goods, but not one which significantly curtailed buying expenses. Some income in kind, however, was so voluminous as to alter household purveyance vastly, eliminating almost wholly the need to buy certain items. Much of this bulk receipt of goods appears to be demesne produce, though it is possible that some of it is rent in kind. Such items were entered in the stock accounts as received from a local bailiff in one bulk entry, and it is impossible to descry their actual source for certain. They were not entered in the charge section of the account, which means they were not conceived of as income, unlike purveyance by estate officials and cash direct from estates; nor yet were they entered in the discharge. One is hard put to interpret such entries as other than demesne produce.

Two sorts of demesne produce may be differentiated: that sent from outlying estates, and that produced from the home manor. Distant demesne holdings were often largely devoted to grains: wheat, barley and prepared malt, rye, and maize. The greater landowners seem to have farmed out their demesnes extensively, and indeed to have commuted payments in kind to cash more readily. As with lesser landowners, however, they usually had at least a small demesne around their principal country dwellings which produced a richly varied, if smaller, income in kind, such as doves, rabbits, pigeons, and game birds. Heronries, and clutches of swans to cull, are mentioned, as are small vineyards, fisheries and orchards. While these products were seldom produced in large enough quantity to make an appreciable difference to expenditure, they provided a welcome variation to diet and removed some difficult items from the shopping list of the caterer. Herons and swans, for instance, were expensive to purchase and difficult to locate. The home demesne, aside from these items, seems to have been in most cases chiefly meadow land, providing as it did grazing and also a partial hay supply for the stables and for stock animals kept for eventual household consumption. Some households

Plate 9 A nobleman and his servants and companions hawking – a source of game meat for the household. George Turbervile, *The Booke of Faulconrie or Hauking*, London 1611. 4to. P. 69, (1) Jur. Page 112. Courtesy of the Bodleian Library, Oxford.

had occasionally to rent such meadow land or buy hay; but in the main the home demesne was able to accommodate a household's grazing needs. Some home demesnes, on the other hand, were essentially farms: this is true of many monastic bases, and for lords such as the LeStrange family and Robert Melton. These farms supplied their owners' houses with most of the grain and meadow they needed, and also supported permanent herds of cattle and sheep which the household culled for its table rather than having to buy stock animals elsewhere.

Income was also obtained by the household from sources other than the lord's lands and estate officials. The lord himself, in fact, and his private treasuries, could be a useful source of cash. Gifts received were entrusted to various appropriate departments. The third Stafford duke's small profits from his Flemish trading investments (64s 3d) were paid into a household treasury.[5] But the most interesting and surprising (if not the most lucrative) of income sources for the household came, not at all from the lord's riches, but from within the household itself, generated by and for it alone, created out of the waste products and unused items in the charge of householders. This created income hints at the efficient, rather than frugal, economy which lay behind the deliberate splendour and apparent extravagance of many noble households.

As we might expect, most households produced staple goods we would now have to buy. Indeed, such items as cheese, beer, butter, wine and bread were easily purchased in the middle ages, but were more economically made in the kitchens, if the resources for doing so were available. As well as maintaining livestock, the household also produced some of its own by the raising of chickens and other poultry, lambs, and some calves; most also had a garden for onions, cabbage, garlic and other vegetables and herbs.

A more positive but also obvious and expected form of income generated by the particular spirit of economy in the household is that of the profitable sale of goods which the household held in overabundance. Any kind of foodstuffs or indeed objects like pots and stools could be sold in this fashion, but stock animals were most commonly so disposed of. Since our knowledge of these sales largely comes from yearly accounts which do not individually date the sales, we cannot be sure of when they took place and the immediate reasons for the sale, but one would suspect that this occurred in the autumn, when the number of the household herds of cattle, sheep and pigs destined for consumption in the hall would have needed to be reduced to what could

[5]Staffs. RO D 641/1/3/6.

be supported over the winter or slaughtered, salted and stored. Such stock was usually sold to local farmers, often at a profit. Ralph Cromwell's kitchen clerk recorded, in 1445, the sale of three pigs for 6s 8d each at a time when they were originally bought for 3d ob (halfpenny) each. Robert Humfrey, cator to Sir William Petre, regularly sold livestock, sheep making a profit of 1s 6d on average. Lords attempting to sell fish, however, often did so at a loss – presumably because of difficulty regarding their freshness. Though not individually effective in counterbalancing household expenses, these examples are indicative of a shrewd and fruitful policy of efficient economic measures.

As well as the relatively simple sale of unneeded goods, the household could also be imaginative in its rendering of waste into by-products of much usefulness, which were utilized in the household or sold. In a smaller establishment we could probably call some of these by-products cottage industries. All households did their own slaughtering of livestock destined for the table; and it is largely as a consequence of this that householders became involved in creating income. The animals, once dead, were first flayed. Their skins had many uses: woolfells and shaven skins of sheep, hides of oxen, cattle and calves could be refined into parchment or vellum, used whole as cart covers or rugs, or cut up into shoes, clothes, thongs and pots. Sometimes the hair or fur was left on the skin; at other times it was removed for separate use as ticking or lining on clothes, or to make thread. Hides frequently were used to make pots and cups of leather; the Radcliffe's cook and the first Stafford duke's laundress prepared rabbit skins for use as trimming on clothing.[6] The wool from unsheared sheep consumed by the household was used to make thread, and woven into clothes for servants. It is not certain whether those hides sold were tanned or not; no record of charges survives for those used in the household to be tanned outside.

Under the skin of the slaughtered animal lay the thick layer of subcutaneous fat. This was cut off, as were more large fat deposits uncovered as the carcass was divided. This fat was then rendered to produce tallow, which was an important ingredient in making candles, and could also be used in salves, or for cooking. It is interesting to note that the rendered fat of sheep and cattle only was called tallow; that of pigs was differentiated as pig-grease or pig-fat. It was produced in great quantities – 120 lbs in a year is not uncommon – most of which went into homemade candles. It was also sold, straight or in the form of candles, to locals. The Luttrells', a most imaginative household in its

[6]Kent RO Cat Mk U1475 A92 and Staffs. RO D 641/1/3/4.

approach to using by-products, used twelve pounds of tallow in 1430 to replace the organs of Sir John's body when he died in late June, in an attempt to preserve the body for the laying out in hot summer weather. Much of the remaining animal was consumed; even Richard II's *Book of Feasts* includes a recipe for 'noumbles', or offal.[7] Even the bones were cracked to obtain the marrow. Some households even dried and segmented the viscera of sheep and cattle to make tough gut cords, for use as twine and as wicks for candles.

The completely butchered animal's flesh was normally prepared for eating by frying or stewing. The fat which floated to the surface of a boiling pot or which remained after the frying was called 'fflottes'. This was used primarily for cooking, as a cheap substitute for lard and butter; but it was also used for tempering metal – the iron parts of a plough or other instrument are less inclined to wear, rust or stick when protected by a film of grease, which is the reason why one should not use soap on modern frying pans – and for the treatment of wood, which benefits because the grease makes it warp and dry out less easily.

Other small industries appeared less frequently in households and involved less bulk and profit. Leftover bran from the bakehouse could be used to make starch. Servants made torches as well as candles, and also oil, for cooking and for lamps, though from what we cannot be sure – perhaps clarified tallow. Most households produced small amounts of vinegar from excess wine. Rushes on their floors were often culled from the lord's own marshes.

These homely items were prepared, in the main, for use by the household, as a substitute for buying other articles. But what could not be used was, like stock animals, sold at whatever profitable price could be got. Most of these items seem to have been sold, not at market, but privately to individual local tenants and farmers, of which many were regular suppliers of meat to the household. Though of rough quality, the items produced by the household were usually cheaper than market goods, and in greater bulk than most tenants and farmers could produce. Homemade candles sold for 2s 3d for two dozen, when a dozen usually cost between 1s 3d and 1s 6d. Household tallow generally sold for a little under a penny a pound, while purchased tallow cost over 2d the pound.[8] Clearly, the buying of these homemade products was as much a boon to the buyer as their selling was to the household.

[7] Lorna Sass, ed., *To the King's Taste – Richard II's Book of Feasts and Recipes* (John Murray, London, 1975), pp. 58–60.

[8] James Edward Thorold Rogers, *A History of Agriculture and Prices in England* (8 vols, Clarendon Press, Oxford, 1876), vol. III, p. 289.

The production and sale of these products was carried out by a wide variety of servants. Obviously much was concentrated in the kitchens and other preparatory departments, as most of the waste material was connected with foodstuffs. But chamberlains and laundresses prepared skins and other things for clothing; general servants and non-preparatory specialized servants such as gardeners made candles; extra stock was peddled not only by caterers but by gentleman-ushers and chaplains. However, the incidence of by-production, just as it was more common among preparatory servants, was greater in some households than in others. Monastic households, small households and settled households were the most productive. Episcopal establishments, the households of dukes and earls, and households that moved about a great deal, neglected even the most basic 'cottage industries'. They bought cheese, bread, ale and butter rather than made it; even tallow was purchased, the fat from carcases being sold directly. Other by-products were put up for sale: skins, woolfells, excess goods. They were not wasteful; but with few exceptions they could not fully exploit opportunities for making or saving money through the household. Home production requires some continuity of place, as products may need a great deal of time to produce – it takes twelves hours, for instance, to render one pound of fat. Furthermore, nobles as rich and as great as these were more interested in the quality of goods rather than unnecessary economies to be made by using clumsy homemade items; nor it is likely that the great quantities of items like tallow which they required could have been met by household production.

Receipts from 'cottage industries' such as we have been examining were almost pure profit, making use as they did of household waste materials. Whether used in the household or sold, each homemade candle and pound of tallow represented a helpful economy. However, such receipts, while a measurable part of household income, were not the major part of the total charges: seldom more than 5 per cent, in fact. We must, of course, remember that these percentages do not include most of the household's negative income from home industry, that is, the free provision of items which would have otherwise been bought. As well, these income percentages are misleading in their appearance of insignificance, to some extent; the 79s 10d earned by the household of Hugh Luttrell in 1422–3 through positive home production would have paid the wages of all his servants for one quarter. One must remember that each household only produced so much waste material in a year; they could not have obtained cheaply more hides than those of the number of animals they needed to slaughter for food. The production of homemade items, moreover, took time which household members and their masters might have been unwilling to spend: even a small animal skin, for instance that of a rabbit, requires several months and some attention to be adequately cured. Finally, and most importantly, household members were not in the business of making money; they were primarily hired to spend it on items needed to make possible the lord's own comforts. Ideally, servants were efficient and thrifty; but the household was chiefly organized around consumption rather than production.

PART III Expenditure

> Call forth my household servants; let's tonight
> Be bounteous at our meal.
>
> *Antony and Cleopatra* (IV.ii)

The myriad functions fulfilled by the household, described in the introduction to this work, demanded a different attitude to money from the one we usually associate with the word 'household'. Phrases like 'domestic economy' and 'the thrifty housewife' spring to the modern mind, and probably lie behind the criticism of extravagance laid at the door of such medieval noblemen as Edward Stafford, John de Vere, Henry Percy, the fifth Earl of Northumberland, and many others, by modern writers. For instance, historians frequently cite – and denigrate – illustrations of apparent extravagance, such as the fact that Archbishop Neville's household, at his enthronement, served up nearly four thousand custard tarts. They fail to take account of the small size (one and one-half inches in diameter) of the tarts, and the number of guests (about six hundred); from which it would appear that the sweet was, in fact, rather meagre.[9] It may be retorted that the good archbishop need not have invited six hundred people; but from his point of view, in the framework he lived in and his position in society, he probably did have to.

The importance and significance of presenting a splendid exterior to the world as a political and social necessity has been described in detail by such historians as Sidney Anglo and A.R. Myers. We need not investigate the subject in detail here; but the premise is apposite to our analysis of household consumption and expenditure. A lord expected a

[9]John Cordy Jeaffreson, *A Book About the Table* (2 vols, Hurst and Blackett, London, 1875), vol. 1, p. 131; Jeaffreson does not give his source.

great many functions to be filled by his household and he expected them to be carried out in a manner befitting his position in society. By keeping a luxurious house and a generous table, by dressing servants in fine livery, by displaying a large following, a lord was able to assert his nobility, proclaim his wealth, and advertise his power, thus attracting clients and gaining respect. The sumptuary legislation passed during this period clearly indicates that people evaluated others by their clothing and their spending habits. To ignore this kind of visual language was to invite social and political downfall. Besides his own person, a lord's household was usually his most obvious and most frequently observed expense. It travelled with him, offered hospitality to his guests, and expressed towards its master the clearest form of respect – personal service. An impudent servant, or a poorly dressed one, did more to undermine a lord's reputation than a recalcitrant tenant or a long list of creditors. The servant was more visible to others, and his insubordination more immediately felt. Georges Chastellain crystallized this principle in the course of describing the Duke of Burgundy's household: 'After the deeds and exploits of war, which are claims to glory, the household is the first thing which strikes the eye, and that which it is, therefore, most necessary to conduct and arrange well.'[10]

The multiplicity of duties meant that a large staff was called for. Even the households of minor gentry required twenty-odd household servants on average, a number that increased going up the social scale and in the later portion of our period. In addition, to fulfill all its functions the household required a good deal of money and effort. The time, organization and cost involved in keeping up a large house or castle and its belongings; of heating and cleaning it; of entertainments and religious festivals and banquets; of travelling expenses for servants riding *in negociis domini* (on the lord's business); of perambulating the countryside on a well-maintained stable – all these required considerable work and expenditure. Moreover, the wages, clothing, feeding and shelter for a staff capable of organizing and performing these tasks became in itself a massive expense, so that it sometimes seems as if the household primarily existed to administer itself.

The English aristocracy was, of course, still relatively wealthy, even if under some economic pressure in the later part of our period; it fully expected to spend money for these necessary purposes, nor was it interested in thrift for its own sake. The household was, after all, the framework through which the lord mainly enjoyed his income. It was

[10]Jan Huizinga, *The Waning of the Middle Ages* (Penguin Books, Harmondsworth, 1979), p. 39.

conceived as a spending, not a saving, agent. Nevertheless, the threats to baronial income in the fourteenth and fifteenth centuries, so thoroughly discussed by K.B. McFarlane and G.A. Holmes, meant that uninhibited expenditure had to be wisely curtailed. Edward IV and his counsellors openly admitted the need for certain economies;[11] others incurred debts which years later their descendants were still attempting to pay off. The reconciliation of magnificence and economy was a chief problem to the fifteenth-century English aristocracy, one that frequently centred on the important but expensive household – itself usually the lord's greatest expense. A principle of accountability was needed to impose restrictions on those spending the lord's money, in order to prevent both deliberate embezzlement and expensive carelessness. Sanctions concerning income and expenditure have already been discussed as they concerned the accounting system; but they also applied to those actually making purchases and carrying out buying policy. Available resources were exploited as much as possible; waste was charged to the personal account of the servant responsible; it was common for a household to set a ceiling on the price of certain items, so that if a purveyor paid overmuch for them the excess would be knocked off his discharge claim. In 1475, for instance, Robert Parker, caterer and kitchen clerk to Joan and Robert Radcliffe, was not allowed to claim more than 3½d for a pig; the auditor reduced all claims outside this amount.

The need to control expenditure by careful husbandry rather than denial, plus the continual problem of careless and sometimes criminal servants such as those of whom the ninth Percy earl complained so bitterly,[12] called for a close documentation of household purchases. Household accounts, especially those after c.1350, are highly detailed documents from which we can discern a great deal about buying habits and the facts which influenced the creation of purchasing patterns. By 'purchasing patterns', I mean a regular and systematic timetable for purchasing (and also hiring) activities in logical, manageable parts; for instance, buying the week's fish each Wednesday, filling the month's grain needs on the first Monday of the month, hiring and paying workmen on Fridays, etc. Most households evolved distinctive, persistent systems, obviously necessary for the satisfactory provision of a large establishment.

[11]A. R. Myers, ed., The Household of Edward IV (Manchester University Press, Manchester, 1959), pp. 89–90.
[12]James Heywood Markland, 'Instructions by Henry Percy Ninth Earl of Northumberland to his son Algernon', Archaeologia 27 (1838), p. 317.

These systems were employed by a number of caterers. The buying staff of the household is difficult to define; it was considerably more amorphous than the staff of, for instance, the chapel or chamber. In fact, anyone in the household, including the master himself, could be deputed to purchase goods or hire labourers. In the smaller households, servants specifically hired as caterers and purveyors were practically nonexistent. While the cook and baker, and occasionally a cator, probably superintended and regulated the majority of food expenses, one can otherwise say little about purveyance staff in small households. Necessary expenses were decided upon by the steward and cook, or steward and chaplain, or steward and master (depending on the nature of the item to be bought or the service hired). The actual job of purveying was handed over, in many cases, to whoever was free, or to whoever was riding in the right direction on other business. Purveyance must often have formed a major part of the general servant's business.

In the larger households, the sheer bulk of necessary provisions required the employment of a more specific catering staff. Nevertheless, even in large establishments the master and other servants who travelled were frequently enlisted to make purchases: in 1473 Lord Mountjoy, the husband of the Dowager Duchess Anne Stafford, frequently bought grain and livestock for household consumption.[13] Even estate ministers, neighbours, guests, relatives and tenants might be asked to purvey occasionally. Advantage was always taken of anyone's travels – a natural consequence of the expense and hazard of transport. Receivers were frequently and regularly employed to purvey wine for their masters' households, probably because of the receiver's constant perambulation, which brought the holder of such an office to ports where wine was available, and because a receiver already had access to the large amounts of cash needed to finance the high cost of a large amount of wine, and of its carriage to the household. Despite this rather malleable catering staff, quite striking buying and catering patterns emerged in the household. Running in weekly, monthly and quarterly cycles, these patterns were the necessary response to the problems of providing for a large number of needs for numerous people.

Catering for large number of people necessitates special arrangements rather different from those made by the average nuclear family. Feeding a group of over fifteen, as opposed to one of under ten, is not merely a quantitative difficulty, but a qualitative one. The simple multiplication of the procedure for the smaller group does not convert it well. Problems of transportation, of considerably more time spent in

[13]BL Add. MS 29,608.

purveying, of finding items in large enough quantitites, of arranging for constant fresh supplies, immediately arise. Large modern institutions – hospitals, nursing homes, restaurants, etc. – deal with the purveyance problem by the organization of a schedule, which allows the buyer to make the most of his time and of available resources. Medieval noble households, also, seem to have relied upon a time-based system of purchasing and hiring as the most efficient way of dealing with the problem of catering for establishments of between 25 and 160 individuals. Surviving, day-to-day household accounts often show strong weekly patterns in the buying of foods and goods to be consumed within a short period of time, and in the hiring of short-term or piecework employment. Such patterns are highly idiosyncratic, varying considerably in detail from one household to the next; but all are marked by three basic elements which unite their variations into an understandable system.

First, we notice that transactions were concentrated on certain days in the week, buying and hiring being restricted to three or so days a week, usually the same ones. Weekly patterns are also marked by the tendency to divide up types of purchases between the various days: for instance, the Luttrells of Dunster bought nearly 90 per cent of their fresh meat on Sundays, and all their candles for the week on Fridays. Finally, in most households one day a week stands out in the accounts as the heaviest buying day, and the day on which business was settled. These sorts of weekly patterns may be absent from the accounts of the greatest households, those of dukes, earls and bishops, despite the immense detail and great care with which their accounts were compiled. Less obvious patterns emerge because buying in these households was on such a vast scale that continuous purveyance of basics was necessary. Goods and services were not always relegated to their own days by type, but might occur nearly every day. What these bigger households do tend to exhibit, however, this time in common with their smaller brethren, are monthly and/or quarterly patterns.

Long-term patterns manifest themselves in the purchase of stock goods, special purchases (that is, of goods not requiring regular replenishment), long-term services, and items daily used in small quantities, such as grain, spices and carting services. Service of indefinite length, and goods which were daily used but seldom spoiled, were often for the sake of convenience renewed over even longer periods, at quarter-yearly intervals. Wages of household servants, and the purchase of wine and ale, were almost universally managed at quarterly intervals. These quarters were usually fixed within, though they varied between, households. Most households used the traditional quarter-days employed by the Exchequer: the Annunication (25 March), the Nativity of John the Baptist (29 June) or Midsummer, Michaelmas (29 September), and Christmas; while some few employed a quite different set of dates: All Hallows (1 November), Candlemass (2 February), Easter, and probably the Feast of St James (25 July). The Staffords, from Henry son of the first Duke of Buckingham to Edward the third duke, experimented with at least three different quarter-reckonings. Despite variations, the basic principles of weekly, monthly and quarterly consumption patterns persisted in almost all households.

What caused such patterns? In determining buying and hiring patterns, we need to consider three compounded and simultaneous factors, which must have influenced systems of purveyance: the types of items and services required; the nature of their purchase – fresh or stock, piecework or long-term hiring; and their source.

The reader will notice that the majority of items consumed by the household are foodstuffs of some sort. Three large categories of consumption are best distinguished, as they often are in household accounts themselves: foodstuffs, non-food goods, and services. Food was without doubt the single greatest expense, not only of the household (as it is in most modern homes), but of the lord's whole concern; any discussion of household consumption is necessarily preoccupied with food, since it is required for the maintenance of a large establishment, and is also the most basic and primitive of hospitable offerings, entertainments, and ways to illustrate splendour and largesse. Nineteenth- and indeed many twentieth-century discussions of the household have become engrossed in and eventually subsumed by descriptions of the staggering amounts, odd nature, strange preparation and splendid presentation of the food purveyed by and served in the household. Such descriptions can be initially interesting, but eventually lead to tedium, and they often lead to historical misconceptions. The gluttonous, overfed English aristocrat with his penchant for honey-laden dishes served in innumerable courses, and his permanent indigestion, is portrayed in book after book of serious historical inquiry. A. R. Myers, in his introduction to *The Household Book of Edward IV*, assumes this attitude on the part of the reader and is constrained to draw attention to the subject.[14] One, at least partially serious, explanation of what is sometimes seen as the irritability and resultant readiness to fight on the part of the fifteenth-century English noble is that his high meat diet made him chronically constipated.[15]

[14]Myers, *Edward IV*, p. 1.
[15]Lawrence Stone, *An Elizabethan: Sir Horatio Palavicino* (Oxford University Press, Oxford, 1956), pp. 33–7.

One must admit that Jones and Furnivall, Jeaffreson et al., had some reason for this portrayal. The modern mind canot help but be appalled at the high amounts of food consumed under such as the fifth Earl of Northumberland: in one year, 16 932 bushels of wheat; 27 594 gallons of ale; 1646 gallons of wine; 20 800 pounds of currants; 124 beef cattle; 667 sheep; 14 000 herring.[16] The sheer amount of food, and also its variety – with swans, boars, sixty different kinds of spices, twenty-eight flavoured waters from 'water of columbine' to 'water of fennell' – stagger the modern imagination. Like the speed of light and the age of the earth, these are numbers which we have great difficulty assimilating, as they have little in common with the pantry of the modern family. We must, however, think of the household in institutional terms, in institutional proportions. Small hospitals and nursing homes cater in similar amounts to the above, without being accused of gluttony. For instance, in the Percy household in the early sixteenth century, 27 594 gallons of ale equalled one and one-half quarts per person per day; as this was the chief water-substitute, the amount is not unusual – most humans today require a minimum of two quarts of liquid *per diem*. The 798 animals providing red meat to the Percy household would have yielded 166 household members in average of somewhat less than a quarter-pound of meat daily – about the modern recommended requirement; and the nutritional and calorific value of food was less in the middle ages. We need not, then, become involved in recounting the amounts of food consumed; but some account of the varieties of medieval food as these affected consumption and purveyance patterns would be useful.

Eight basic categories, common to most households in England during the period from 1350 to 1550, can be discerned: grain, meat, poultry, fish, dairy products and eggs, vegetables, spices and fruits, and ale and wine. The grain most commonly used was wheat, in bread especially but also in porridges, pastries, stuffings, batters, and the like. Wheat probably out-bulked all other foodstuffs in its use. Barley, malt, rye, and various pulses were used in coarser breads, meat cases, brewing, and feed for horses and poultry. Red meat was probably the most expensive item of consumption. Beef cattle, and sheep, were the most common source of protein; but calves, oxen, lambs, pigs, boars and even occasionally a milk cow were also consumed. Venison, oddly, seldom enters the accounts, probably because it was hunted rather than purchased. Most red meat was bought as livestock, either for immediate slaughter or for pasturing as a pantry on the hoof; but dead animals,

[16]*NHB*, section I.

whole or butchered, were obtained occasionally. As well as red meat, the more delicate flesh of poultry and wildfowl varied the medieval diet. Chickens, capons and pullets were the most common domestic bird consumed, and duck was a frequently enjoyed wildfowl; but geese, pigeons, swans, herons, occasional peacocks, larks, sparrows, and such sea birds as gulls and terns, were also eaten. For at least a third of the days of the year, however, meat was forbidden by the church; in the more pious households, not only Fridays and Lent, but Advent, Wednesdays and Saturdays were observed as days of abstinence. The alternative source of protein utilized was fish: river, sea, fresh, salt, or pickled. It would be impossible to recount the huge variety of fish types, well over 150, consumed. Salmon, fresh or preserved herring, sprats, trout and plaice most commonly graced the table. All manner of seafood – lobster, crab, crayfish, mussels, oysters – can be found, though more frequently and in greater variety in some households than others.

Certain purchases recurred daily: various dairy products, and eggs. Milk (and cream), though not used as a drink, was necessary to the cook, who might use several gallons in a day. Eggs were used in numerous receipes, and were also eaten on their own, especially at breakfast: eggs, ale and a 'dish' of butter constituted the standard morning meal for Anne and Edward Stafford.[17] Butter, of course, had numerous other uses. Cheese figures in few accounts. William Langland in *Piers Plowman* called it 'the poor man's meat', which nobles did not deign to use; but it is more likely that cheese – soft new cheese being considered more digestible than the harder, mature variety – was made by the household and hence does not require entry in the accounts. Vegetables have been put in the same category as cheeses, because they seldom appear in accounts or recipes – a food of the poor, unfit for the finer table. In fact, certain manuscripts of the *Liber Niger*, the Black Book of the household of Edward IV, list vegetables among necessary items to be purveyed, and they are commonly featured in accounts of castle gardens, along with such herbs as rosemary, sage and thyme. Like cheeses, vegetables were 'home-grown', not usually requiring purveyance, and so do not enter the accounts. While vegetables were not eaten on their own as commonly as now, they were essential ingredients in many soups, stuffings and dressings. Onions, leeks, garlic, turnips, mushrooms and parsnips are especially common; vegetables such as carrots, cabbage, kale and lettuce are never mentioned.

Besides the common, garden-grown herbs and vegetables, more

[17]BL Add. MS 34,213 and Staffs. RO D 1712/2/6.

exotic spices and fruits were demanded by the medieval palate, both for purposes of preservation and for their own sakes. The variety of spices – about sixty different kinds –is staggering; from such common modern ones as cinnamon, mustard and ginger to items we can today scarcely identify: cubebs, 'graynes of paridyse', erringo root. Fruits such as oranges, lemons, figs, dates and raisins were imported; English goods – apples, rose hips, various berries, and numerous edible flowers such as rose petals, dried elderflower, and sunflower stalks (called Jerusalem artichokes) – were also purchased. By the late fifteenth century, conventional sweetmeats such as biscuits, suckets (boiled sweets) and comfits also enter the accounts.

Water was no more convenient and considerably less safe to drink than alcoholic beverages; ale and various kinds of wines were commonly drunk at all meals. Some households brewed most of their own ale from malt and barley; others purchased most of what they required from local producers. Ale came in several grades, depending on alcohol content, clarity and the quality of the grain used; most households kept a 'best ale' and a 'second ale' in their cellars. Belying the famous ditty, hops for beer first appeared in the 1480s but were not in general used until the early sixteenth century. By the 1520s, beer was as or more common than ale in the household.[18] While some vineyards did exist in the southern parts of England, which were exploited by their owners – mainly monasteries – to make wine, their yields were small; so most wine was imported from Europe, generally France, but also Spain and Bavaria. In the end of the fourteenth and the early years of the fifteenth century, wine was usually only differentiated as 'red' or 'white'; but by 1450 such distinctions as Bastard (a sweet Spanish dessert wine), Rhenish, and occasionally Malmsey appear.

This very cursory tour of foodstuffs generally consumed in English households gives some idea of the varied diet and resulting complications in purveyance with which the household had to cope. Determining where these foodstuffs could be got, in what quantities, how long they would remain fresh, and how often they were needed, had probably the greatest influence upon the development of household consumption patterns.

Other goods, however, non-edible stuffs, had also to be purveyed by the household. These vary considerably in type from household to household, and include many special items not requiring regular replenishment, such as fire irons, chairs, bells, etc. In general,

---

[18]H. S. Corran, A History of Brewing (David and Charles, Newton Abbot, 1975), pp. 50–3.

households used several wide ranging categories to deal with non-food goods: cloth and clothing (the largest non-food category); candles, wax and wicks, torches and other lighting implements; coal, wood, rushes, and other fuel; ironmongery; and building materials. The heating, lighting and maintenance of a castle or large manor house, and the dressing of, often, over 100 people, required considerable organization – especially when such bulky items as rushes, or hard to locate goods such as red satin, had to be purveyed – and affected purveying systems.

As well as goods, even the largest and most self-sufficient households required certain services, short-term or long. Households which oversaw a demesne farm often hired full-time and seasonal agricultural labourers; constant maintenance required not only materials but builders and labourers. Most households in England, except some mainly monastic ones, had to rely on smiths outside the establishment; in some cases households, such as Lady Margaret Long's in 1542, saved up numerous jobs and then hired a monger outright for a week or more's labour. Finally, in most households, carters had to be employed to supplement household transport services, and especially in the carriage of consumables to the household from the place of purchase. These services, many of them intimately involved with the getting of the goods described above, were largely financed out of the household's pocket, and were generally adapted to the system of purveying and accounting for goods.

The nature of the goods and services required by the household was the initial factor in the evolution of purveyance patterns, depending on what each household ate or used. But the manner of purveying such items was particularly affected, through the nature of the goods and services involved, by the chance of spoilage, bulk, and the frequency with which the items were consumed. Items which were eaten daily and spoiled quickly had to be purchased frequently. Goods which kept well, or were bulky enough to require special transport, were purchased in large quantitites at long intervals. The buying of 'fresh achats' and 'gross emptions', and the balance between them, exercised considerable influence over the purveyance pattern of a household.

Fresh achats include those items bought for more or less immediate use, and in most cases were a repetitive purchase of items frequently and rapidly consumed. Goods were probably purchased fresh for several reasons. Firstly, quickness in spoiling might force the house necessarily to buy certain goods in small amounts at frequent intervals: eggs and butter, for instance. Eaten nearly every day, these items were bought on average about three times a week in nearly all the households I have examined. Milk and cheese were less frequently consumed, but, probably due to their rate of spoilage, were always bought as fresh achats. Items which probably lasted rather better, but were used in such quantities and so frequently that stock had to be continually replenished, were also purchased in this way: butchered meat, some livestock, poultry, and fresh fish. These items consituted the daily shopping list of household purveyors. Certain services can also be conveniently grouped with fresh achats – short-term and piecework labour. Builders doing minor repair work, wives hired to weed the castle garden, seasonal agricultural labourers, and in some households stablehands, were paid once a week, although their wages were computed *per diem*.

Fresh achats, because of the frequency of their purchases, were often paid for by a credit system, similar to many modern milk delivery services. Instead of paying for daily purveyed eggs and butter at each transaction, the household paid in one lot for all those items consumed over a week. This system prevented the household from having to keep an open supply of small coinage, and allowed financial officers to organize payments on a single day, which they could then oversee. Positive evidence for such a credit system exists in the accounts for the households of Hugh Luttrell and the Cromwells of Tydd, and is implicit in many other day-accounts. While, for the individual from whom the goods were purchased, such a system could create a backlog of payments, it also meant that they might bring about a virtual monopoly on provisioning the household in question. A credit system meant reliance on a limited set of providers with whom credit agreements were made.

Some goods and services were better bought as stock or gross emptions – that is, items got for the larder, purchased in bulk to last over a period of at least a month and often longer. Items fashioned to remain usable over a long period of time, such as pickled and salted meats and fish, were naturally purchased as stock. One would expect stock to be of primary importance in the winter months, but in fact little evidence exists to show that this was the case. Items of consumption show little change throughout the year, regardless of the seasons – calves and lambs, despite price fluctuations, were consumed the year round in steady proportion to the rest of the diet. Grain was not purchased in greater quantities during September, though cheaper then. Somewhat more salt meat and fish was consumed in the winter months, but freshly slaughtered meat was as common. Seasonal variation seem to have made little impression on the aristocracy's consumption, though household servants may have lived off salt beef over the winter months.

Livestock formed the greatest part of the household's pantry – a larder on the hoof. Quite large herds of cattle and sheep were grazed or in winter fed on hay near the household, to be culled periodically for the table. Chicken coops and rabbit hutches, ponds for ducks and fish, and freerange geese in the park, are mentioned in whole or in part in the records of many households. Frequently used but exceedingly bulky goods, which took time, money and organization to purvey and cart to the household, were also usually bought in large amounts, to keep the household supplied for between a month and a quarter year at a time. Candles, cloth, fuel, rushes, wine, ale and grain were most often purchased in this manner. Daily or even weekly purveyance of the wheat and ale used daily would have required considerable needless energy; therefore caterers contrived to use the storage space of cellars and granaries to keep the household supplied with these goods.

Other items which were used frequently but in very small quantities were also most easily bought as stock items. Cinnamon, ginger and other spices, salt, dates, fish oil, vinegar, and other condiments could be stored almost indefinitely, and a relatively small amount might suffice for a year. This explains why, in addition to a daily routine, caterers made special but regular expeditions to get these major items. Certain services were also handled in the manner of stock items – at long intervals, to cover up to a quarter's service. Continuing labour of indefinite term was frequently paid in this way. Household servants are the most obvious example; in every wage list I have seen they were paid at every quarter. Also some carters and agricultural labourers who worked regularly for the lord were reimbursed every month, or more often each quarter.

Stock purchases were also sometimes assisted by standing credit arrangements, so that the caterer did not have to be trusted with truly large sums of money, and so that he could continue to purvey more necessities even if his cash had run out. While creditors could and did have difficulties in obtaining payment, they were also assured to some extent of continuous patronage.

Thus we find that, depending on what the household tended to consume, caterers had a double buying and payment system: a daily/weekly routine of fresh foods to purchase, and a less frequent but more strenuous system of stock replenishment. Some households relied much more on fresh produce than stock, and some vice versa, depending on their dietary basis and size. Whether favouring fresh or stock buying and hiring, however, the establishment of particular days as buying days within the pattern was largely determined by the available sources of foodstuffs, goods, and labour.

The great majority of goods and services required by the household, especially as fresh achats, could be obtained within the locality, within half a day's ride from the household base. This was, of course, necessarily the case for certain items, especially milk and eggs; no household could have survived for long in a wasteland, regardless of their carting facilities. The centres of noble establishments, castles and manor houses, were from the earliest times strategically placed where supplies were easily obtained. What is perhaps surprising is the extent to which households with transport and large nearby market towns continued to rely on the rural locality for goods and services; and surprising too is the ability of that area to fill household demands. One common explanation for the movement of noble establishments is that such households stripped the countryside of available goods over a few months and then moved on to another area whose supplies were not exhausted. However, as I have previously indicated, households came to achieve a great stability, beginning in the late thirteenth century, without creating deserts in their immediate vicinity. Clearly, it was possible to create a balance of production and demand within a relatively small area. Local purveyance was divided into two methods: purchase at market, and direct from farmers.

Many small households relied almost entirely on several local, weekly markets where they could obtain most of the household's fresh achats and some stock goods. Here lies the explanation of buying day variations. The Dunster town market was held on Friday, when we find the Luttrell household bought most of its provisions, especially red meat. In the larger nearby town of Minehead, the market was held on Wednesdays, when most of the week's fish was purchased. When we further consider that Dunster's was chiefly a cattle market, and that Minehead is still a renowned fish port, the distinction of types of food purveyance for different days becomes fully understandable. This correlation of chief buying days with local markets occurred in every single household with appropriate surviving records.

Markets were less satisfactory for supplying the fresh achats of bigger establishments. The buyers for abbots' households usually purveyed for the monastery as well, which a market might not be able to supply in full; and peripatetic households, such as those of bishops, did not always travel in synchronization with market days. Also, the sheer quantity of daily requirements often precluded total dependence on markets, especially those of smaller towns which were noble bases. These were simply not large enough to produce regularly the quantities of livestock, fish and butchered meat required by the great noble establishments. It is rather like attempting to obtain, regularly, ten

Plate 10 A local market. MS Gough Liturg. 7, f. 11. Flemish, c.1500. Courtesy of the Bodleian Library, Oxford.

pounds of cheese from a corner shop each week; ultimately one is better off getting closer to the initial suppler.

Big households – and small households to a lesser degree – relied directly upon local farmers to supply them with certain goods. The majority of nobles obtained fresh meat from regular circles of six to ten farmers around their main country homes, and, relying upon wider circles of perhaps fifteen farmers, probably established some informal agreement about supplies; the animals were exchanged and driven to the household area as needed, so as not to exhaust the grazing lands. Similarly, fresh fish could be got from the fishing boats themselves. Other fresh achats which required replenishment daily, such as milk, eggs and butter, might be obtained from local farmers, often by a regular arrangement – I have already discussed credit systems. Stock goods such as grain and ale were also obtained direct from farmers, who could supply them in the necessary bulk. The major exceptions to this purveyance arrangement are those monasteries and episcopal establishments endowed with lands which were farmed direct or those whose fees were still paid in kind. Some ecclesiastical establishments, such as Durham Priory, were practically self-sufficient in grain production and did not need to purvey from local farmers.

Finally, the great majority of the labourers, skilled and unskilled, who were hired by the household, came from the locality. Wage labourers, and peasant farmers outside the busiest harvest season, were taken on for building repairs and demesne husbandry. Household members, as we have already seen in chapter 2, were frequently of local stock, as far as can be shown. However, certain goods and services were simply not obtainable within half a day's ride of the household centre. Fine cloth, ready-made clothing, wine, spices, goldsmiths' work, and master masonry could not be located in the relatively small, country areas in which most households had their primary abodes. For such, recourse was made to bigger, urban centres.

Some households, because of their closeness to such centres, relied on them even for some fresh achats and regular stock food, particularly if they had a house in London or a similar major urban centre, such as Bristol, which they frequented. Chiefly, however, households seem to have relied upon the larger towns for items and services which could not be obtained locally. Wine, spices, jewellery, clothing, fine cloth, special candles and torches, armour, dried fruit and sweetmeats had to be got in a large town; the services of goldsmiths, drapers, mercers, and shoemakers were more readily available there. The extent to which the household relied upon the towns was determined in part by its particular demand for luxury goods. Wine, spices, and good quality cloth, because they were generally imported from overseas and because they were quasi-necessities – no gentleman's standard of living excluded these – were bought in the nearest large town. As well as London, places like Bristol, Boston, Colchester, Chelsmford, Norwich and Coventry provided nobles with imported and skilfully made goods.

The accounts of merchants such as the Celys bear out the importance of noble and gentle patronage in their garnerning of income via luxury goods.[19] The purveyance of consumables varied, depending on the household. Nearness and ease of access to large towns influenced how often they were used, and determined how visits to them fitted into the purveyance pattern. In most cases, items from the towns were bought in stock quantities. Those such as spices and wines, due to the latter's bulk and the former's daily use in small amounts, lent themselves to stock buying; but cloth was also purchased in bulk. Visits to these centres from most households, therefore, seldom occurred more than twice a quarter, and often less. Unlike local stock purveyance, however, such shopping expeditions were not always regularly arranged occurrences, but were more often made in conjunction with the receiver's business or the master's travels.

In some households we also find that purveyors had a direct overseas link. As with the direct trading with local farmers, foreign contacts could have been exploited for the easier and cheaper garnering of the many ells of velvet and gallons of wine and pounds of spice consumed yearly, circumventing the retail profits of the shops. The maintenance of such a contact, however, required its own full-time employees, involved sizeable speculative shipments, and ultimately entangled the household in a trade system which was not its chief object. Overseas contacts, then, tended to be largely fortuitous. The recently published Lisle letters show most clearly how a noble might use an official position or a trading link to import luxury goods and foreign necessaries, especially wine and cloth and spices, more easily and cheaply for household and personal use, either himself purveying while in Europe or using a servant stationed permanently in Europe to do so.

The consumption rate of the household as a body was, as we have seen, formidable. Six hundred and sixty-seven sheep *per annum*, even when placed in proper perspective, is still a great many sheep. Naturally, the noble household affected trade in England, on a local and also a wider level. The decimation of a countryside was doubtless occasionally the case in a superficial sense – Peter of Blois frequently

---

[19]See especially Alison Hanham, ed., *The Cely Letters* (Early English Texts Society, Oxford, vol. 273, 1975), nos 31, 40, 42, 55, 83, 123.

mentions the exhaustion of an area's immediate supplies by a visitation of King Henry II and his court[20] – but the more settled households of the later middle ages, to survive, must have reached some sort of equilibrium between supply and demand. The effect of the household on some aspects of overseas trade is obvious. Such items as sugar, pepper, dates, wine, silks, velvet, German armour, Flemish horses, and other luxury items were almost wholly consumed by the aristocratic classes and their households. Without these noble establishments, Italian merchants who specialized in such terms would have had little business in Britain. While it had little effect on the staple English international trade of wool and wool cloth, the luxuries market strongly affected the character of London, and also the provincial metropolises on which many nobles depended for the attainment of luxury goods. Households created steady demands on these trading centres, and utilized their sophisticated services on a regular basis.

But the real effect of the household was felt on a local level, in those small towns and villages wherein lords established their largely permanent homes. The presence of a noble and his household created a demand for numerous local products in bulk, serving in effect as an economic stimulus to the area. Moreover, it was a regular source of demand, increasing, if anything, throughout the later middle ages as households tended to get larger. Regardless of war, political crisis, plague, etc., the household had people to feed, a house to maintain, and a status to keep up, which meant that its consumption level was unlikely to fluctuate drastically. Just as the growth of towns created an increase in secondary consumers who did not produce their own food and by whom a surplus was required from primary consumers, so the noble household was a cash source for farmers. The latter, however, was a more immediate stimulus; it required less outlay in terms of time, carting expenses, etc. As well as local goods, the household demanded and sought local services – carting, building repairs, woodcutting, garden and demesne agricultural labour, and numerous other chores, as well as the skills and crafts of the tanner, smith and brewer. During the less than fruitful times of the year – in winter, and in June before the first crops sprang – the extra income provided to locals via household work must have helped to even out the tenor of medieval rural life; through the household, at least some of the money collected by the lord through rents and fines found its way back into the hands of those from whom it came originally. Many medieval markets were created by the

---

[20]Petrus Blesensis, *Opera Omnia*, ed. J.A. Giles (4 vols, I.H. Parker, Oxford, 1847), vol. 1: *Epistolae*, no. 14, pp. 49–52.

aristocracy's receipt of royal charters to establish such trading centres near their chief homes, chiefly from the eleventh to the thirteenth century. This explains the existence of markets in such small places as Dunster, Castle Hedingham, and Tattershall, while none were ever established in considerably larger towns nearby.[21] The establishment of a trading centre, to which the household continued to supply demands for local produce, not only stimulated the production of surplus goods and services, but stimulated demands for these. As well as for householders, the market became a supply centre for those from the area within a day's ride of it; they came not only to sell, but to buy. Such markets, serving their rural surroundings, created trade communities which formed the basis of medieval internal trade in England.

There was, of course, significant damage which a household could inflict upon a countryside's economy, too. Even a relatively stable establishment might, especially with a change of master, suddenly take to a new home, depriving the area of accustomed demands. A household might also demand and get labourers at a time when farmers could ill afford to lose extra hands, such as at harvest season. By the early sixteenth century, extensive enclosures had begun to eat away at wasteland which an expanding peasant population could have colonized. Households could, and distressingly often did, purvey on credit, building up huge debts which they were in no hurry to pay; and few local farmers or tradesmen would have been willing to act against noble customers. Elizabeth Phillips, a London silk-woman to whom Edward Stafford owed several hundred pounds outstanding for nearly a year, wrote numerous dunning letters to his caterers in 1519 and 1520, but continued to deal with the Duke's servants and allow them credit.[22]

Nevertheless, in order to survive in stability, any household ultimately had to balance its drain on the local community with the latter's ability to fill its demands. As a result, the household acted as an economic institution, both internally, as a way of the lord's controlling his income and expenditure, and externally, as an organization through which some international, but especially local, supply and demand was modified. Alan Macfarlane, in *The Origins of English Individualism*, has remarked upon the strong evidence of regular surplus production by English farmers as early as the thirteenth century, and argues that an exploration of this phenomenon might help to explain that great puzzle of economic history, why 'capitalist' methods of economy developed at

---

[21]J.A. Chartres, *Internal Trade in England, 1500–1700* (Macmillan, London, 1977), pp. 47–50.

[22]BL Royal MS 14B XXXV D.

all. The beginnings of stability among English noble households in much the same period may very well have been one of the stimuli to surplus production and a market economy.

4

In Negociis Domini:
Politics and the Household

The Earl of Worcester
Hath broke his staff, resigned his stewardship,
And all the household servants fled with him
To Bolingbroke.

Richard II (II.ii)

Political history is probably that area of study with which we most readily associate the noble classes. The part of the medieval nobleman in the form, organization, administration, defence and government of his particular social order has exercised the wits of many scholars. This book has so far been chiefly concerned with other aspects of noble households. The involvement of the household in what was one of its master's chief concerns must now be considered. The medieval noble household has seldom been examined in this light, yet it played both a passive and an active role in its master's administrative duties, parliamentary activity, military endeavours, and intrigues at home and abroad. The part of the household in political affairs is discerned in the frequency of the phrase '*in negociis domini*' in household accounts and other household records. The part of the household *in negociis domini*, upon the lord's business, is revealed in a surprising number of varied and important functions, through which the household and household members could come to exercise important if discreet powers, helping or betraying their masters in times of crisis, and vicariously participating in the political life and government of the county and kingdom. While the nature and extent of this involvement was naturally dependent upon the lord's own status and the expectations and origins of individual household members, an examination of these varying roles will exhibit the importance of his household in the career of the medieval nobleman.

The most obvious and the most superficial role of the household in its master's political career was the performance of those duties which made possible the lord's involvement in local and national affairs: the mechanics behind the exercise of power. Much of this includes the ability to absorb odd payments into the household's economy and also to provide ready money when required. Accounts reveal numerous payments of annuities and the provision of liveries for the lord's clients, retainers and allies. *Regarda* were handed out to visiting messengers and the servants of other nobles. Fees of legal advisers were paid. Gentry and others who rode to meet the lord to give and take counsel were reimbursed for their expenses. In most households, such payments amounted to about 9 per cent of the household's yearly expenditure.

The household also supported the lord's political life by the provision of necessary services. The suitable entertainment of people important to a lord's political position was certainly an important detail; much value was consciously attached to the showing of honour and worship as an outward recognition of power and influence. Providing food, entertainment, accommodation, stabling, and sometimes clothing and fresh horses to visitors was often crucial to the development of a working relationship between the lord and the recipient of these favours. Such diplomatic hospitality was not merely extended to officials or men of obvious personal stature. Many a lord daily entertained townspeople, tenants, merchants, and local farmers, building up ties of good will and mutual assistance between local communities and himself.

The household also could be used to organize, as well as finance, political manoeuvres. However, these roles, important as they were, did not in themselves convey to household members a direct or responsible role in political action. If this organization of the mechanics of power were the sole function of the household in its master's local and national involvement, it could be quite legitimately ignored. In fact, the noble household also occupied more directly involved positions in its master's political career, which deserve the attention of the historian.

Perhaps the simplest active role played by the household was in the provision of messengers. Unlike the royal household, nobles had no official messenger service. From the performance of mundane secretarial tasks of buying, preparing, providing for the lord's political requirements – probably often without full knowledge of the significance of such provisions – individual servants could be removed temporarily from the normal sphere of household activities to carry and receive letters, to convey and return instructions, and to assess the attitudes of opposite parties. While this activity could be called a rather mechanical one, involving little initiative or involvement, one must remember that an unscrupulous or careless messenger was a dangerous thing; and at times his judgement as to how, when and before whom he might deliver a message, especially an oral one, was extremely important. Moreover, a messenger might be asked to make observations and deductions from what he saw and how he was treated. George Cavendish, acting as a harbinger for Wolsey in France, attached much importance to, and was always careful to report to Wolsey, the manner of his reception, as it reflected the host's attitude to Wolsey himself.[1] Several of the Paston and Stonor letters also exhibit the importance attached to how a messenger was received, such as John Malpas's report, to his master the Earl of Oxford, of Paston's good treatment of him in a land transaction.[2] The servants of William Cromwell and Hugh Luttrell, in their letters to their absent masters, conveyed their impressions of affairs abroad and at home.[3]

In some cases, a servant's role of messenger changed to that of ambassador or deputy for his master, enabling him to treat with others concerning the message carried, and to make decisions, agree to undertakings, and perform duties on the lord's behalf. Such deputizing could occur on several different levels. Lords serving as sheriffs often deputized their servants to make arrests and carry out distresses. When lords such as Cardinal Wolsey, Sir Anthony Brown, the Lisles, Gilbert de Clare, the Earl and Countess de Warrene, Hugh Luttrell and William Cromwell were absent from the realm, they employed servants to ride *in negociis domini pro consilio*, taking counsel with various local gentry and sometimes acting upon that counsel. This allowed the household member considerable responsibility and scope for initiative in making important decisions about estate administration, legal matters, etc. *in loco domini*.

Perhaps the most interesting and informative evidence concering such deputization is that contained in the third Duke of Buckingham's letters of instructions to his chancellor, Robert Gilbert, when the latter was in London in November 1520.[4] Gilbert was instructed by his master to deliver various 'letters of credence', to speak with Wolsey and all others to whom he took these epistles, and to determine and affect the recipients' attitudes to these documents' contents, of which Gilbert was fully cognizant. Most of these concerned the duke's desire to go to his Welsh estates with an armed retinue, for which he wanted Wolsey's consent and the support of others such as Sir Harry Owen, the royal

---

[1]George Cavendish, *The Life and Death of Cardinal Wolsey*, ed. Richard Sylvester, (Early English Texts Society, London, vol. 243, 1959), pp. 54–6.

[2]Norman Davis, ed., *Paston Letters and Papers of the Fifteenth Century* (Clarendon Press, Oxford, 2 vols., 1871 and 1976), vol. II, no. 837.

[3]Kent RO Cat Mk U1475 A83 and Somerset RO DD/L P/37/13–17.

[4]BL Cotton Titus Bi fos 171–4.

household's comptroller, and Sir Thomas Lovell; others involved Gilbert's getting information about the French king's and the emperor's activities. Gilbert was also ordered to take counsel with such as Lord and Lady Fitzwalter, arrange for various loans, hire servants, mollify creditors, check up on various land sales and trading interests, order Christmas gifts for the royal court, and make personal calls on the duke's friends and relatives. Clearly, Gilbert, and such other servants who acted as deputies for their masters, were crucial to a nobleman's ability to keep his finger on the pulse of developments at court and in the country, especially when the lord himself was not able to be present.

Such exceptional duties required exceptional men; and we must examine the sorts of household members who became involved in these functions. The simpler messenger services can be found to be performed by servants, and by every variety of servant. Cooks, valets, purveyors and even pages carried oral and written notices; but purveyors – probably because of their wider knowledge of the country and the convenience of using them – and personal chamber servants were perhaps employed more frequently than other sorts of servant. Servants employed in conciliar deputization and undertaking delicate ambassadorial functions, however, were almost wholly drawn from the upper ranks of the household staff. Higher servants were generally the more trusted people in the household, and were usually more cognizant of their master's plans and policies. They reached and held their positions because of their facility in organization and administration, and probably also because of their ability to communicate with and please the noble class employing them; all attributes necessary to the servant deputy. And, of course, many of these upper servants were themselves from the gentle classes. This not only increased their masters' trust in them and allowed them greater facility in working with other nobles and gentry, since their own prestige and influence worked in the master's favour; it also gave them a natural desire to participate in such employment, which could further the interests of their own families and foundations and allow gentle servants the luxury of a kind of vicarious power.

These gentle servants were one constituent of one of a noble's most important political weapons, his affinity. Broadly, this was his network of peers, patrons and clients, fellow nobles and gentles with the same interests, pursuits and needs, who worked together for mutual benefit and support, generally centred on local power bases. The ties between them ranged from the carefully specified and legally recognized, to the most tenuous and vaguely defined. Traditionally, the affinity was drawn from the feudal system of land tenure and was related to feudal

Plate 11 Sir Richard Beauchamp and his personal following at the Battle of Shrewsbury. *Pageant of Richard Beauchamp*, Cott. Ms. Julius E iv, art. 6, f. 4. English, c. 1465. Courtesy of The British Library.

obligations of military service and protection, and many lord–client relationships in the fifteenth century still had a feudal background; but the gradual commutation of feudal duties, the outlawing of subinfuedation in 1290, and changes in the composition and power of county families led to a much more complex situation. From the fourteenth century at least, clientage and affinity had little to do with strictly feudal relationships. The retaining of followers by the payment of annuities and the granting of livery, called 'bastard feudalism' or (in the statutes against it) 'livery and maintenance', was a relatively straightforward way of assembling a power base, and its popularity is shown by the frequency of laws passed against it from the time of Richard II until the 1530s. The payment of fees and annuities was not in itself illegal, however, and lords generally spent a proportion of their income in yearly sums paid to local families whom they hoped might support them in peace (for example, on county commissions) as well as in war. Lords not only gave annuities to their followers but received payments from nobles greater than themselves, often from more than one source. This tended to produce a deeply complex tangle of vague alliances, with much sought after clients often holding the balance of power between rival lords, from both of whom fees were obtained.

Nevertheless, tried and true relationships of support and service reinforced over several generations often existed between particular clients and particular patrons. Ties between such families were commonly made stronger by the inclusion of client family members within the patron's household, itself the tightest bond of service available legally to nobles after Richard II's reign. Only resident, household servants were allowed to wear livery and to be subject to life contracts. Thus, many of the gently born servants responsible for political duties were taken from families that already had clientage ties to the lord, or families whose allegiance the lord hoped to attract or strengthen. Due to the maintenance laws, therefore, the household stood as the bedrock of the lord's wider affinity.

Both gentle servants and nonresident allies of the master's client network were members of noble councils. We know remarkably little about baronial councils and how they worked; they have left almost no records of their activities, and surface but briefly in the documents of other administrative bodies. Indeed, the existence of such private councils was hardly recognized by historians until 1925, when A.E. Levett first presented her paper on 'Baronial Councils and their Relation to Manorial Courts'.[5] While modern scholars have rejected Levett's

[5]Published in Ada Elizabeth Levett, *Studies in Manorial History* (Clarendon Press, Oxford, 1938), pp. 21–41.

view of the domestic council interfering with the work of manorial courts, introducing a 'strong professional element which ultimately overthrows the older traditional system', her description of conciliar composition and concerns still forms the basis for later books on the private council. Since Levett's paper was published, a number of historians have written briefly on specific baronial councils, and it has become increasingly obvious that by the mid-thirteenth century at least some form of conciliar body was common to most nobles and knights. Intimately connected with the feudal obligation to give counsel, by at latest the fourteenth century (when more information begins to appear) councils had acquired an executive as well as an advisory role, in administrative, legal, personal, estate and political affairs, and included officials and servants as well as magnates.

Nevertheless, baronial councils can still only be studied through a glass darkly, due to their peculiar nature. Unlike the King's Council, or other administrative baronial individuals and bodies like receivers-general and manor courts, the private council kept few or no records and had very little formal structure: it was essentially an indeterminate body of varying size with irregular meetings and membership. Yet a definite, it not well-defined, idea of conciliar counsel and action did exist, separate from individual sanction or informal advice. The council could advise and act as an extension of the lord himself. The peculiar formation of the baronial council was closely linked with, and perhaps sprang from, the conception of the household, and in some instances parallels the development of the King's Council.[6]

While some few peers – notably John of Gaunt and the fifth Earl of Northumberland – required counsellors to take an oath and appointed them to the office by a patent or indenture, the great majority of lords defined the membership of their council much more informally, simply requesting the persons desired to attend at each separate meeting; and even Lancaster and Northumberland had counsellors who never took an oath or received a letter, or were counsellors for several years before receiving any such formal confirmation. Some idea of the medieval conception of private counsel can, however, be discerned from existing oaths, compensation paid to counsellors, and the laws against livery and maintenance. Northumberland's counsellors were bound to give advice and make executive decisions concerning all Percy's interests. In return, they received payment in a yearly fee of 100s, equal to and listed in the chequerroll with that of the chief officers of the household, and/or an annuity, plus bouche of court (allowance of victual) when with

[6]R. Virgoe, 'The Composition of the King's Council, 1437–61', *Bulletin of the Institute of Historical Research* 43 (1970), pp. 134–60.

the lord, and a suit of his livery appropriate to the counsellor's rank: in the *Northumberland Household Book*, equal to the dean of chapel. Northumberland's riding household included two counsellors, each allowed a servant and several houses as the other upper servants, giving the impression that some counsellors were almost always in attendance. Between 1438 and 1455, the first Duke of Buckingham listed his counsellors' fees – which in his case varied with the status of the counsellor – in the yearly chequerroll of the household, fees which follow the same gradations as household wages. Except for bishops and abbots, who relied more heavily on benefices to fee counsellors, most lords retained a large number of counsellors in this way. Such retaining was legal, as the statutes of livery and maintenance exempted household members from the restrictions, and also counsellors, who are, it is posited, to be counted as part of the household.[7]

As indicated above, the persons invited to sit on baronial councils fall into three categories, one of which includes household members. People of what Rosenthal calls 'independent prominence' – that is, other peers, knights, esquires and gentlemen – are probably the oldest element of the baronial council: the friends, relatives and comrades in arms on whom he relied for advice. By at latest the mid-fourteenth century, however, two other elements had complemented and eventually superseded the baronial element. As the council became more of an executive body, feed lawyers and the lord's own salaried servants swelled its ranks. The salaried servant, as a sort of technical expert, was able to explicate and advise upon matters of counciliar concern, such as the advisability of pressuring recalcitrant tenants, the paying off of large debts, and the ins and outs of organizing a military campaign. Estate and household officials, with intimate experience in such matters and the eventual responsibility for carrying out many conciliar decisions, were an important part of the baronial council. An individual council meeting averaged between eight and twenty members,[8] though over a year's gatherings a great magnate might pay as many as fifty to seventy-five people *pro consilibus suis*. The number of counsellors tended to decrease over the span of the fifteenth century; but the importance of the household element remained strong, if anythng increasing. The nature of servants' involvement as baronial counsellors is worth examining in greater detail.

In most councils, it was the chief officers of the household who attended: the steward, chaplain, comptroller, treasurer, and secretary.

[7]*SR* II 74.75 (1390) and *SR* II 426 (1461).

[8]Joel T. Rosenthal, *Nobles and the Noble Life, 1295–1500* (Allen and Unwin, London, 1976), p. 77.

As well as their special knowledge and expertise in areas concerning the council, the personal backgrounds of such officers often made them important men in themselves, whose opinion was worth seeking because of their own influence and authority. But higher servants of yeoman stock were as active in the councils as their better born fellow household members, and it was probably for their professional knowledge and advice that they were invited to take part in baronial council sessions. But other household servants besides these top officials were to find a place on the council. Gentleman-ushers, valets and other chamber servants frequently were regular council attendants. Often well born and always in close proximity to the lord, such personal servants are obvious choice as confidants and councillors.

Some evidence exists to show that household members became the most influential and active baronial counsellors by the late 1400s. J.R. Lander and others have shown that in the King's Council under Edward IV and Richard III, household officials were probably the greatest single element at any one meeting, and that at the majority of meetings household members were all but the only members present, handling the most mundane, day-to-day duties of that body. Something similar may have occurred in baronial councils. Certainly by 1507 the third Duke of Buckingham, for whom much conciliar evidence survives, was relying chiefly upon his household men for advice and executive personnel. For three of the meetings held at Thornbury in 1507 and 1508, seven of the fourteen present were household servants; a paper describing one of the last of the duke's council meetings, on 26 October 1520 (contained among the papers gathered for his trial), shows that all those present were servants, with the exception of Thomas Cade, the receiver-general who had but recently served as a household member to the Duke.[9] T.B. Pugh makes much the same point for the counsellors of Jasper Tudor.[10] Certainly servants, being intimately involved in the carrying out of many conciliar concerns, and often of landholding families of influence with similar problems, were well able to advise their masters on most things. Moreover, a lord, knowing these men with whom he lived from day to day, was able to gauge their interests, foibles, abilities and prejudices with some clarity in considering the merit of their advice. Furthermore, they were easily available to the lord, unlike busy and peripatetic estate officials and lawyers, or other nobles with their own problems and concerns.

[9]Staffs. RO D (W) 1721/1/5; *L & P H VIII* vol. III, pt, 1, no. 1284; and Staffs. RO D 641/1/3/9.

[10]T.B. Pugh, *The Marcher Lordships of South Wales 1415–56: Select Documents* (University of Wales Press, Cardiff, 1963), pp. 290, 295.

The baronial council, then, was not ideologically attached to the household, but was often heavily recruited from household members, particularly by the late fifteenth and sixteenth centuries, and especially with regard to the most routine and regular meetings. Greater barons and bishops at times used the term 'privy council' for these meetings, probably in imitation of the royal privy council, which noble usage seems to postdate. Counsellors, as an extension of their lord's mind and desires, could also stand *in loco domini* out of his presence, conferring with others for the lord and having the power to make some decisions independently. Most fifteenth-century valors were prepared by conciliar commissions, and household members were often represented on these. Indeed, evidence that such practices were becoming widespread exists as early as the fourteenth century, when peasants can be found claiming that baronial councils were forcing them to bring their claims thither rather than to more traditional judicial bodies.[11] This supports Levett's hypothesis of the weaking of manorial courts through the actions of the council, but is not generally upheld: baronial commissions, while not unusual, were generational events usually instituted after a long minority or absence, in order to tighten up resultant slackness and confusion.[12]

Individual counsellors could also represent their master in various capacities. James Goldwell, Bishop of Norwich, summoned to the King's Council in 1520, was bidden to send one of his own counsellors if unable to attend personally.[13] Nobles seem to have exercised a similar option in negotiating with fellow nobles, particularly over land disputes and to obtain advice, and in many cases the counsellors they sent were household members: the records of the Staffords, of Elizabeth de Burgh, Lady of Clare, of Ralph and William Cromwell, of John de Mauduyt, and of many other nobles indicate this. Lords who were often abroad, such as Hugh Luttrell and Lord Lisle, and abbots in particular, frquently trusted their lay servants to stand in their place.[14]

Councils also managed their masters' domestic and personal affairs. It was the Duke of Lancaster's council that appointed household officials in the late fourteenth and early fifteenth centuries. The hiring of estate and household stewards especially was often referred to the

---

[11]*Rot. Parl.*, vol. III, p. 285.

[12]See Kenneth McFarlane, *The Nobility of Later Medieval England* (Clarendon Press, Oxford, 1973), pp. 214–17.

[13]Levett, *Studies*, p. 25.

[14]Evinced particularly in Durham Priory's relations with Finchale Priory, and in the records of Selby Abbey. See especially R.B. Dobson, *Durham Priory, 1400–50* (Cambridge University Press, Cambridge, 1970), pp. 116, 121.

council; and it was the fifth Percy earl of Northumberland's council that drew up the *Northumberland Household Book*, establishing household policy and organization. Where evidence is available, it is everywhere apparent that household members were particularly active in this sort of council business. Often counsellors were also among the witnesses, executors and feoffees of their masters' wills. In the case of the heir's being a minor, they became an extremely important body, though they governed under the guidance of a widow or other relative or guardian. Once again, higher servants of the household were often among the counsellors so appointed. Such conciliar wardship was one reason behind continuity among secular noble families in land tenure practices, householding methods and personnel, and administrative policies, despite long minorities. Perhaps the best indicator of the council's political influence lies in the warnings of men like Sir John Fortesque in *The Governance of England*, or Lord Strange,[15] who believed that a lord could become a cat's-paw of his own council, whose members 'served themselves and told the lord what he wanted to hear'.[16]

Higher household servants were probably less influential in the council than figures such as the lord's legal advisors, who were involved in almost every aspect of conciliar business, or the lord's closest peers and clients, who probably had more influence as regards major political decisions, especially during the civil wars of the fifteenth century. Nevertheless, the regular presence and large percentage of household members at council meetings suggests that their influence over conciliar decisions might be greater than is immediately obvious.

The household as a whole, as well as responsible individuals, had an important part to play in its lord's political career, by its very existence forming a crucial element in the master's public image. Sidney Anglo and others have written recently and at length about the motives behind conspicuous consumption in medieval and early modern Europe, and it is inappropriate and unnecessary here to introduce a prolonged discussion of the significance of pagentry and spectacle. Indeed, the use of clothing and other ornamentation, and of displays of prowess and massed groups of people, in order to impress allies and foes in common to all cultures, primitive and complex, and is not far removed in spirit from the mating dance of the peacock or the aggression displays of the baboon, though it is perhaps more complex in method and motive. In

---

[15]Charles Lethbridge Kingsford, *The Stonor Letters and Papers, 1290–1483* (Camden Society, London, vols 29 and 30, 1919), vol. 29, no. 30; 'I will not be overmastered by one of my feed men.'

[16]Rosenthal, *Nobles*, p. 77; from a fifteenth-century verse.

the fifteenth century, however, royal and noble constructions of self-images were of a particularly extravagant and obvious nature, and moreover directly involved their households. All nobles used their households both to create and to represent a visible, tangible expression of the lord's power. As in so many other aspects, the medieval noble household financed and organized displays of pageantry calculated to impress. The Duke of Buckingham's magnificent appearance on the Field of the Cloth of Gold in 1520, his own dress covered in little silver bells and his train hardly less sumptuousy attired, was purchased, designed and constructed by the wardrobe of the household. In large households such arrangements required specialized servants: musicians, players, tumblers, fools, and in some cases, the equivalent of the king's master of revels.

Besides the role of stage hand, however, the household also had a main acting part in the exemplification of noble power. Because of the closeness of the household to the lord, it was at once the most obvious and easiest, and the most significant, group of people on which the master could illustrate his *magnificentia*; this body, frequently seen and closely associated with its master, gave to the world a telling picture of what it might expect from the noble in question.

Lords used their households to display their magnificence in a number of ways, of which perhaps the most obvious is livery of cloth. By the comfort and grandeur of these garments, and by the massed effect of numerous servants all in the lord's colours, livery promised generosity and good living to the prospective retainer, and exhibited the extent of the master's influence and charismatic drawing power, as well as his potential force of arms. This was especially so in those households where the cut of cloth indicated – thanks to the frame of mind which created sumptuary laws – gently born servants whose own families and friends might provide a further network of influence and support. The extreme nervousness evident about the abuse of the wearing of livery reflects in a very real sense the symbolic and the actual significance of uniforms. Laws of livery and maintenance strictly limiting and controlling the wearing of livery, however, never extended to household members; and all lords dressed their domestic servants in the livery of their various individual colours.

Domestic arrangements could be manipulated to impress the observer, and were, especially in the larger households. The sheer number of servants could impress, as the Pastons make clear, writing to each other about the thirteenth Earl of Oxford in 1470–1, in their descriptions of his large retinue.[17] Generous hospitality was, however,

---

[17]Davis, *Paston Letters*, vol. I nos 245, 345; vol. II, no. 915.

probably the most useful and widespread form of nobles' conspicuous consumption; putting up, feeding and entertaining guests. The efficiency and gentility (or lack thereof) offered by the household in the provision of such hospitality, as well as the quality of the hospitality itself, would affect those whom the lord was attempting to impress.

But perhaps the medieval noble was best able to use his household as a token of his strength when he was on the road with them. The sight of anything from 30 to 200 people on horseback and in carts, moving in cavalcade, must have been impressive; if that massed body was armed, liveried, well horsed, and proceeded in good order, how much more impressive. Nobles were fond of using travel to their advantage, particularly when they could make political capital out of it. Not only the greater peers, but men like Hugh Luttrell and John Paston, purchased new livery, horses and accoutrements for their household to enter London in style, especially when coming to Parliament. Bishops, the most peripatetic of nobles in the later middle ages, were particularly impressive in their riding retinues; Cardinal Wolsey's household procession is, of course, legendary. Such displays, probably the single most attractive form of pageantry practised by the household, both enhanced a noble's public image and provided a popular barometer by which his power could be measured. Indeed such parades accompanying lords into Parliament were believed to intimidate that gathering and were eventually regulated by statute which restricted their size and arms.[18] When the household of the beheaded Lord Hastings transferred their allegiance *en masse* to Richard III, he issued them with his badge and flooded London with them, putting fear into the hearts of nobles perhaps too complacent about their followers' loyalty. Conspicuous consumption, pageantry, and spectacle worked not merely by bedazzlement, by some sort of irrational stimulation of pleasure; it provided a kind of language by which the observer could make practical assessments. By such displays, nobles were able to advertise quite accurately the extent of their wealth and status; they could, especially when riding, make known their potential armed strength; they could exhibit through the persons of their servants the extent of their affinity; and to prospective retainers their generosity was apparent in the size, fine attire and bearing of their immediate followers – the household.

In war, as in other aspects of a lord's political career, the household and household members participated. They frequently purveyed and arranged transport for armies very much as the king's wardrobe of the household might take over the treasury of wars; but also, household

---

[18]A.S. Turberville, 'The "Protection" of Servants of MPs', *English Historical Review* 42 (1927), pp. 89–106.

members actively participated in battle, as attendants, administrative staff and soldiers, though in no household of the fifteenth century can servants employed specifically as part of a standing army or bodyguard, or indeed anything more aggressive than a porter, be detected. Among the litigious nobility, property squabbles and personal grievances, labouring through the law courts, could erupt into violence; and in these petty wars servants were often the chief militia. Margaret Paston's valiant defence of the manor of Gresham against Lord Moleyn's men in 1449–50 is well known to historians; and her letters show that the billhooks, arrows, javelins, etc. already in Gresham and sent from London were employed by her household servants. The besiegers, as well, seem to have been composed chiefly of Moleyn's own servants.[19] Fifteenth-century statutes on retinues attending masters at Parliament speak of riots between such rival groups. While it would be wrong to suggest that such full-scale attacks were typical of the everyday duties of the fifteenth-century household members, they seem to have been perfectly able and willing to take part in these personal battles: and in all likelihood they were made particularly adept by that sort of minor violence and threat required to subdue recalcitrant tenants, which they employed in the supposedly more peaceful aspects of their varied duties for the baronial council – collecting rents and debts, subduing creditors, and performing missions for their masters as sheriffs and justices. With cooks and ushers of such violent capabilities, it is perhaps not surprising that no specific bodyguards or house guards were required in the noble household.

Household servants could also become active participants in warfare on a national scale, both at home and abroad, much as the royal households were involved in the king's financing and running of wars. Evidence of such activity can be found in many household accounts and other relevant records. John Mowbray of Berkeley Castle relied heavily upon his household for his involvement in the French wars of 1416–17, and the outfitting of the household for these wars is still on record. So are the war payments of Thomas Beauchamp and Philip de Courtenay, for 1372–4, payments made by their households and in part for their households in prepartion for going to war with the lord. Many other examples may be cited. A lord's gentle servants were of course particularly valuable (or dangerous) in war; not merely because they themselves were likely to be well trained in its arts, but because they might have significant connections with allies or enemies, and because they might be able to bring their own affinity into the lord's ranks.

[19]Davis, *Paston Letters*, vol. I, nos 36–9, 130–3; vol. II, nos 443, 444, 454–8, 486.

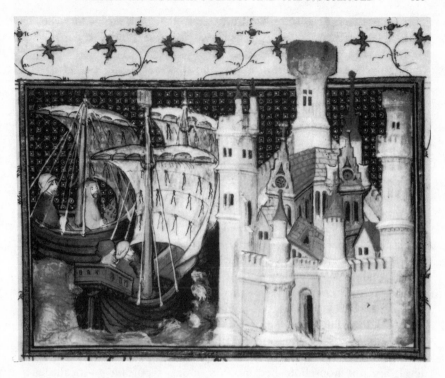

Plate 12 A lord and his servants on a diplomatic mission – the Earl of Salisbury arriving at Conway. Harley Ms. 1319, f. 14v. French, early 15th century. Courtesy of The British Library.

Surely this was the import of the third Duke of Buckingham's reassurance to Wolsey in 1520, concerning his projected expedition into Wales with a force of 300 men in order to assert control over his estates: that they would merely be 'myn own officers, tenants, gentleman servants of smalle stature'.[20] Certainly Wolsey may have had good cause to fear: in 1486 one of the Earl of Oxford's 'gentleman servants of small stature', John Aynthorp esquire, was able to bring six men to fight for the Earl.[21]

The French wars, combined with a lack of political stability at home, probably contributed to the great increase in average household numbers from the 1380s and throughout the fifteenth century. Those lords who fought or served in an administrative capacity in the

[20]BL Cotton Titus Bi fos 171–4.
[21]Soc. Ant. MS 77.

continental territories often had to expand their households, in order to staff and run their English possessions, to purvey and carry messages between France and England, and to serve the lord personally abroad. The Luttrell, Talbot and Stafford accounts, as well as those of Henry IV when he was Earl of Derby, show around the turn of the fifteenth century sudden increases in numbers of household members which correlate with expeditions abroad. The civil wars of the fifteenth century also certainly contributed to the rise in household numbers; the establishments of the Staffords, Richard, Duke of York, the Stonors, the Howards and the Courtenays exhibit sharp increases in household numbers, particularly in 1461, 1471, and 1483–5. While the numbers rose, however, it is interesting to note that the overall composition and organization of the household did not alter greatly, which reflects what has been said earlier: that all members of the household, not just individuals particularly designated as armed supporers, were of use to the lord in wartime. This reflects the political role of the noble establishment as a purveying and supply machine, a vehicle for the extension of significant hospitality, and an expression of the lord's *magnificentia*, as well as an engine of war. All these roles of the household became more important as the master rose in power himself, and as the domestic situation became less stable. Nobles scrambled to establish and/or safeguard their own positions on a local and national level, and the household became even more important politically as a result.

It is significant that the one change in household composition observed during these troubled years is a tendency for a higher number of servants to be drawn from the lord's broader affinity, particularly for jobs such as steward and treasurer, formerly the total reserve of clerks. While this probably reflects a general improvement in the standards of education for lay nobles, it certainly also suggests a need to tie client families as closely as possible to the patron in order to cement local alliances and ensure a following in the face of actual battle. The Courtenay, Howard and Percy families, in particular, exhibit a rise in the number of annuities paid to clients through the household, which also may indicate a closer connection forged between affinity and household, although the overall financial picture of estate administration is too complex to allow us to ascertain the exact significance of this development.

The role of the household in its master's political career was advantageous not only to the masters but to the servants, in a number of ways. The sumptuous livery and splendid foods which helped to bolster a lord's political image also gave his men a high degree of comfort and a great deal of personal prestige, equalling or increasing the standard of living into which they were born. A lord's political influence could obtain for a favoured servant useful personal and professional advancement, such as that accorded to Thomas Denys, a servant of the twelfth Earl of Oxford, who in 1457 managed to marry a Norfolk heiress of considerably higher rank than himself through Earl John's efforts.[22] The patronage of a head of household could also extend to a servant's family, particularly when the servant was already from a family whose members were clients of his master, as happened so frequently; good service strengthened their affinity (or strained it, in the case of a rogue younger son) as well as affinity encouraged service. The political collapse of a noble seldom seems, however, to have brought down permanently his household members, who switched their loyalties rapidly and, it seems, without stigma. William Hastings' men immediately attached themselves to the second Duck of Buckingham in 1482;[23] and everyone is familiar with the career of Thomas Cromwell, whose rapid desertion of Cardinal Wolsey after years as his chief personal assistant and secretary was equalled only by his swift rise under Henry VIII following Wolsey's fall from influence.

For many servants with ambition, especially those with genteel backgrounds and expectations, involvement in their masters' political schemes must have provided a kind of vicarious power. While their influence and authority was at best second-hand, servants could and did receive personal respect and interest from other syncophants, reflected from master on to servant. As in many other areas in which the household was an important factor, the close domestic bond trans-cended the boundaries of birth and afforded to household servants a modicum of political pretensions; and sometimes allowed them to cast down the mighty from their seats. Drawing client families into the central political machinery was, of course, a calculated risk as well as a potential advantage. William Stonor, the second Duke of Buckingham, Lord Hastings and probably many other lords were betrayed, during the fiasco of the first rebellion against Richard III, by members of client families who had become servants in their households.[24] Privy to political secrets, household members were in a perfect position to use their knowledge to advance themselves and their families, often at the expense of the one they had promised to serve.

[22]Davis, *Paston Letters*, vol. I, no. 49; vol. II, nos 452, 490, 491.

[23]W.H. Dunham, Jr, *Lord Hastings' Indentured Retainers, 1461–83* (Transactions of the Connecticut Academy of Arts and Sciences, Hartford, Conn., vol. 39, 1955).

[24]Carol Rawcliffe, *The Staffords, Earls of Stafford and Dukes of Buckingham* (Cambridge University Press, Cambridge, 1979), p. 35.

Both the contemporary recognition of a household's special knowledge of a lord's private attitudes and secret manoeuvres, and the effective use household members could make of such knowledge, illustrate the extent to which households were involved in the political careers of their noble masters. If the rise in numbers of household members between about 1380 and 1490 correlates with a rise in political importance for the household due to the needs of war and of nobles' to consolidate their power in the face of national instability, the decline in household numbers from the late sixteenth century may also have political signficance. While this will be discussed more fully in the conclusion, it is worthwhile to note here that this decline is concomitant with the much discussed decline in the authority of the aristocracy from the late Elizabethan period to the Cromwellian interlude. Clearly, the role of the household as an expression of noble magnificence, as a facilitator of political activities and as a participant in war was associated with the ambitions and potential powers of its master.

5

The Household as a Religious Community

Blood will I draw on thee ...
And straightway give thy soul to him thou servs't.
I Henry VI (I.v)

From the earliest days of christianity, the domestic community has served as a unit of worship. The New Testament letters of Paul, and the writings of such church fathers as Augustine and Jerome, assume that religious training and celebration was based in the household. In the middle ages, the English aristocracy, lay as well as episcopal and abbatial, also accepted that their household should be a religious as well as a domestic communtiy, and took steps to see that this should be put into practice. The household existed to serve its master, and he had christian duties to fulfil, whether through a sense of obligation, self-aggrandizement, or personal piety; lords used their households to administer those duties. Thus the household paid out alms and annuities to religious foundations, saw to the arrangement of major festivals, and financed and organized a regular liturgical system.

The personalization of christianity, especially among the aristocracy – as expressed in the astounding increase in private Books of Hours, portable altars, statutary and relics owned by the laity, etc. – and particularly towards the latter end of our period, seems to indicate a general movement in religious feeling. People required a more intimate and personal relationship with God, perhaps in the face of pre-occupation with the fear of death and concern with the afterlife, especially escape from purgatory, so prevalent in Europe during and after the great plague years.[1] The aristocracy used their households both as passive organizers of such practices as daily office, mass, and prayers for the dead, and also as active participants in these, adding their prayers and good works to the lord's. In his manner the household

[1] For an exposition of this subject, see T.S.R. Boase, *Death in the Middle Ages* (Thames and Hudson, London, 1972), p. 98.

could become not only a simple administrator of its master's pietistic duties, but in itself could function as a religious community for its own salvation, and that of its lord.

The third Duke of Buckingham posited in his chequerroll of 1519 that all household members were to attend mass daily, as 'no good governaunce in politik rule may be had, without service to God as well'. The fifth Percy Earl of Northumberland, in his book of household ordinance, expressed a similar sentiment; several fifteenth- and sixteenth-century royal ordinances, and most courtesy books for young courtiers, also echo this. The difficulty lies in showing whether this ideal remained unfulfilled, or whether the medieval household did indeed have a specifically christian as well as a domestic identity. In the end we have little unambiguous evidence; but we can examine the means of religious observance available in the household, and study some of the motivations to use these means.

In the nineteenth century, morning and evening prayers were often said in the dining room, where the family and servants could congregate most easily. In the middle ages, the gentry and nobility had far more elaborate accoutrements available, indeed the means for a particularly full religious observance: the building, the implements, and the staff. Even Robert Melton, a yeoman farmer, had a small room set aside as a chapel for his tiny household;[2] one would be hard-pressed to find a gentle or noble establishment devoid of a building or room for worship. Technically, private chapels required a licence from a bishop before mass could be celebrated in them; but episcopal registers do not appear to be a very good guide to the existence of such chapels, as it seems that in many, mass was regularly held without any licence being purchased, or at any rate recorded. For instance, the Luttrells had two active chapels within the walls of Dunster Castle in Somerset, but no licence for either is traceable in the near-perfect set of registers for the diocese of Exeter. Despite the low incidence of registered private chapels, therefore, one usually finds that aristocratic households contained at least one chapel, with all the liturgical paraphernalia needed for mass.

These chapels could be anything from a 'closet' or small room adapted as a chapel, to a separate building in the size and style of a parish church; and often, within a single castle or manor house, there was more than one. The oldest known are those in keeps, dating from 1100 to 1300 approximately; they are largely similar in concept to those more well-known royal ones at the White Tower in London, and

---

[2]Lady Caroline Kerrison and Lucy Toulmin Smith, eds, *A Commonplace Book of the Fifteenth Century* (Trubner, London, 1886), pp. 10–12.

at Castle Rising in Norfolk. While many of these are architectural gems, they are generally extremely small, being fitted into the little space available in a thick-walled keep designed for warlike, not religious, exercises, and often measured no more than ten feet square. Before 1350, some larger, generally wooden chapels were constructed in baileys; but it is generally after this date that large stone chapels were erected, such building being especially common during the fifteenth century. Often freestanding or but partly attached to the main body of the dwelling, these are distinguished by their surprising size, comparable to a parish church.[3] Some of the best surviving examples of the domestic chapel are, perhaps surprisingly, those attached to priors' and abbots' quarters, such as the abbots' house at Nettley (Hampshire) and the prior's house at Wenlock (Shropshire).

The size of these later medieval chapels may tell us something about attendance at mass in the household; they generally coincide in date with the beginning of a steady increase in the number of household servants.[4] While the fifth Earl of Oxford in c.1290 may have been able to fit his household of around forty-five into the tiny keep chapel at Castle Hedingham, the 120 employed by the thirteenth Earl in the 1480s would never have managed. The much larger bailey chapel may have been built to accommodate a growing congregation. On the other hand, such chapels may be explained by a growth in personal religious practises, the prestige value of a new and obvious chapel, and/or the general domestic building phenomenon of the fifteenth and sixteenth centuries, which was marked especially by an increase in space and luxury. The older chapels were not, however, de-sanctified, but continued as active houses of religion. In the same year (1405–6) that he finished the new bailey chapel of St Lawrence at Dunster, Sir Hugh Luttrell spent 2 li 7s 5d on the repair and refurbishing of the old keep-chapel: he later supplied it with new vestments and plate.[5] Throughout the fifteenth century, other additional chapels, besides the old keep-rooms and the new, larger buildings, were set up, many of them 'privy' or 'closet' chapels in which the lord said prayers with his chamber servants or alone. All these chapels required outfitting in vestment and plate, and such purchases occur as a significant expense in most accounts. The stock account for Sir Henry Clifford's new chapel, 1515–16, is a particularly revealing record of the extent to which lords were prepared to go to keep their domestic chapels in sumptuous array.

[3]Margaret Wood, *The English Medieval House* (Phoenix, London, 1965), pp. 227–40.
[4]See chapter 2.
[5]Somerset RO DD/L P37/7 and 10–A.

Plate 13   Ladies at prayer in a private chapel – Margaret of York with her ladies. Ms, Douce 365, f. cxv. Ghent, 1465. Courtesy of the Bodleian Library, Oxford.

As well as the physical means, the household also had the animate means for celebration. One would have difficulty in finding a household document which does not mention at least one resident chaplain and numerous *clerici*. The chaplain might have other priests as well as clerks to assist him; at least one sacristan, certainly, to look after the upkeep of the chapel and its accoutrements; and, in the very largest households, a singing-school, comprised of both boys and men. Unfortunately, it is difficult to say a great deal about any household's clerical element, with the possible exception of those of bishops, where benefices may be a useful help.

The incompleteness of episcopal registers (in themselves and as sets), the commonness of many names, a lack of sureness as to where such clerics might have been ordained, and the generally low social origins of many religious, means that biographies can be compiled only for a very few. However, as indicated in chapter 2, the term *clericus* does generally seem to be applied, in household parlance, to those in holy orders; though one may not assume that *clerici* were priests unless specifically designated as such. Despite these reservations, we often find households with more than one resident cleric who was capable of saying mass. The Stonors were, rather unusually, licensed to have six chaplains;[6] but normally only the households of dukes and earls contained so many. Two priests in a moderately sized household of forty-five or fifty members was not unusual. Abbatial households also follow this pattern but episcopal households usually had a larger number of priests. However, most of these were not employed as chaplains but in other capacities, as stewards, secretaries, etc., and bishops seldom had more priests employed as chaplains than in lay households. These priests, while some were employed in accounting capacities, were in the main hired to function as chaplains. As such, their duties comprised saying daily mass and perhaps divine office; such requiems, twelve-month-minds (marking the anniversary of a death), and pentitential services as the lord required; and constructing and directing these services in the chapel. More generally, they seem to have been charged with the moral and spiritual welfare of the household community, in particular that of other clerics in the household.

Household clerks must have posed something of a problem to bishops. They frequently moved around the country with their masters, in and out of dioceses, and hence in and out of the authority of their spiritual overlords. Those paid by benefice in the lord's granting must have required a perpetual leave of absence. Some evidence exists to show that, as far as the household was concerned, the senior chaplain had a special authority over other household clerics. The fifth Percy earl's dean of chapel occupied such a position.[7] As well, in most chequerolls, the servants are grouped in departments, within which they are ordered by rank; the clerics, of the chapel and of other parts of the household such as the kitchen, are all grouped together and are headed by the chaplain, who is placed in relation to them similarly to the way in which subheads of departments are placed in relation to their staffs. Thus it appears likely that the senior chaplain was recognized, within the household at least, as being in a special position of authority as far as other household clerks were concerned. The form this authority took is harder to determine, but practically, it probably involved much the same responsibilities attributed to the dean of the royal chapel: such

---

[6]R.J. Stoner, *Stonor* (R.H. Johns, Newport, 1952), p. 88.
[7]*NHB*, section 42.

things as seeing clerics fulfilled their religious obligations, and that they were not indulging in moral and/or theological error.[8] The senior chaplain may also have drawn upon non-chapel clerics for liturgical ceremonies, such as chanting, reading the lesson, etc.

The chapel staff proper, however, could also contain laymen. Most households employed at least one sacristan or verger, usually classified as a valet or groom, who was charged with the upkeep and guarding of the chapel and its valuable goods. The Earl of Northumberland also had two 'yeoman pistelers' who were employed solely to read the first lesson from the New Testament Epistles at daily mass.[9] In the greatest households, *scholae cantorum*, in imitation of the king's chapel royal, enriched the household's religious life. Such chapel choirs appeared in the royal household as early as 1135. The first instance of a *schola cantorum* in a noble household, however, does not occur until 1360, when we find that Henry, Duke of Lancaster, employed six adult singers in his chapel. Henry's son-in-law, John of Gaunt, employed such a chorus too, but with boys' voices as well. John, Duke of Bedford, also had a choir for his household chapel in 1435, as did Humphrey, Duke of Gloucester, who left annuities in his will to his numerous *schola* members, boy and man. However, these *scholae* do not seem to be a general trend among the nobility in the early fifteenth century, but offshoots of the royal chapel choir. Margaret Beaufort, as much as the tradition of the chapel royal, may have encouraged Henry VII in his extensive patronage of polyphonic composers; she also had a *schola cantorum* in the late 1480s and may have had one earlier.[10] Edward Stafford, Duke of Buckingham, was almost certainly imitating Margaret Beaufort, his guardian and mentor, in his own *schola*, as he had imitated her household administration in other ways. Certainly no earlier Staffords had employed a choir. Both Edward Stafford's and Margaret Beaufort's choirs consisted of about twelve boys and around four gentleman-singers under the direction of a master of the children of chapel.[11] The low number of adult male voices is probably due to the greater expense of maintaining them and a greater scarcity of such professional singers. Boys were cheaper; and, as they received an education as well as a stipend, such positions were probably coveted.

But such choirs were established by other nobles not intimately

[8]A.R. Myers, eds., *The Household of Edward IV* (Manchester University Press, Manchester, 1959), pp. 133–5.

[9]*NHB*, section 42.

[10]Frank Harrison, *Music in Medieval Britain* (Routledge and Kegan Paul, London, 1958), pp. 17–25.

[11]Ibid., pp. 172–4.

related to the crown. John, thirteenth Earl of Oxford, also employed a *schola* consisting of a master, about twelve boys and at least two adult male voices, in 1490.[12] By 1512, and probably earlier, the fifth Earl of Northumberland patronized a large household choir.[13] Cardinal Wolsey and a number of other bishops also had private choirs in the early sixteenth century.[14] Such were obviously restricted to the greatest nobles, who alone had the wealth and prestige to support such schools of singing properly.

The choir members came from all classes of society. Unfortunately, we have few names of the masters; but those whose identity is known seem to have been respectable musicians, even minor masters of the art of polyphony and the English melodic adaptation of plaingsong. William Excestre, John of Gaunt's *magister* in 1393, became master of Henry IV's chapel royal, and probably wrote some or most of the pieces now known from the Old Hall manuscript; Thomas Farthyng, Margaret Beaufort's choirmaster, has left numerous compositions which exhibit his skill and illustrate his importance to the development of English music.[15] Men like Farthyng and Excestre are of obscure origins and clerical backgrounds, which took them to the great cathedral schools where they learned and perfected their singing skills. In the case of both these men, noble patronage proved a stepping stone to royal favour: Farthyng, like Excestre, became master of the Chapel Royal under Henry VIII. Those singers of relatively humble origins perhaps showed youthful promise at a cathedral school or other educational establishment – music training being a requisite part of late medieval learning – and were commandeered by their noble patron. Other 'children of the chapel', however, were actually henchmen; they came from well-established gentle families, often from those tradition-ally allied with the employing lord. Edward Stafford's *schola* included, in the years 1485 to 1521, several Brays, de la Mares, Pointzes, and other gentle family members from the Welsh Marches. Along with the other henchmen of the household these choirboys received a gentle-man's education.

As adults, these children often retained their connection with their fosterhome. The Brays' and de la Mares' old ties with the house of Stafford continued throughout the career of the third Duke, and were probably strengthened by such fostering. For boys of lesser rank, a position in the *schola* often led to a lifetime profession. Some, like 'litel

---

[12]Soc. Ant. MS 77.
[13]*NHB*, section 42.
[14]Harrison, *Music*, pp. 174–6.
[15]Ibid.

Fraunceys', an otherwise unknown protégé of the third Duke of Buckingham, entered the University of Oxford and later the church with their patron's assistance.[16] Others, such as the thirteenth de Vere Earl's choir boy, John Hewett, remained in the household on a gentleman's pay of 53s 4d per annum; some even formed the adult voice corps of the *schola* if their youthful promise persisted.[17] In 1512, the fifth Percy Earl's two 'yeoman pistelers' were ex-choir boys.[18] Some singers, however, entered the household choir as adults. Like their young colleagues they covered a wide social stratum, from the younger sons of gentle families to gifted commoners, who could have received their musical training in a cathedral school or grammar school.

Obviously, nearly every aristocratic household, large or small, had the means for creating a religious community. However, our picture of courtly life, both royal and noble, is one of considerable worldliness, pomp, show, and splendour. We may easily picture those Puritan households of such as Oliver Cromwell,[19] living a strict life of common prayerfulness; we have a harder time imagining the sort of religious community which might exist under a great lay nobleman of the middle ages, or even under a bishop like Wolsey or Bogo de Clare. We need to look at the motivation present in such a household, which might, through the regular pattern of worship shared by the community, encourage the formation of religious zeal in individuals, and in the group as a whole; for the lord, and for his household members. A great deal depended on an individual lord's own sense of piety. Acts of charity were almost a social duty of the aristocracy, as were attendance at mass and the initiation of other religious services. Certainly chroniclers cite such pietistic practices as synonyms of good lordship; and we would be hard-pressed to discover a noble who never gave alms or endowed a chantry. But such activities could, of course, be turned largely outward, or they could be expressed not only through but in the household. As in most other spheres of consideration, religious activity tended to vary considerably from household to household. But, perhaps in the majority of noble establishments, numerous factors stimulated a particular kind of piety, which worked to bond the household into a spiritual unit.

I have already mentioned the intensely personal aspect of religious

---

[16]BL Royal MS 14B XXXV D.

[17]Sir William St John Hope, ed., 'The Last Testament and Inventory of John de Vere, Thirteenth Earl of Oxford, *Archaeologia*, 66 (1915), p. 301.

[18]*NHB*, section 42.

[19]H.F. Lovell-Cocks, *The Religious Life of Oliver Cromwell* (Independent Press, London, 1960), pp. 20–3 and 68–70.

feeling in the later middle ages: a kind of mystical yearning for closeness to God which ran as an undercurrent through much of fifteenth-century theology, especially. Few people, of course, had the spiritual concentration of St Vincent Ferrer, or the emotional violence of Jan Hus. But for nobles, in particular, the personalization of religion helped to mitigate the conflict between Christian humility and poverty, and worldly display, by identifying Christ in themselves and their possessions. Books of Hours are one manifestation of this trend. These guides to prayer provided a formula for religious experience. Moreover, they could be handled and touched; the sacred word was further familiarized by the drawings of arms and donor's portraits, and the inclusion of family trees and of patron saints' pictures and prayers. The personalization of the sacred also naturally encouraged the practice of piety within the household. To have one's own services, one's own priest, one's private liturgical adaptations and celebrations, was a way of controlling and coming closer to a distant godhead. One could in a sense bring Christ into the living quarters, within the very heart of one's life, by the creation of a private chapel. This craving for the personalization of religion was not peculiar to the aristocracy. Household members, as well as their masters, were susceptible to this religious trend. The chapel, the priest, the ornaments, the liturgy intended especially for these relatively small groups of people united in a common service, were spiritually reassuring and satisfying to everyone involved, and perhaps similar in intention and effect to the religious activities of craft guilds.

The importance of strongly personal religious feeling, then, could motivate close-knit groups such as noble households to be drawn into their own pattern of piety, to which the individual could relate as part of a community; though the extent to which such feeling was present or recognized in England is difficult to gauge. More practical motives, however, also encouraged the practice of religion in the household. We have mentioned the status value of a new chapel; and certainly such magnificent buildings and their accoutrements were one way of advertising one's splendour. What better way for the noble to exhibit his strength and munificence further than by utilizing religious festivals and processions to display his personal following? Such a display was thereby given an acceptable excuse, rendering it less likely to be inflammatory; politics was hidden by piety. This was a ploy which Italian princes in particular were also heavily exploiting in the fifteenth century, using the liturgical calender to create a pattern of festivals for the celebration of the Medici, the Uffizi, the Visconti. In fact, it was used by all princes, though perhaps less unambiguously; English nobles can hardly have been immune to its value. Certainly the third Duke of Buckingham's household expedition to the burial place of Prince Edward, son of Henry VI, in April 1508 was but a thinly disguised advertisement of his sympathies,[20] meant to remind Henry VII of his family's attachment to the Lancastrian cause.

Finally, the creation of the household as a religious community was of benefit to the household as an organization. Lords recognized the value of group worship: Edward Stafford, George Duke of Clarence, and Henry Percy, in particular, have all left specific notices urging enforced attendance of mass. As Paul V.B. Jones posits, 'Not a noble master, but felt that his control over the servants was fortified, and a difficult management made smooth, through the attendance of the entire house, compulsory if necessary, at religious services.'[21] For the sake of morale and what we would today call the encouragement of 'teamwork', group worship must have been an ideal way of uniting the household and incorporating it into the hierarchical structure of society encouraged by medieval christianity. Shared worship, shared belief – especially for a society whose people were caught up in the personalization of piety – was (and for that matter still is) a very useful way to create a loyal, closely knit community. The practical unification of the household was not just in the lord's interest, however. Group worship was as much an expression of, as a causal factor in, household 'teamwork'. Any community of individuals wishes to express and confirm its unity through some kind of ritual; whether this be the crowning of a monarch, the yearly celebration of Mother's Day or a community street party. Daily worship is one obvious way to do so. Individual household members were probably motivated to attend the household mass provided for them because it reaffirmed each day their place in the community on which most of their lives centred.

Considerable incentive existed, therefore, for the creation of the household around its lord as a religious community. In each household, however, worship varied enormously in terms of what was actually done and how, depending on size, means and individual interests. In general, however, the medieval English nobility, like most elite groups, tended to be fairly conservative in their attitudes and deeds, remaining close to the traditional patterns of thought and action. Nobles did not convert their personal households into monasteries even if they were abbots or priors, nor did they approach extremes in their search for an

---

[20]PRO E/36/220.

[21]Paul V.B. Jones, *The Household of a Tudor Nobleman* (University of Illinois Studies in Social Sciences, Chicago, vol. 6, 1917), p. 183.

intimate and secure relationship with God; nobles and gentry largely confined themselves to the exercise of traditional forms of pious practice, adapting these to suit the requirements of an individualized form of institutionalized religion. We can conveniently divide noble household religious activity into four categories: daily worship patterns; observance of the liturgical year; generational ceremony; and general charity. In these four spheres the lord acted through his household, which organized these events, and also in most cases participated in them.

While it seems likely that daily mass was common in households, we cannot really be perfectly sure that it was celebrated daily, or whether, if so, individuals actually attended. We must remember that weekly mass, even, was beyond the religious exertions of most people, and that the church only required attendance at mass twice yearly. Once again, much depended on the lord's intensity of religious devotion. The general impression is that the aristocracy were fairly fastidious about their religious observances, either out of piety or duty. We can probably assume that the lord and his family, at least, felt an obligation to hear mass frequently. Moreover, some useful economic evidence exists for supposing that daily mass was celebrated. Wardrobe costs in household accounts with enough detail break down to reveal that nearly a third of the candles, torches, etc. used in the household were expended in the chapel. Since candles are an essential part of mass and divine office it seems reasonable to draw the conclusion that fairly regular services were held in domestic chapels. In a number of households with records of servants on board wages or acting as a skeleton staff, this candle consumption continues even in the absence of the master.[22] (Indeed the Ordinances of Eltham and the *Northumberland Household Book* make provision for the keeping of community meals and daily mass in the absence of the Lord.)[23] Therefore, one can probably assume that a daily mass was said in most household chapels; and that the motivations previously described, and in strictly run households the insistence of the master, ensured some sort of congregation. In the larger households especially, the music, fabulous ornamentation and release from duties must have made even a low mass an attractive diversion, at the least.

Several ordinances also specify other daily services: in particular the divine office and masses for the dead. Henry Percy, and the governors of the little Edward V when he was still a prince, made provision for the

[22]Cf. the Luttrells, Somerset RO DD/L P37/7, 10, 11, 12; Margaret Beaufort, WAM 12185; and the Petre day-books, Essex RO D/DP A 1–4.
[23]Soc. Ant., eds, *A Collection of Ordinances and Regulations* John Nichols, London, 1790), pp. 160–1; and *NHB*, sections 39 and 46.

Plate 14 An ecclesiastical household saying a mass for the dead. Ms. W. 287, f. 149. Harvard Hannibal Master, *c.*1420. Courtesy of WALTERS ART GALLERY, Baltimore.

chapel staff, including the *schola*, to say the office in part – probably lauds, terce and vespers – each day.[24] Edward V and his young henchmen were supposed to attend the office, but naturally the rest of the household was not expected to do so. They were, of course, too busy with their primary duties. The same is true of the requiem masses. In affect some lords endowed chantries in their private chapels, usually for the souls of their parents. In the fifth Earl of Northumberland's household chapel, a Lady mass was said daily for the good of souls, and in the chapel of George, Duke of Clarence,[25] but these were not intended as congregational masses, nor was the household community expected to attend.

Religiously inspired abstinences and bounty were also regular observances that coloured the life of the household. In nearly every household account we find a scrupulous observance of the Friday abstinence from meat; in a few others, abstinence on Wednesday and Saturday – recommended but not required by the church – was observed. Abbots' households generally followed the fasting regulations of the order involved, but neither abbatial nor episcopal households are noticeably more scrupulous than lay establishments in attending to general ecclesiastical rules. The purveyance patterns of most households show that these penitential days were countered by a day of joy, Sunday. In all households, spending and consumption were particularly large on this day, increasing the total expenditure over a normal meat-day such as Monday or Thursday by as much as 50 per cent. Unusual or exotic foods also occur frequently on Sundays – herons, dolphins, peacock, wine even for the lower servants, boar, and a high percentage of wildfowl.

As well as these regular observances, the annual cycle of the church calendar probably exercised a strong influence over the life of the household. Of course, it can be argued that the liturgical year impressed itself on any medieval mind; but in the noble household, as in the monastery, or convent, the church calendar could be much more intensely experienced than it was, for instance, by a small village. Despite the closeness of this latter community and the importance to it of the local priest, the farmer's year was much more likely to be influenced by the seasons and their vagaries than by the cycle of the church. This is not to suggest that the two were incompatible, or mutually exclusive. It is certainly true that the liturgical year played a part in a farmer's life; for instance, Good Friday was used as the sowing

[24]Soc. Ant., *Collection*, pp. *24–*33, and *NHB*, section 42.
[25]Soc. Ant., *Collection*, pp. 89–91, and *NHB*, section 42.

deadline. But this is due more to the link between Good Friday and the vernal equinox than to the symbolic tie between sowing and the crucifixion, though the latter was the interpretation of the theologian. On 25 March a farmer, unless it was a Sunday, would probably be busy ploughing. He was not required to attend mass. He would probably eat no better that day than any other, nor would he be likely to have any more leisure or entertainment.

Compare this with the experience of the average household member on the feast of the Annunciation. A vigil was kept on 24 March; on the feast itself a solemn high mass and almost invariably a banquet were held. The chapel was in the same building inhabited by the household member, near the hall where he ate his meals. If not himself, at least some of his fellows would have been involved in the preparations. A special preacher was frequently imported, as were singers and/or tumblers. In a household attached to a bishop or abbot, the household attended services in the great church as well as the domestic chapel.

The differences between these two modes of celebrating the Annunciation give us some idea of the religious atmosphere pressing on the household member. He would have had actively to avoid the celebration of this feast. Whatever the household member's religious convictions, he could hardly help taking part in, and being moved or excited by, the ceremonies and festivities; they were a quite unavoidable part of his life. Much more than many others, noble household communities were likely to be affected by the liturgical calendar, if their Lord's devotions or political interests prompted him to order its keeping, because the household was both means of celebration and congregation. A look at the account books of most households show that the major festivals of the year – what are now called solemnities, feasts and holy days of obligation – were almost without exception celebrated as feasts.

The Annunciation is one of these, often occurring as a (probably welcome) break in the austerity of Lent. Accounts show conclusively that during Lent complete abstinence from meat was strongly enforced, though not extending to such items as eggs; a complete fast was observed on Ash Wednesday, Maundy Thursday and Good Friday. Easter Vigil and Easter Sunday were solemnly celebrated at all the households with records remaining, with high mass and a banquet. The majority of lords also distributed largesse in honour of the day, and special preachers, most often Dominican or Franciscan friars, were invited. During Eastertide, Ascension Day, Whitsunday or Pentecost, Trinity Sunday and *Corpus Christi* were solemnly celebrated at all. The Birthday of St John the Baptist, which coincided with Midsummer, and the Assumption of the Blessed Virgin (29 June and 15 August respectively), were the only common summer feasts. St Michael the Archangel's feast (Michaelmas) was not only of fiscal importance, but was generally celebrated as a religious holiday, on 29 September. All Saints' and All Souls' (1 and 2 November) were kept with numerous requiem masses and the saying of the office for the dead.

Then, as now, Christmas – the whole season as well as the day – was probably the most important holiday of the year: not only religious, but as 'secularized' and 'commercial' as a modern Christmas. Buying for it began in October and November. Special torches and candles, fowl and stock cattle for fattening, and supplies of such dainties as figs, dates, and sugar, are entered as Christmas *empciones* as early as 15 October in many accounts. Christmastide officially began at the first Sunday of Advent, but in fact the Immaculate Conception of the Virgin on 8 December marked the heightening of household preparations for Christmas, as yet more supplies were purchased and guests poured in for the holiday. Guests were an important feature of the Christmas season, especially relatives. It was also celebrated with entertainment: waits, companies of players, 'clerks of St Nicholas', musicians, gymnasts and fools; even the smallest households managed to import a peripatetic lutenist. Nevertheless it was not, certainly, devoid of religious sentiment: daily high mass with sermons, as well as daily banquets, were celebrated. The Christmas holidays followed the traditional pattern of twelve nights in most households, the chief high points being Christmas Eve, Christmas Day, St Stephen's Day (26 December), the feast of the Holy Innocents (28 December), Twelfth Nigh, and Epiphany or Twelfth Day (6 January). A generous exodus of guests on the morning following Epiphany marked the end of the festivities. In *Sir Gawain and the Green Knight*, the celebration of Christmas, though poetically exaggerated, follows a similar pattern. All these religious festivals were organized in and through the household; but also for and with householders. The best illustration of this can be found on the celebration of the Presentation of Christ in the Temple and the Purification of the Blessed Virgin (2 February), on which feast candles were issued to every member of the household so that they could participate in the ceremonies.

Each household, besides those main feasts, also had its own particular set of feast days which filled their liturgical calendar. Patron saints' days, dedication memorials, and other obscure solemnities with special meaning for the family, were celebrated with solemn high mass and a lavish meal. The variety of these feasts is endless, and no real pattern emerges. Our knowledge of these yearly cycles varies, of course, from family to family, depending on the number of daily accounts surviving. These, by recording in detail expenditure, number of guests, etc., tell us a good deal more about holidays than the yearly summaries. Letters where they survive also provide useful insights. Most establishments were, not surprisingly, devoted to the feast of the patron of the domestic chapel (as well as to the monastic patron in the case of abbatial households, and the saint of the cathedral for bishops), though whether the devotion or the naming of the chapel came first it is impossible in any case to day. Personal devotions on the part of a lord or a member of his family often turn up as feasts celebrated by the whole household, in particular name days, and in some, usually sixteenth-century, examples, actual birthdays.[26] The will of the thirteenth Earl of Oxford lists twenty-three statutes of St John the Baptist; nearly all the Earls of Oxford were named John, and two in one set of siblings were not uncommon.[27] A large number of households kept all the Marian feast days, including the more obscure ones, such as the feast of St Joachim and St Anne, parents of the Blessed Virgin (26 July). One wonders if these celebrations, which honoured the noble family involved as much as the saint specified, had the same sort of meaning for the household as a whole. We cannot know, but the theory is a tempting one. In a household which functioned as a religious community, such patronage feasts could have easily been used to express, through religious ritual, the unity of the household.

Constant exposure to the pattern of the liturgical day and year, as organizers and participators, and the fact that this calender was celebrated outside the normal parish system by an organization with its own liturgical traditions and its own clergy and chapel or chapels, must have strongly reinforced the sense of religious community within the household. As well as these regular, cyclical patterns, however, generational events marking the passage of a linear time, and involving church ritual, were often organized by and partipated in by the household: in particular, baptisms, marriages and funerals. These rites of passage were – for that matter, are – highly significant occasions; ritual allows one to control, understand, and maintain continuity through unsettling changes in status. We find continually that lords and servants participated in each others' generational rituals.

In the middle ages, godparents and other sponsors were chosen carefully; they were meant to take their position seriously, and indeed were often the child's first patrons and aids. The regular inclusion of

[26]The third Duke of Buckingham's in 1520, for example – PRO E/35/220, 7 September.
[27]Hope, 'Last Testament', pp. 275–348.

household members in the christening train is therefore, perhaps, significant; perhaps it symbolically pledged them to serve the heir of their master, providing a rationale for continuity between the generations. A great deal of information about baptisms survives in numerous records. It is a feast commonly recorded, and several lists of directions for it survive. Typical is a Stonor paper of 1482 which includes a list of directions for a christening, probably for the baptism of William Stonor's son, John. This was organized through the household and took place in the domestic chapel at Stonor. Of the twelve priests involved, several were household chaplains; and a number of other household servants, alongside relatives and influential local gentry, were involved in the ceremony – Christopher Holland, then household steward, held the basin and salt.[28]

A more elaborate and less well-known set of directions for a christening survives in a peculiar Percy manuscript now in the Bodleian.[29] This book, a sort of second volume to the better known *Northumberland Household Book*, details the ordering of special religious ceremonies and their accompanying secular festivities. Many of the occasions detailed are generational, and include the lying-in of a countess, and the christening of the children of an earl. While the rules laid down in this book are extremely elaborate and detailed, down to the number of cushions to be placed on the benches of the church porch, and may never have been followed with any exactness, the book expresses a kind of ideal of how such affairs should work, and therefore deserves considerable attention. And this book specifies quite clearly that household members should set up and supervise the ceremony, and that household members – particularly the gentleman-ushers, the lord's closest servants and often companions – actually take a major role in the christening procession.

Such involvement also held good in the opposite direction. Lords frequently stood as godparents to their servants' children, later acting as their patrons. Noble wills regularly record bequests to such god-children, and personal account books frequently mention gifts to servants for the christening of their infants.

Marriage must have affected household life and practices more immediately and distinctively than any other major shift in status; and we know, from the Stonor, Lisle and Hoby letters, that it could create

[28]Charles Lethbridge Kingsford, ed., *The Stonor Letters and Papers, 1290–1483* (Camden Society, London, vols 29 and 30, 1919), vol. 30, no. 358.

[29]MS Eng. Hist. b 208, which I am presently preparing for publication. D.M. Barratt identified it as a companion to the *NHB* in 'A Second Northumberland Household Book', *Bodleian Library Record*, 8 (1967–72), pp. 93–8.

tensions in the household. Thus it is unfortunate that no household accounts for the years when any heads of household married can be found to survive. We do have some late information about the marriages of daughters. These often took place in the chapel of the bride's father. In addition, the Percy ordinances for religious ceremonies record details to be observed in the marriage of an earl's daughter, and the dressing of the chapel for the marriage of an earl's child (presumably either male or female). The marriage of the daughter of Sir William More of Loseley (Surrey) in 1567 is particularly well documented.[30] These occasions were organized through the household members, who handled the catering, entertainment and decoration, and were present at the ceremony, though not, as far as can be observed, part of the actual ritual. Perhaps the marriages of sons, who might one day take over the household, were differently arranged. On the marriages of servants, however, lords often attended the service, providing a substantial marriage-gift and often a dowry for the bride. This is as true of bishops and abbots as of lay nobles.

But it is in death that the household particularly involved itself in the rite of passage. For the servants, especially, natural sorrow was accompanied when a lord died by great insecurity as the household changed hands, even though many lord stipulated in their wills that their servants were to be kept on for at least six months after the funeral. Household members organized and participated in their masters' funerals, arranging for the procession, burial, and largesse, and also for the wake afterwards, usually following the instructions of the will. Servants normally took part in the procession, following after the chief mourners and in some cases carrying or leading the body. Their numbers were not restricted; all household members were issued with livery and expected to join the procession. Through the funeral ritual servants were able to express their grief, perform a last act of service for their dead lord, and perhaps, by their privileged position in the ceremony, identify themselves with the chief mourners – usually the lord's heirs or successors in office. At a time of trauma and insecurity such indentification may have had career as well as psychological benefits for servants and masters.

The almost orgiastic wakes common to some cultures are explained by anthropologists as an effort to affirm life in the face of death. After the solemn funeral, such wakes seem to have been common in medieval England; Ralph Stonor's lasted over a week. That of Thomas Stonor II,

[30]John Evans, 'The Wedding of Richard Posted and Elizabeth, Daughter of William More of Loseley, Surrey', *Archaeologia* 36 (1855), pp. 35–52.

in 1474, cost 74 li 2s 5d. ob, about two-thirds of which was expended in food, including such delicacies as venison, brawn and 'surloyne'.[31] *Hamlet*'s 'funeral bak'd meats' take on a new perspective. The anniversary of the death was celebrated in the twelve-month mind, which involved both a religious service and a feast. Households organized and participated in those, not only for a dead master or one of his relatives, but occasionally for servants. Abbatial households were particularly diligent in the keeping up of masses for deceased servants.

Our information on generational rituals is perhaps rather slender, but suggestive. Householders not only organized such rituals for their Lord, but participated in them, with their master, and he participated in theirs. Again, this intimates the importance of the household institution as a crucial framework for the lives of master and servant.

Apart from liturgical ceremonies, lords chiefly fulfilled their christian duties by dispensing alms, and founding and supporting religious houses. When discussing the role of the household in charity, one may distinguish between the great, planned, charitable action and casual almsgiving. The former was largely organized through the lord's will, or, if he wished to make a grant during his lifetime, through his receiver-general, or by judicial procedure. Of such grants we thus find little or nothing in the records of the household. What we discover of them usually reflects on the consequences of that patronage, such as a former servants' admittance to a master's foundation, the head of a foundation's place on its benefactor's council, or the hospitality of such foundations to their patron's travelling servants. We know considerably more about casual almsgiving and largesse.

As well as major, expensive charitable schemes, the aristocracy was also generally expected by others and themselves to exhibit their munificence by the frequent distribution of largesse. Though this was, at some religious feasts, a set custom, with a specific amount handed out year after year, in essence such almsgiving was casual and spontaneous. Beggars on the road or at the door, clerical guests and poor students, were seldom turned away empty-handed. Most lords had certain biases in their almsgiving. Despite the claim that the mendicant orders had fallen into disrepute in the fifteenth century, the most frequent recipients of alms from our noble households were friars of one sort or another. Impoverished university students were frequently favoured, and many lords were particularly charitable to lepers. These preferences notwithstanding, all accounts mention numerous 'powre men' met on the road, to whom alms and a request to pray for the donor were

---

[31]Kingsford, *Stonor Letters*, vol. 29, no. 138; vol. 30, nos 342, 343.

distributed. Such alms were financed by the household. Hospitality was paid for by the steward or almoner; simple alms were usually dispensed via chamber servants who accompanied the lord, but any nearby servant could be told to open his purse. The accounts of Elizabeth of York, Henry VII's Queen, show her gentlewomen being reimbursed for providing her impulsive gifts, *per mandatum dominae*.[32] Many similar entries occur in all private accounts.

One occasionally finds, however, a dispensation alms not given *per mandatum domini*, but *pro hospicii*, or *in nomine hospicii*. The evidence, slender but unambiguous, seems to suggest that household members, as a group and as individuals, had the right and the duty to dispense charity. Almsgiving was an accepted function of household members and householding, as christian individuals and as a religious community. Also, servants themselves could benefit from their master's charity through the household. Many servants ended their days in a foundation patronized by their master; since a lord's support of an ecclesiastical establishment often resulted in his ability to influence the appointments in its gift, clerical servants often got benefices and other career boosts through their own patron's patronage.

While this sort of casual charity involved a minute percentage of household income – seldom more than two pounds per annum – it was in most households frequent: two to four times per week on average in lay households. Bishops' and abbots' households record more frequent giving in general but not much more cash expended on alms as a whole. Widows regularly appear as the most generous givers. Tuppence, the normal rate for a single gift, constituted a day's wages for an agricultural worker, and surpassed that of a household valet (40s per annum, about 1d ob qua (farthing) a day). This sum does not reflect well, perhaps, on the charity of the aristocracy (though we shall recall that household-based alms were only a very tiny percentage of their annual charitable expenditure). But the frequent distribution of alms, equalling per donation about twenty pounds in modern purchasing power, and between forty and eighty pounds a week on average, indicates a much more substantial level of giving than at first appears. This allows us to gauge better the character of medieval charity and its physchological effect upon the household member. The treasurer of York Minster, Bogo de Clare, who between 1284 and 1289 gave about tuppence a year according to his accounts, is an untypically miserly example. The average household member would have been aware that the establish-

---

[32]Nicholas Harris Nicholas, *Privy Purse Expenses of Elizabeth of York and Wardrobe Accounts of Edward IV* (Frederick Muller, London, 1872).

ment in which he lived gave enough to keep together the bodies and souls of a number of poor people, and some of this was distributed in the name of himself and his fellows, for whom it would reap a harvest of prayer.

Much of the available evidence on household piety is ambiguous and uncertain. We know, from ordinances and chequerrolls such as those of Edward Stafford, third Duke of Buckingham and George, Duke of Clarence, that lords wished to see their households operate as a religious community, daily worshipping in a body; but such sources reflect the ideal, rather than the real, household, and must be used with circumspection. The means for the existence of such a community were present, but how, and how much, these means were utilized is less sure. Implicit and explicit motivation for the formation of such a community can be argued, but is more difficult to prove in entirety. Finally, the pious actions of households can in many cases be discerned; but the evidence of such action is sometimes ambiguous in nature, and its real significance – such as whether households actually did attend the daily masses which were probably held in most households – is difficult, often impossible, to ascertain.

In the end, we must rely on quantity as much as quality of evidence; on the steady accumulation of information, which, though each item by itself is perhaps insignificant, achieves *in toto* a kind of persuasiveness. Few medieval English households under the aristocracy could have reached the ideal aspired to by such nobles as George, Duke of Clarence, who ordained: 'sith that alle wisdom, grace, and goodnesse, procedeth of veray love, drede, and feythfulle service of God, withoute whose helpe and socoure no good governaunce ne politique rule may be hadde; it is ordeyned therefore . . . one of the chapleyns shall be redy to saye matyns and masse to the householde, and also evensonge; and that every (one) . . . be at the seid dyvine service.'[33] Nor could all servants have attained the spirit of religious zeal enjoined upon them in *The Lytylle Childrenes Lytil Boke*, addressed to servants and youths:

> Aryse be tyme oute of thi bedde,
> And Blysse thi brest and thi forhede,
> Than wasche thi hondes and thi face,
> Keme thi hede, and Aske God grace
> The to helpe in All thi werkes;
> Thow schall spede better what so thou carpes.
> Than go to the churche and here A messe,

[33]Soc. Ant., *Collection*, p. 89.

> There aske mersy for thi trespasse . . .
> Blysse bi mouthe or thou it ete,
> The better schalle be thi dyete.[34]

Moreover, behind this idealistic front lurked the less exalted motives of order and control, and the manipulation of religious spectacle for political purposes. Nevertheless, accumulated evidence seems to indicate that the noble household of the later middle ages was united under its lord as a religious community – not as a monastery or as a city of the saved *à la* Mount Tabor, but as a cohesive body which attempted regular daily worship and frequent charitable practices as a 'familye [that] may live together in love and kindness'.[35]

[34]F.J. Furnivall, ed., *The Babees Book* (Early English Texts Society, Oxford, vol. 32, 1868), p. 17.

[35]Braithwait, quoted in Jones, *Household of a Tudor Nobleman*, p. 186.

6

Family and *Familia*

My master, my dear lord he is; and I
His servant live, and will his vassal die;
He must not be my brother.

All's Well That Ends Well (I.iii)

The myth of the extended family dies hard, even amongst historians. While since 1972 documentary evidence has more than proved that nuclear families were the norm among peasant families in Britain and western Europe,[1] very recent books on the history of the family still find it necessary to reiterate at some length the relative smallness of households and their lack of kin outside the conjugal family under a single roof. This has led to some scholars stressing the importance of wider, extra-household ties of kinship and neighbourliness, but nevertheless the immediate unit of living was the conjugal nuclear, or biological family – parents and their offspring. Curiously enough, family history has reversed the normal historiographical order and concentrated on 'peasant' or small landholding families, rather than upon the aristocracy, particularly with regard to the period before 1500. This is probably related to the fact that the first family studies were of the English smallholding and village families; many historians have also held that magnates moved so frequently that determining who dwelt under a single roof was a difficult if not impossible task. More probably, however, the different structure of noble households with their large bodies of servants have made them difficult to evaluate and classify in the same way that has been evolved for poorer families. Moreover, with the noble family the whole question of the extended household again raises its head.

Although simply not enough research has been done to allow one to

---

[1] See particularly Peter Laslett, ed., *Household and Family in Past Time* (Cambridge University Press, Cambridge, 1972).

make pronouncements about the aristocratic family in western Europe, the accepted if rather tentative wisdom is that for nobles some sort of extended household structure remained, even after the gradual introduction of patrilineality, primogeniture and a dynastic sense of kinship, as a necessary concomitant of power. It is possible that the presence of kin around the hearth served as a basis for a wider network of kinship and affective ties by which the aristocracy maintained its political and economic ascendancy, the presence of kin also providing a rationale for religious and social practices. Whether this was truly the case still remains to be fully researched, though historians such as Jaques Heers and Georges Duby have gone some way towards establishing the household arrangements of certain groups.[2] But this scenario just does not fit the social world of the English aristocracy. As has been established earlier, nobles in England, with the exception of some bishops and abbots, very seldom kept their kin around them either as family members of servants. Therefore it might be worthwhile to examine the English noble household along historio-anthropological lines for understanding the family as a basis for controlling the world and as a framework for interpreting experience, while also comparing what is known of western European and Scottish noble households with their English counterparts.

Early European power-holding has a strong basis in the *geschlechte* or *sithe*, a clan or tribe of relations with cognate connections (that is, both matrilineally and patrilineally derived), living together as much as their semi-nomadic existence allowed, who supported each other in their battles and political alliances and worked closely together for economic advantages in the control of trade and agriculture. Whether the counts who appear in the tenth century are direct descendants of such ancient Frankish collectives, or are new blood who replaced them, it is now probably impossible to ascertain. The kin reckoning of such groups was ego-centred – one traced one's closest relationships and most important ties through oneself, so that a sibling or sibling's child was closer than a grandchild – and this seems to have been more concerned with the generation contemporary to the ego, with horizontal rather than the vertical blood ties. Descent from a common ancestor, however, and indeed forms of ancestor worship, often united all the members of the *geschlechte*. Since the qualification for living together

[2]Jaques Heers, *Family Clans in the Middle Ages*, trans. Berry Herbert (North Holland Publ. Co., Amsterdam, 1977); Georges Duby, *The Chivalrous Society*, trans. Cynthia Postan (Edward Arnold, London, 1977); see also, for example, David Herlihy, *Medieval Households* (Harvard University Press, Cambridge, Mass., 1985).

was cognateness, such groups seem to have been made up of diversely connected people of varied social composition. Many kin may have been essentially servants to their more powerful relations.

The changing political nature of Europe and particularly of the Frankish empire in the period around 900 to 1050 also changed visions of kinship, and, it would appear, household structure. As counts won autonomy from the great territorial princes, castellans appropriated fortresses, *milites* of the royal household broke away and were established with a landed base, and generally all forms of feudal tenure became more obviously hereditary, 'the position of . . . aristocrats crystallized around the privileges attached to their qualifications.'[3] That is, power came to lie not so much in the holding of a wide network of relationships defined by kinship, but in the holding by hereditary right of a piece of land and its concomitant privileges and duties. In such a situation, the need to keep the holding intact encouraged the practice of primogeniture, and the need to establish hereditary rights from one male to another enhanced the importance of agnatic connections and linear descent. By the early thirteenth century, Lambert, chaplain to the Count of Guisnes, is describing a house built to encompass only a single conjugal couple; there is no real place in it for married children, even for an elder son and his wife, nor indeed for any adult children.[4]

Nevertheless, Lambert was himself kin to the master, and he was also a married man. Despite the demise of the widespread noble *geschlechte* structure, the household remained a place of kinship by blood. Europeans in the fifteenth and sixteenth centuries considered strict English primogeniture bizarre, cruel and a threat to family connections,[5] particularly with regard to the lack of provision for younger sons. While the middle ages in England saw the end of any extended kin household among the nobility that had previously existed, it appears that in Europe some such forms survived as basic to noble householding practice.

English notions of primogeniture extended to the inheritance of nobility. The peerage proper consisted only of those who actually held title; their children and kin were commoners, albeit accorded courtesy titles. In practice, as we have noticed, it is not really possible to distinguish between gentry and nobility in terms of way of life and

[3]Duby, *The Chivalrous Society*, p. 148.

[4]Georges Duby, *The Knight, the Lady and the Priest: The Making of Modern Marriage in Medieval France*, trans. Barbara Bray (Allen Lane, London, 1983), pp. 255–6.

[5]Jack Goody, Joan Thirsk and E.P. Thompson, eds, *Family and Inheritance: Rural Society in Western Europe, 1200–1800* (Cambridge University Press, Cambridge, 1976), p. 185.

circles of influence and interest. Nevertheless, the technical lack of nobility, combined with the tendency for younger sons to be excluded from the major part of the inheritance of their father, meant that the children of nobles, and indeed of gentry, were more or less inevitably caught in a downward social mobility that could only be reversed by a favourable marriage. English parents did attempt to provide for their children and were often successful, though from 1500 at latest economic factors began to make this more difficult; nevertheless it was possible for the youngest son of the youngest son of a peer to disappear completely from the ranks of the gentry.

European practice was rather different. Although primogeniture was widespread by 1300, the tradition of partible patrimony died hard in Europe (whereas in England primogeniture had been customary from 1066 at least and quite possibly was also a Saxon custom), and non-divisible inheritance was modified by a number of practices. Younger sons were often provided with small seigneuries, either purchased for them or carved off from the central inheritance, often ringing the main estate like satellites or buffer states. Moreover, the notion of nobility in western Europe was different from that in England. Nobility was conferred not by title but by descent, and all the children of a peer, and their children in turn, would be considered in some sense noble. This led to great variations in wealth and influence amongst the gentry. Indeed, the 'popular nobility', as they are sometimes called, were often no better off than peasants, though they were of course free. (It has been suggested that this popular nobility in its earliest manifestations was in fact simply a synonym for the state of being a freeman).[6]

Under two such different conceptions of nobility and provision for children, kin relationships are bound to differ as well. In the English system the concentration on the heir and the dynastic line, often to the detriment of younger children, was not likely to make the nobility particularly well-disposed towards their cousins, nephews, nieces, aunts, uncles, and more distant relations in terms of providing for them; and because such relations, by the harsh laws of primogeniture, were often not particularly wealthy or influential, there was very little incentive for a noble to rely on his kin for political or economic advantages. It would be very easy to overstate the case here. Of course the grandson of a peer was generally better off and more favourably regarded than the grandson of a butcher; naturally affective ties often overruled political or economic considerations; certainly nobles and gentry in England did rely to some extent upon blood relationships to establish connections.

[6]Heers, *Family Clans*, p. 25.

But with a system of non-divisible inheritance, brothers, let alone cousins, were seldom natural allies in the defence of territory and position. Alliance by marriage proves, in English kin claims, to be as important as relationship by blood, and more frequently used and more important than both is the appeal to good lordship, to ties of clientage and patronage. In Europe, by contrast, the modified nature of primogeniture and the broad definition of nobility made of one's kin, one's natural peers.

Differing kin relationships also led to different household structures. The continuation of forms of partible inheritance in Tuscany was concomitant with the presence of *consorzi* or *sorterie*, mostly urban by the fourteenth and fifteenth centuries but most probably with a rural background. These were very large, wealthy family groups living under one roof and banding togther to protect, amalgamate and increase their rural domains, to create strong trading and commerical links in the cities, and often to support each other in private wars and political intrigues. In Sestri Levante in 1467, the census counted 135 households with two to five heads of conjugal families, and 87 with more than five heads.[7] It is important to note that the size of such *consorzi* was directly related to the wealth of the family.

Outside the Italian city-based states, however, such massive extended families were not common. While *frereches* and *paraiges* forms of extended households survived in which adult siblings cohabited, particularly in *lange d'oc* France and Alsace-Lorraine, most nobles lived in households with a single conjugal couple at its heart. But the body of people living with them seems to have a strong kin element. Preliminary examinations indicate that many of a lord's and lady's servants and attendants would be related to them in different degrees. Fourteenth-century Genoese households of the aristocracy and the wealthy traders have been found by Jaques Heers and others to contain large numbers of kin both as servants and hangers-on.[8] W. Zaniewicki discovered that in Poland and Castile domestic servants were often called 'nobles in attendance', could form a useful political dependancy, and were often kin to their master by blood or marriage.[9] J.B. Ross, considering the Erembald clan of Bruges, found that their military power, local authority, and variety of revenues were related to the close communal life of many levels of kin.[10] Georges Duby, in his researches into the

---

[7]Ibid., pp. 41–2.

[8]Heers, *Family Clans*, p. 41; also Herlihy, *Medieval Households*, pp. 151–5.

[9]W. Zaniewicki, *La Noblesse 'Populaire' en Espagne et an Pologne* (Lyons, 1967), no publisher.

[10]J.B. Ross, 'The Rise and Fall of a Seventeenth Century Clan', *Speculum* 34 (1959), p. 385.

lives of the Counts of Guisnes, has indicated that kin appeared to form a large part of the household, particularly as higher servants.[11] In societies where inheritance patterns were kinder to those not directly in the line of primogeniture, and where the whole notion of nobility was widely interpreted and crossed boundaries of wealth and status, the use of kin to cement the foundations of the noble house, the basis of noble power, remained a possibility. The employment of family in varying degrees of closeness appears to have been neither embarrassing nor difficult, and was in fact probably a natural extension of the already existing alliances between the head of the kin structure and the various descendants of younger sons holding small seigneuries in the same locality. More research needs to be done into the exact kin relationships of household servants in Europe to their masters, but at the moment they appear generally to have been cousins in varying degrees – younger sons of younger sons for whom no monetary or landed portion was possible.

In complete contrast, as we have seen, English nobles almost never employed kin as household members. It might be thought that strict primogeniture would encourage the retaining of kin, which would provide the best chance for cadets of the main line to maintain their social status. After all, servants of nobles were almost *de facto* gentlemen and their chances of upward social mobility were considerable. However, one must remember that in England the definition of the peerage was very strict indeed and, while there was no clear boundary between a gentleman and a non-gentleman, the range of possibility was a good deal narrower, particularly as regards wealth and land, than it was in Europe. A servant might be regarded in courtesy as a gentleman, particularly if he was by blood or wealth entitled to such regard, but it would be peculiar to regard such a person as part of the body of gentry, unless he entered it as well by means of land acquisition. While a Frenchman, Italian, Spaniard or inhabitant of the German lands could speak of himself as a noble whilst living like a peasant – or a servant – the boundaries of gentility in England were simply not so loose. Given such a mental attitude, the notion of living in the house of a kinsman, particularly a close kinsman, would have been seen as an immediate step downwards, and probably would have created an atmosphere of tension and anxiety not compatible with the smooth running of a household.

What was possible, if a younger son could not be otherwise provided for, though, was to take service with a patron or lord, possibly one with

---

[11]Duby, *The Knight*, p. 227.

whom one's family already had a tradition of clientage. Just as a peer could serve in the bedchamber of a king without worrying about this status, so the younger son of a gentle family could happily serve in the household of a peer or a wealthy gentleman, particularly if a relationship of good lordship already existed to help define the connection. If kin stood at the foundations of European noble household structure, good lordship took its place in England.

It might be, indeed has been, said that good lordship was a more efficient grease to the wheel of alliances and interlocking networks of control than was claim to kinship. Certainly, contemporary appeals in England for help and support are more frequently couched in terms of good lordship and patronage than in reminders of blood or marital ties. Later medieval practices, such as 'bastard feudalism' and private indentures, frequently call upon memories of services rendered to lords, and protections and favours extended to their followers, which created ties of loyalty and duty at least as effective as those of kin. At the foundation of any good lord's affinity lay his household, which provided the mechanism by which he organised his political, economic and social life. This work has already discussed the way in which the noble household functioned for its master politically and economically, taking on roles which, on the continent, might have been more frequently undertaken by associations based on kinship. It is also interesting to note that, in attempting to create a religious community, the household religious practices of lords in England recall both the pagan tradition of ancestor worship amongst the earliest *geschlechte* kin groups, and also the Christian European household's devotion to saints who in family legend are associated with an ancestor.[12] In English households the *penates* are more usually the patron saints of the lord currently head of the household, rather than the ancestor's holy mentors or the ancestor himself. The medieval notion of the patron saint is not without parallels to the idea of good lordship, once again suggesting that in England patronage rather than kinship was the basis of household loyalty.

What all this seems to suggest is that kinship as the basis of ties in the household of a noble or gentle, the norm in Europe, was in part at least replaced by links of clientage and patronage with few kin elements in England; and that for the aristocracy some of the traditional functions of kinship which persisted in Europe were taken over in England by a household body not made up of kin. It is fairly easy to accept the working of this in relation to political and economic interests, the more

---

[12]Heers, *Family Clans*, p. 242.

'commercial' and self-interested functions of kin. As Duby stresses, 'Were they not impelled by forces which ever since their childhood had been slowly transforming the highest nobility from which they sprang into a motley assortment of families, companies of vassals, "houses", to conceive of political relations as family relations?'.[13] It is more difficult, however, to turn that conception on its head. How far can ties of loyalty and mutual help stand in for kinship in affective and emotional relationships? How far were household members able and even willing to fulfill such bonds, generally accepted as familial? If lords could conceive of feudal ties as like bonds between father and son – a common category conceit – did they also interpret practical relationships in the light of their feelings and expectations about families?

For the historian of the family the determination of affective bonds between individuals is fraught with difficulty. The little material that is amenable to such an analysis is generally ambiguous and complicated. Determining, for instance, in a letter from a husband to a wife whether he 'loves' her, or what his personal feeling and hopes concerning her may be, is notoriously difficullt even when dealing with modern documents, let alone when faced with the different conventions of the middle ages; and many historians have fallen prey to the urge to air their personal and admittedly unproven beliefs about the affections of medieval people. However, a closer look at some traditionally familial functions and the part of the English noble household played in them will perhaps yield some clues as to just how far the household could replace the kin group, as a primary social organism.

The familial relationship at the heart of the household, the nucleus of husband, wife and children, remains as puzzling as it is compelling for the inquisitive historian. However, since this nuclear family is the unit the household was constructed to serve, the affective relationships involved deserve some attention, as they must have helped determine the emotional ties of the wider household. Historians interested in affective kinship have concentrated on two sorts of evidence. The emotional bonds expressed in letters and wills can, when used cumulatively, lead one to some impression of the strength of family ties, but documents of this sort which are of use are rather rare prior to *c.*1530. Historians have also extrapolated hypotheses from the facts of family life, its structure and patterns, often basing their arguments upon psychoanalytical notions. While the evidential value of this sort of speculation is doubtful, its logical force can be persuasive.

[13]George Duby, *The Three Orders: Feudal Society Imagined*, trans. Arthur Goldhammer (University of Chicago Press, Chicago, 1980), p. 71.

One aspect of the medieval and early modern family which has given rise to considerable scholarly discussion is its lack of privacy and continuity, in other words its lack of exclusivity. Modern families are typified by the ideology of the private circle of familial existence, which almost forces family members to define themselves in terms of their nuclear kinship, as this group provides the opportunity for the most intimate and long-term relationships in modern society. In contrast, the family between 1250 and 1600 furnished neither privacy nor continuity, especially for noble families. Domestic life was in fact public, due both to lack of facilities such as individual apartments for the family only, and to the use of domestic occasions such as meals and the morning *toilette* for purposes of display and political manoeuvering. The introduction of private dining halls and bedchambers into fifteenth-century architecture may be the first indication of a need for privacy that grew into our modern concept of the enclosed family.

Families also lacked continuity in their relationships. Nobles were frequently absent from hearth and home, separated from their wives and children; children were generally put out to nurse and once weaned were cared for and raised by servants and left home in early adolescence; mortality rates were high, and those adults who survived past the age of forty generally had had more than one spouse and had seen numerous offspring die. Death in the family, so disturbing to modern nuclear kin groups, was a common occurrence. Lack of continuous association would seem necessarily to militate against tight family bonding, both by failing to provide the opportunity for close relationships to evolve, and by making it too emotionally traumatic for the individual to risk such ties.

That said, it must also be stressed that religious ideology dwelt heavily upon the mother–child relationship, which would not have been effective if it failed to strike any cord in the medieval breast; and the pragmatic nature of marriage as a financial arrangement was mitigated by the insistence of the Church upon its consensual, affective basis. Moreover, it is clear that even in arranged marriages the characters of the prospective spouses were considered, and their compatibility and chances of generating affection in each other were taken into account. Lawrence Stone, Michael Mitterauer and others have frequently suggested that in fact it is possible that the looser nature of medieval family ties may have led to less emotional trauma in the family context, making families more psychically healthy than the inverted modern nuclear groups.

In any case, the structure of the nuclear noble family does seem to have been much less rigid, enclosed and defined than ours. This implies that it was within the bounds of possibility for familial relationships to spread beyond that immediate nuclear core, and to include relationships with servants who lived no less continuously and closely with the family under the same roof than did siblings, spouses and offspring. And, indeed, we find suggestions that the noble household did take on traditional familial roles.

Recent anthropological studies of kin groups have made much of their function as a system for the process of social reproduction: 'the domestic domain is the system of social relations through which the reproductive nucleus is integrated with the environment and the structure of the total society.'[14] The household's part in fostering and educating those who will ensure its own continuation is worth examining if we want to consider how far households filled the functions of kinship.

The role of noble households in education has been discussed in previous chapters, in particular those describing household members and organization, considering social training and trade apprenticeship as well as academic instruction as it occurred in the household. However, there is little concrete information about how the household's educational role was manifested, nor the extent to which it was an institutionalized phenomenon; it is usually very difficult to obtain detailed knowledge of how household children were educated, in whatever sense of the word. Specific information about academic instruction, beyond its existence, is scarce or nonexistent. The learning of a trade by children within the household seems to have taken place through general example and observation rather than a formal apprenticeship. While we can sometimes see its results, social training was not a matter of coursework so much as a kind of osmosis, and the sources we have do not permit our tracing of its processes in any given household. Recently interest has been expressed by scholars such as Nicholas Orme in the function of the household as a provider of education, academically, in trade terms, and socially. While it is important to stress that the household was not a child-centred institution, which may explain the scantiness of references to their education and upbringing, nevertheless families may not be child-centred either. Since it was particularly common for the children of nobles and gentles, especially the boys, to serve in a great household during their prepubescent and adolescent years, it is worth looking at the evidence available on education in the household.

[14]Jack Goody, ed., *The Developmental Cycle In Domestic Groups* (Cambridge University Press, Cambridge, 1971), p. 1.

Plate 15 The baptism of Sir Richard Beauchamp. *Pageant of Richard Beauchamp*, Cott Ms Julius E iv, art. 6, f. 1v. English, *c*.1465. Courtesy of The British Library.

Certain distinct and recognizable means for educating the young in households can be discerned. Nobles who had young children of their own generally kept tutors for all their wellborn charges. The third Duke of Buckingham's wardrober has left us a rare account of some of the books he bought for the children in the duke's care in 1503–04: courtesy books, primers and grammar books, as well as pencases and penknives. The same account, however, also includes bows and arrows, armour, and other martial equipment for the duke's son, wards and pages. There was also a female 'nursery governor' for the duke's daughters in 1517. Clearly, the noble children in the Stafford households learned knightly and probably domestic skills, as well as academic studies. The Staffords also kept singing masters for their children of the chapel, who not only directed these young singers but taught basic music and liturgical knowledge which they could use as adults, as singers or in other positions. The male Stafford heirs were also given practical training which they later put to good use: Humphrey and Henry served their father, the first duke, as estate agents while still in their teens; and the third duke's heir, Henry Baron Stafford, was appointed his father's estates steward in 1519, when he was eighteen.[15] Such administrative training doubtless lies behind the undoubted ability of the Staffords to squeeze the maximum profit out of their lands.

Great lords of the higher peerage were particularly likely to provide formal teachers for the young in their care, but even among the minor gentry, those with children of their own usually employed at least one servant, who often was the chaplain as well, to see to the academic and moral education of all the household's children. Hugh Luttrell employed schoolmasters for his own offspring and fostered children, and a 'master of henxmen' in 1405–06, the Luttrells' six kitchen and stable boys being grouped as the 'henxmen'. Their master was presumably in charge of their discipline and training. In addition, Hugh's eldest son John was achieving practical experience in estate administration from about the age of fifteen, like the Stafford sons, helping to collect rents and eventually taking over the running of the manor of Carhampton.[16] Payments to tutors and purchases of pens, paper and books for the children of Sir Henry Clifford (later Earl of Cumberland), during the reign of Henry VIII, are to be found in the Clifford documents at Chatsworth. John Ffouke, governor and tutor to the sons of Edward Courtenay, Earl of Devon, has left a detailed

[15]Staffs. RO D 641/1/2/23 and D 1721/1/1 fo 382.
[16]Somerset RO DD/L/P37/10–A.

expense account for the years 1395 to 1400, which includes books, paper, and miniature weapons for the children's use. Further down the social scale, the accounts of Lady Margaret Long of Hengrave Hall (Cambridgeshire) include a book of charges for Thomas Kytson, a ward of the Longs in 1571–2. Even more interesting are the payments made by Robert Melton, a yeoman farmer, for the support of his wife's young brother; the commonplace book in which these payments are made includes a 'courtesy book' or poem detailing social mores for the enlightenment of children.

Some households, however, seem to have made no provision at all for the children under their care, though whether the concomitant expenses are merely hidden in the accounting system and other servants doubled as teachers is not certain. But it is significant that those lords whose records show no obvious provision for their children, their own, fostered or child servants, are very frequently those with no children of their own or whose children are grown up or in service in other households, and presumably being educated there. The Cromwells of Tydd and Tattershall (Lincolnshire), for instance, show no sign of having had any forms of education within the household. William and Margaret Cromwell, and Ralph's heirs, the Radcliffes, had few wards or child servants, but Ralph, Lord Cromwell, had a number of wards and an average of five child servants between 1444 and 1451. The one offspring of any of these families, Robert (who died in 1441), son of William and Margaret and later a ward of Ralph, never has a tutor recorded among his attendants. It is difficult to be sure, but he seems seldom to have resided with his uncle; perhaps he was at service in a household elsewhere, or possibly boarded with a tutor, as did Edmund Stonor's son Edmund, who was sent to a grammar school at Ewelme (Oxfordshire), not far from Stonor; the Thomas Stonors I and II lived with their guardian Thomas Chaucer at Ewelme and, one might infer, most probably attended the same establishment. Thomas Stonor I's papers include an agreement for the education as well as the maintenance of his daughter Isabella by her grandparents,[17] though giving no details of what this education should consist.

It is possible that some of the Stonor's young charges, in particular the girls, may have received academic instruction from one of the numerous chaplains. William Stonor, like John Luttrell and the Staffords, was from his early teens given practical experience in estate administration, looking after the Stonors' Devon holdings under the

---

[17]Charles Lethbridge Kingsford, ed., *The Stonor Letters and Papers, 1290–1483* (Camden Society, London, vols 29 and 30, 1919), vol. 29, no. 56.

watchful eye of his uncle. William's unmarried sisters were fostered by the Duchess of Suffolk. Similarly, the Paston and Plumpton letters tell us more about the fostering of these families' offspring in other households rather than education in the parents' home; as do the accounts of Sir William Petre for his daughter Thomasine (1554–6) and his son John (1567–70).

The *Northumberland Household Book*, on the other hand, includes numerous provisions for the education of common and noble children in the household of the fifth Percy Earl of Northumberland: singing masters, disciplinary governors, sergeants for military training, and academic tutors – probably the most comprehensive example of anything like a household educational system, though its actual implementation is not certain. Perhaps more typical would be the arrangements made for Anne Talbot, daughter of Gilbert, Lord Talbot, who had a governess and a tutor, but who was also given practical experience in handling household money and overseeing the daily account book, between 1402 and 1411; or for Sir Henry Willoughby of Wollaton's young charges in 1549, whose tutor bought for them Thomas Elyot's *Boke Named the Governor*, a treatise on the education of those young nobles destined to hold authority.

It will be noticed that the education of the young in households did not only consist of basic academic skills and domestic achievements, but laid stress on moral and social learning. Literature purchased for the education of children relied heavily upon 'courtesy books' such as *Stans Puer Ad Mensam* and *The ABC of Aristotle*, which had a wide circulation – there are at least fifty extant copies of *Stans Puer Ad Mensam*, dating from the early fourteenth to the mid-sixteenth centuries. They are as much or more concerned with behaviour and social rules as with academic matters, and many are quite clearly written for the benefit of children living in a great household. Some, like *The Babees Book*, instruct noble children in service to their lord, such as holding his washbasin for him before meals, and also such differing points of etiquette as blowing the nose at table and holding conversation with one's betters. Others, like John Russell's *Boke of Nurture* or *The Wise Man's Advice to His Son*, teach skills like carving, waiting service and proper serving order to youngsters making a career of household service.

Those households most likely to have formal provision for the education of household children were those of influential peers with large households, and families of wealthy gentry who were heavily dependent upon county society. Peers depended upon education to extend their and their children's patronage and to create a generation of servants. The wealthy gentry may have had relatively small, basically practical households, but the provision of an educational centre could give them the vital edge in extending patronage and consolidating social ties.

The existence of such a system, however, might well have been cyclical. In the households of the greater peerage and episcopacy, which took in large numbers of adolescent children from good backgrounds, tutors were probably provided all the time; but in households further down the scale of nobility, the stimulus or spark encouraging a formal provision appears to have been the state of the lord's own nuclear family. Even a great lord such as the first Duke of Buckingham had more wards and childservants in the 1440s, when his own children were young, than in the 1450s, and it is from the earlier manuscripts that the tutors are recorded. Similarly, the thirteenth Duke of Oxford is recorded as employing a boy's choir, singing masters and tutors only from the 1490s, when his nephew and heir became his ward. During this period of their lives, lords were probably most naturally concerned with the whole question of education and training of the young, and they seem then to have been the most amenable to instituting it themselves, whether their own children were living at home or were fostered; while childless or older heads of households, like Ralph Cromwell and Elizabeth de Burgh, were less interested in the advantages concomitant with the household playing an educational role. Though there are exceptions to this rule, most families do seem to exhibit this tendency.

Undoubtedly children in the household received as their main education the whole process of socialization into the household, in learning to survive as servants and among their peers in such a way as to prepare them for life as heads, or as members, of households. In this sense any group of people among whom children live can be said to have a familial function, regardless of the intentions, interests and wishes of the authority figures in charge of them. The fact that it took the presence of the biological children of the lord to kindle interest in and attention to the education of all the children in the household's care probably indicated both that education still had strong links with biological kinship in medieval England, and that in this area the noble household had not entirely assimilated the functions of the family. One's responsibility to the children living in one's household was not the same as one's responsibility to one's own biological offspring.

As well as responsibility for education and training, anthropologists define familial associations as 'jural units'. That is, those living together tend to define themselves by doing so as subject to a common authority, though this authority need not be a single person. It is this aspect of the family which most frequently leads political and religious leaders to refer to those for whose welfare they are responsible as a family. A common and early name for the household, the *familia*, clearly echoes this sort of metaphor. How far the household simply mimicked or paralleled certain facets of the family as a jural unit, and how far it actually took the place of jural kinship, is a difficult question to answer; but large numbers of courtesy books, ordinances (most, unfortunately, dating no earlier than the fifteenth century) and lists of rules, as well as the fate of servants in law courts, may give us some idea of the nature and scope of household authority.

A great deal of evidence, even if most of it is rather oblique, suggests that the household could be an exceedingly unruly place. References in poems, plays and chronicles often refer disparagingly to the wanton activities of some hapless lord's 'feed men' – a good many of whom turn out to be household members, both at home and abroad – while acknowledging the difficulty of controlling such large bodies of men. But the authority to control and punish them was also publicly (if not always by statute) recognized to be their master. John Hardying's *Chronicle*, in a section of doggerel poetry advising the king on how to rule, complains that feed men should not be above the law; but he also recommends that it is the master who should control and chastise his followers, and bonds to keep the peace generally enjoined that a lord was responsible for his servants' keeping the peace as well. When a servant was brought to law for his micreancy he was nevertheless often released into the master's care, owing to heavy and sometimes probably threatening lobbying on the part of the lord, but probably also because the lord was believed to be the appropriate authority: as Edward IV is made to say in *Richard III*, 'But when your carters or your waiting-vassals / Have done a drunken slaughter, and deface / The precious image of our dear Redeemer, / You straight are on your knees for pardon, pardon; / And I, unjustly too, must grant it you.'

Whether a master could, or would, control his followers is another question. It has long been recognized that certain elements in the violent acts of lords' followers are not unrelated to older traditions of vendetta, usually the province of kin groups. If two lords were in conflict their followers would carry on their disagreement among themselves. Also, if such conflict escalated into homicide, revenge for the dead man could be achieved by killing any member of the opposite following, not necessarily by the death of the one who actually did the deed. The indiscriminate harassment of the servants of the Pastons by those of the Duke of Norfolk when Paston and the duke were contesting the Fastolf inheritance is one example; another, more famous and extreme, is the murder of the eldest son of the third Baron Stafford by John Holland, purportedly due to the death of an esquire of Holland's caused by a Stafford archer.

While such hostilities were most common and most violent in times of unrest, and particularly during the fifteenth century, servants certainly pursued vendettas, fatal or trivial, in earlier and more settled centuries. Disputes over inheritance and boundaries between lords often prompted their servants to attack one another. Undoubtedly masters often fueled and encouraged their turmoil for their own ends: Henry II and King John were not the only peers of the realm to muse aloud on the death of rivals. In their identification of a rival lord's household as a legitimate focus of attack for his misdeeds, in their identification of themselves as prosecutors of their master's disagreements, and in their failure to discriminate between individuals in the pursuit of vendetta, household servants do seem to have classed themselves as a jural unit with many of the characteristic duties and responsibilities of kin groups in dealing with aristocratic feuds. The passion and violence of these battles between households may indicate something more than purchased or hired loyalty.

Lords were not, however, always pleased by the rumbustiousness of their followers, which did not reflect well on their own honour and worship. Since lords were willing to stand surety for their servants, it is perhaps reasonable to assume that they felt capable of disciplining them. The way in which household servants may have been controlled and chastised seems to indicate the acceptance by them and their masters of the household as a jural unit with its own rules and powers. A number of fifteenth-century ordinances contain sets of prohibitions and exactions with fines and penalties laid out for non-compliance which suggest a systematic attempt to keep unruly servants in line.[18] These ordinances are all those of royalty or very high nobility, and do not find parallels in their disciplinary procedures with earlier ordinances, so their evidence must be evaluated carefully. Their disciplinary procedures may reflect particular fifteenth-century problems, such as the political situations which often seem to have set off servant violence; they may also reflect the growing numbers in households in the fifteenth century generally, numbers which were becoming increasingly unwieldly and hard to control, particularly in the households of great magnates. Keeping an eye on the activities of thirty or forty servants is

[18]Soc. Ant., eds, *A Collection of Ordinances and Regulations* (John Nichols, London, 1790), contains many of these.

quite a different proposition from regulating four or five hundred, which may explain why George, Duke of Clarence, set out his household rules in an ordinance and gentlemen like Thomas Bozoun or William Vredale do not appear to have done so. But this does not mean that such gentlemen were incapable of effectively disciplining their servants. Nor are the problems which such rules were set out to solve necessarily peculiar to the fifteenth century. They might reflect a common group of noble rules and regulations for the household whose actual writing down and codifying reflect the conditions of very large late medieval households.

Many of the regulations set out are concerned to prevent the waste or theft of food, embezzlement, theft of other items, etc., problems closely connected to the business of purveying and accounting for a large institution. But a good many of the rules have to do with general behaviour. Gambling with dice or cards was forbidden (George, Duke of Clarence, allowed it at Christmas, however); regulations against swearing were oft repeated, Edward IV objecting particularly strongly to swearing by the mass; and tellers of ignoble stories, and 'users of ribawdry', were also discouraged. The chief servants, particularly the steward and marshall, could dismiss those described as 'backbyters' and common troublemakers. Drunkenness and fighting were also taken very seriously. For all these misdemeanors a first offence could earn a fine; a second several days' pay; and a third, dismissal from service. The drawing of a weapon in the course of a fight usually merited immediate dismissal, though in the household of Edward IV's sons such an offender earned a day in the stocks. But perhaps most importantly, most of these ordinances provide an arbitration service, stipulating that quarrels between servants are to be settled by appeal to the household statutes and the decision of the lord, or his chief servants as deputies. Whether such authority was accepted or not is of course another question, and one difficult to answer; but the provision of such a method for dealing with problem servants indicates that public assumptions about the lord's right of authority over his servants had a basis in fact, and that household statutes, while not binding in law, may have been regarded as a jural system of discipline by lords and household members, whether they were written down or customary.

Ordinances do not only forbid certain types of behaviour, but attempt to reinforce others. Three areas of household rules were used to enforce the 'pollytique, sadde and good rule' or tenor of household life: the treatment of servants' menials and dependants, chapel attendance, and dining regulations.

Servants, not only gentlemen servants but yeomen and grooms, frequently had personal attendants who looked after their possessions and helped them in their work. Lords were clearly concerned, from the evidence of the ordinances, with the character of these menials, the way in which they were treated, and the sort of work they did. Ordinances hastened to ensure that servants' servants were vetted by the chief servants to see that they were honest, presentable and of the right sex and age. In some households children and women were forbidden; in most it is assumed that such servants will be men (the ordinance of Edward IV's son speaks out against the mistreatment of maid or man by a servant, though whether this refers solely to servants' servants is not really clear), and the presence of women in servants' chambers 'without a cause reasonable' is punishable by a fine on the first offence. Servants' servants were also forbidden to do their master's chores in the household as a substitute for him, and they were regarded as under the jurisdiction and pleasure of the household officers. Servants were not allowed to set up their own mini-households.

Attendance at chapel was in all households supposed to be enforced by the exaction of penalties which could be either fines or even restriction of diet to bread and water. George, Duke of Clarence, required his household members to bring proof of their having been shriven and received the sacraments at Easter, on pain of being dismissed. Ignoring normal dining hours was also a misdemeanour. Princess Cecil, mother of Edward IV, was praised by the author who described her household for having set meal times strictly enforced. 'Dining of noblemen in corners', as Henry VII's ordinances of Eltham put it, was strictly forbidden with the exception of those who worked in the kitchens or those who were ill, and taking your meals privately instead of in the hall with your household peers is reiterated over and over again as a serious offence. Like chapel attendance, communal dining was an important way of creating a community out of a disparate body of retainers, and its lack was believed to breed riot and disorder and lack of deference to the authority of the household officers. Just as modern and not so modern family sociologists have pointed to the decline of the family meal and family worship as elements in household disintegration, so medieval English nobles clearly saw lack of coherence in praying and eating as a threat to their household's stability. Whether or not such activities have anything to do with establishing community in fact, the stability of households was being evaluated along the same lines as that of families. Noble households seem to have functioned as a jural unit in ways not unlike those of kin groups, and the authority of the household was maintained by the enforcement of practices commonly ascribed to families.

Worshipping and eating together reinforced the community spirit and links between household members, but also served to limit servant autonomy and independence of action, by orienting basic human activities towards the group.

The control of servants' servants was not simply a means of protection for menials and for the household; it was also, as has been suggested, a way of keeping servants from setting up their own mini-households, an act which, like eating alone or refusing to participate in group worship, challenges the authority and unity of the householding structure. Another way of preventing the creation of satellite households was to keep servants from marrying. Anthropologists in particular have pointed out that heads of households are generally not only jural authorities, but control the means of reproduction in the household: hence the tensions which arise once there is more than one conjugal couple under the same roof, and why the onset of adolescence can create so many problems in families. We have already seen how a married child tended to leave the family roof while an unmarried adult child might continue to live with this or her parents in some harmony. In Britain and northern Europe, the household, however composed, almost never had more than a single conjugal couple at its heart. Thus the marriage of servants, either kin or as in England in the place of kin, threatened to create another centre of conjugality, another focus of unity at least for the servant couple, which might undermine the central unity of the household. While only a few ordinances actually state that servants might not marry (and even these cannot afford to refuse service to gentle married servants; George, Duke of Clarence, can only dismiss pages, scourers and turnbroaches who marry), we have already seen how in most households married men did not rise as high in service as unmarried and clerical men, and their wives and families lived outside the household. It is interesting to note that the few married couples who served in tandem in the household did so generally as reflections of the central conjugal couple; she as personal servant to the lady, he as a personal servant or proxy master to the lord. While it is difficult to generalize, it seems that the marriage of servants set up the same sort of tensions in the household as the marriage of sons.

The affective relationships of masters and servants still remain among the most difficult areas of research for the household scholar. But the possibility that English noble households took over some of the functions of the kin-based aristocratic households of western Europe and Scotland, and in turn some of the functions of kin, makes it less surprising to find, in wills, letters and personal documents, affections and tensions not unlike those found between family members. The

Plate 16 The death of Sir Richard Beauchamp. *Pageant of Richard Beauchamp*, Cott. Ms. Julius E iv, art. 6, f. 26v. English, c. 1465. Courtesy of The British Library.

indignities suffered by Byrdescrytte, a scribe of Hamon LeStrange's household, whose fellows consistently altered his name to Byrdeshytte in the accounts, and the friendly exchanges of letters between the Stonor servants, are reminiscent of brotherly relations. The care, gratitude and love expressed in bequests to longstanding servants in wills are often as tender as those sentiments addressed to near relatives.

It is generally in the households of bishops and abbots that direct comparisons between family and household are made, where the establishment is referred to as 'my family' and the servants as 'my sons'. These lords, without a conjugal family at the heart of their great households, depended more exclusively upon their servants for affective relationships. It would be wrong to suggest that the secular lords in the household replaced the family in affections; children and probably siblings as well as spouses come first in terms of endearment and loyalty. But the line between *familia* and family, as *familia* came to assume some of the functions and roles of the wider kinship in the absence of close extended-family ties, was often very thin indeed. John Husse wrote to his dearly beloved employer, Lord Lisle, in 1534,

> not to use company of mean personages, nor to be conversant with some persons which he saith useth daily company with your lordship sounding highly against your honour. I trust your lordship will take no displeasure with me because I write so plainly, as I was desired, but I take God to record, I would your lordship as much good as my own heart.[19]

Whatever self-interest may be said to lie in his devotion, it is nevertheless an attachment not far removed from that of a kinsman.

[19]Muriel St Clare Byrne, ed., *The Lisle Letters* (6 vols, University of Chicago Press, Chicago, 1981), vol. 2, no. 260.

Conclusion
The Demise of the Household

Was this face the face
That every day under his household roof
Did keep ten thousand men?

Richard II (IV.i)

This study of the household has allowed us to reach a number of conclusions highly relevant to our understanding of such concerns as the English family, noble politics, the exercise of authority on a local level, the internal organization of certain economic systems, and the various functions of religious activity in the life of a community. I began with the internal makeup of the household, studying the lord and his family, and the servants working within or with the household: their status, social background, geographical origins, training and patterns of activity. The mechanisms by which these individuals were coordinated – the accounting systems, hierarchies, and organizational schemes which contained household members within specific forms and overall patterns – were examined. But, having analysed the component parts of such a machine, and discovered how these worked together, one must study what actions and reactions this structure produced. In the four chapters that followed the basic analysis, I discussed the role of the secular noble household as an important part of economic systems, in particular within localized trade, but as a consumer and producer; as an organization through which lords exercised their authority, on a national as well as a local level; as a group within which social and religious activities worked to cement household members into a community; and as a substitute for extended kin groups. Now all the clockwork must be fitted into its case and wound: that is, we must reassemble the aspects of the medieval household which we have been studying separately, in order to understand its full signficance.

The household was a framework upon and through which individuals and groups organized and controlled their lives. It acted as a system through which nobles, their servants, local tenants, farmers, and a noble's wider affinty could initiate and control a local economic balance, exert or seek escape from authority, and filter community experiences of piety and affection. The household cannot be dismissed as a mere domestic organization, nor yet as a simple political tool of the noble classes. It functioned as an important structure in helping men and women in the later middle ages to conceive, comprehend and carry out their existence. Like the family in later and earlier times, the noble household served many authors as a paradigm or microcosm of wider relationships and abstract principles of community: Giovanni della Casa, Baldesar Castiglione, George Cavendish, Geoffrey Chaucer, Sir Thomas Elyot, Richard Fitznigel, Sir John Fortesque, John Hardynge, William Langland, Palladius, Oliver de la Marche, Machiavelli, and many other writers of the period studied here, used the form of the noble household as a vehicle to criticize, support, analyse, and explain the workings of the world at large. Castiglione insists that what makes a perfect courtier, makes a perfect man;[1] and it appears probable that for many people between 1250 and 1600 this assessment was a true expression of their experience of living. The household explained the world to those who experienced the world through it.

Kenneth McFarlane posits that 'Institutions sometimes seem to have a life of their own',[2] and certainly the secular noble household often has this appearance, owing primarily to two factors. Households survived as institutions as living beings survive: by being self-supporting and self-perpetuating. I noted in chapter 3, on consumption, that the household sometimes seemed to exist solely for the purpose of supporting and administering to itself; while its chief function, certainly, was that of serving the lord as he desired, indubitably household members spent much time and energy in keeping the household staff and appurtenances in some kind of order. The greatest percentage of household expenditure went towards servants' wages, clothes and food, and the upkeep of utensils, furniture and buildings. Though numerous servants and well-appointed rooms were of course meant to serve the master, nevertheless probably only about 10 per cent of household income was spent directly on the lord and his family.[3] Like a living organism, the

---

[1] Baldesar Castiglione, *The Book of the Courtier*, trans. George Bull (Penguin, Harmondsworth 1980), pp. 284–5.

[2] Kenneth McFarlane, *The Nobility of Later Medieval England* (Clarendon Press, Oxford, 1973), p. 280.

[3] Since the ultimate end of certain products purchased is not always clear it is difficult to be sure of such figures; but an examination of appendix B illustrates this principle to some extent.

household devoted considerable effort to self-preservation. A crucial part of such survival techniques, however, as much for households as living beings, is the adaptability to fit into an ecological niche. Between 1250 and 1600, the noble household adapted to changing circumstances in order to remain a viable institution, dependent as it was upon the noble patronage which created and sustained it. After 1600, when the lives and requirements of nobles ineluctably changed, the household stumbled and collapsed, like the dinosaurs, with the change in climate.

Also like the dinosaurs, the household in its heyday grew to monstrous dimensions. The basic form of structure of the household, in terms of the departments and basic accounting systems, was in place by 1250. Even in the very earliest surviving household records, we find the noble establishment regulating noble expenditure, processing noble wealth, and filling noble stomachs. The household's first identity was as an administrative unit which facilitated the relatively smooth and pleasant course of its master's existence, requiring companions, spiritual counsellors, accountants, valets, and cooks: all of the personnel types we find in place 350 years later. But the fully feudal nature of English noble life in 1250 meant that the lord found his political identity amongst his vassals; and, quite apart from the need to find new sources of food in a land still in places typified by subsistence farming, lords needed to circulate through their scattered holdings to maintain a sense of their presence and power. The peripatectic nature of the very early household, as well as its chiefly administrative function, dictated its size. Early households are small; that of an earl might number thirty-five or so, large enough to fill his needs and make a good show on the road, but small enough to move around and feed efficiently.

Between 1300 and 1380, however, noble life altered. Feudal obligations and structures changed, the methodology of power shifted, and households adapted to new conditions. Firstly, they settled down. This process can first be glimpsed in the early years of the fourteenth century, and by the time of Richard II is universal. In every household document, I have found, instead of regular movement once or twice a month, a long steady habitation of from four to six to sometimes eight months at a time in a single dwelling, and moreover, a strong tendency to move between only two or three estates, even when the lord has widely scattered lands.

Precisely what caused this century-long settling down is difficult to say. Certainly nobles attempted to consolidate scattered holdings, but they were seldom able to form geographically extensive blocs of manors and estates.[4] Again, the farming out of demesne lands, the growth of a market economy and the move to production of cash crops may have been in part stimulated by, as well as a cause of, the permanent presence of a noble lord and his household with their demands for supplies. Nobles may have abandoned the peripatetic life, however, because the development of an efficient estates administration system obviated their regular attendance, and because the breakdown and commutation of feudal duties made the establishment of a noble power base more dependent upon non-feudal ties of clientage. The best way to ensure the latter was probably to develop control over a local area rather than over far-flung locales. It must have been easier to practice non-feudal good lordship and political control over those with whom contact was relatively easily established and maintained, especially when it came to managing county commissions and the choice of MPs. In any case, the household settled down; and this allowed for the possibility of household growth, freed from the constrictions and necessities of continual travel.

Yet another factor worked in favour of household growth. The breakdown of feudal ties was in part replaced by the development of systems of indenture and clientage. In tieing followers to himself, the lord was unlikely and generally unable to reward faithful allies with grants of land. But he could show patronage and good lordship by monetary fees, hospitality and a position in the household. While the paying of fees to indentured followers was by far the most important and common method of retaining, the statutes against livery and maintenance which were introduced throughout the fourteenth and fifteenth ceturies made the provision of a position within the household the main legal way of retaining services for life. This swelled household numbers, inevitably; and it also made the household a more important political tool for the lord and for his clients. Throughout the foureenth century, household posts became much sought after as a source of influence and advancement, particularly for younger sons of gentle families. While even as early as 1250 such individuals were attracted by the standard of living and vicarious power a household position provided, the changes in noble power outlined above gave a new urgency and potential to service in a noble establishment. By 1350–80, the average size of an earl's household had increased to around eighty.

England's political instability and lack of centralized control in the years between 1399 and 1485 must have contributed to the develop-

---

[4]Joel Rosenthal, *Nobles and the Noble Life, 1295–1500* (Allen and Unwin, London, 1976), p. 70.

ment of the household in the fifteenth century. Perhaps, rather than overpowerful lords weakening the king's authority, the weakness of royal control necessitated powerful lords, in order to provide a modicum of stability in a very uncertain world. Undoubtedly, the search for good lordship and firm alliances resulted in complex networks of patronage, and the household played its part in this. In the face of more and more sharply defined statutes against livery and maintenance, the household took a major role in the extension of patronage, expanding to include vast numbers of clients and members of client families able to wear legally and openly the badge of the lord, and thus to represent publicly him and his power. As the household became more central to noble political life it also took on greater symbolic duties: household hospitality, always an important aspect of noble life, took on greater significance, being in itself a representation of good lordship, and the magnificence of the household in its display, largesse and livery was a potent symbol of the lord's power.

Oddly enough this gargantuan growth and development does not appear to have affected the actual structure of the household, which remains in form remarkably like its thirteenth-century precursors, but swollen marvellously. By the 1450s, the average household of an earl numbered upwards of 200, an increase of more than 100 per cent since the period 1350–80. Only the households of abbots appear to have escaped this tremendous quantum leap in size, probably because monastic power was the least affected by fifteenth-century traumas. Because of its peculiar association with noble power at this time, the fifteenth-century household was undoubtedly the climax of possibilities of political importance, structural symbolism and general influence. It is between 1350 and 1500 that the most frequent use of the noble household as a metaphor for the nation occurs, from the writings of Chaucer to those of John Hardynge and Sir John Fortesque. Shakespeare, writing a century and more later, gives full weight to the power of the noble household, real and symbolic, in his history plays of the Wars of the Roses.

The size, omnipresence and crucial importance of the noble establishment meant that it served to filter and condition the needs and expectations of a wide variety of people. Nothing breeds success like success. Nobles, peasants, servants and freeholders utilized the household in the fifteenth century as a consumer of local excess produce, a target for luxury goods, an argument for market status, a source of simple manufactured items such as tallow, an organism for controlling and moderating expenses, in some cases as a parish church, and probably in all cases as a focus for gossip and social excitement. The bigger the household, the more people that passed through it, depended upon it and used it for their own purposes. The use of the household as a religious centre in the face of growing interest in popular, personal religiosity, its replacement of the kin group and its role in education, for instance, have been discussed in chapter 5 and 6 of this work.

By the 1480s, the household had become an at times unwieldy giant. Many nobles enacted household ordinances in an attempt to control and regulate its life, many of which (including the royal ordinances) express concern over the creeping increase in numbers, and attempt to restrict growth. It is doubtful if even the continuation of events favourable to household life and status would have encouraged further increases; the households of 500 strong run by such nobles as the Duke of Buckingham, the Earl of Northumberland and some of the archbishops were probably of the maximum size attainable in terms of actual usefulness and efficiency. It is not therefore surprising that households stabilized in size by 1500 and remained relatively the same throughout the sixteenth century. But the climate of the household also changed as the role of nobles altered. Starting with the reign of Henry VII, the circumstances of English politics so changed as eventually to cause the demise of the household.

If households functioned as institutions, which were used in a wide variety of fashions by numerous different sorts of people, and which necessarily interacted with other forms and concepts governing medieval society in what sometimes seems to be an organic manner, we must remember that McFarlane also said of institutions, 'this [independent life] is only an appearance. They are born, develop, change and decay by human agencies. Their life is the life of the men who make them'.[5] This intimation of mortality leads one to remember that, just as households were changed and developed in order to continue as viable vehicles of noble action between 1250 and 1600, afterwards they were allowed to decay, in a sense, from social institutions to purely domestic establishments. Beginning with the Tudor monarchy's often successful attempts to subdue and control English nobles, through heavy fines, recognizances and on occasion outright persecution, the gradual centralization of authority in king and Parliament eventually moved much of the political impetus of nobles towards the royal court, where they could seldom bring their entire entourages, and away from their traditional provincial centres of support, where their households tended to remain. Consequently the role of the household as a kind of petty court was inevitably lessened, and more and more noble establish-

[5]McFarlane, *Nobility*, p. 280.

Plate 17 Sampson pulling down the magnate's house. *Queen Mary Psalter*, Royal Ms. 2 B vii, f. 46v. English, 14th century. Courtesy of The British Library.

ments came to resemble that of such absentee nobles as Hugh Luttrell, whose household sometimes disbanded entirely for a year or more. The household's loss of importance eventually resulted in its decline, both in numbers and in the status of its members.

A great deal of literature now exists discussing the role and status of the Tudor nobility, and the time scale over which it changed, as well as the manner in, and the extent to which, aristocratic life and ambition altered. The changes the household went through in this period will not solve the dilemmas of these discussions, but may throw some light upon them. The Tudor monarchs were all concerned to establish a strong and wealthy central government, and indeed this was an interest shared by most nobles, for whom a weak kingship spelt danger and instability as much as a chance to exercise personal power. Despite the spectacular eclipse of certain powerful figures such as the third Duke of Buckingham under the Tudors, royal power did not lead to noble genocide, and aristocratic families were often funded or continued to flourish in the sixteenth century. Nevertheless, it must be said that the foundations of noble power altered through this period, and in ways fatal to the noble household as it had existed previously.

The collapse of rebellions such as the Lincolnshire and northern branches of 'The Pilgrimage of Grace', the Yorkshire plot of 1541, and the Uvedale and Dudley plots under Mary, indicates that the medieval network of noble power was no longer sufficient to ensure aristocratic ascendancy. Throughout the Tudor period, the lords who rose were those who attached themselves in service to the Crown, and those who fell were those who tended to depend on more ancient allegiances. While local disagreements, such as that between the Stanhopes and Talbots which disturbed the peace of Nottinghamshire for many years, were allowed to carry on unchecked for the most part, these local power enclaves were quickly and ruthlessly broken up as soon as any question of treason or rebellion against the crown was mooted.[6] In addition, the positive use of crown patronage served to centre noble aspirations upon public office and court life. This did not necessarily decrease the power of the nobles; in some cases it can be said to have increased their influence. But it did move the focus of aristocratic authority, slowly perhaps but surely, away from their private establishments.

It was neither physically possible nor desirable from the point of view of the Crown for nobles to bring their entire establishments to court, or to London for Parliament. While households tend to remain fairly consistent in size over the sixteenth century, what we do see is an increasing tendency for the household to spend much of its time split into sections: a small part with the lord; another group on 'board wages', effectively unemployed; and small groups of servants stationed at the lord's major seats, caretaking, forwarding food or possessions to the lord as requested and showing hospitality to visitors in his absence. While a household position with a noble was still valuable for a young gentleman, the number of such positions available naturally decreased as the lord spent more time at court with a smaller entourage.

This change in noble life effectively dropped the household as a total organism out of the power equation. It could not longer serve as the nexus of local control and patronage, the basis of its size and significance in society generally. Lordly patronage took on other forms besides that of the entourage, such as obtaining court positions and county offices for their clients. While as late as 1590 great nobles like the Earl of Leicester and Henry Herbert, Earl of Pembroke, might have substantial knights in their personal entourage, this was becoming more and more rare. Strict fines for breaking the laws of livery and maintenance, the courts disapproval of extensive retaining, and finally

---

[6]Lawrence Stone, *The Crisis of the Aristocracy, 1558–1641* (Oxford University Press, Oxford, 1974), pp. 114–15.

the feeling among the gentry that it was not concomitant with their dignity, helped to lessen the role of the household in patronage; but the major reason must have been the shift in the focus of noble power, which made the medieval noble household eventually superfluous. The household did not exactly die out; but, rather as it is posited that as the brontosauruses and tyrannosauruses dwindled into birds, it became a much smaller, quieter and more domestic beast. For example, in 1561 the Stanley Earl of Derby had a household of 120; in 1586, an establishment of about a hundred; but by 1702, the earl managed with a staff of thirty-eight domestic assistants.

The lessening of the status of household servants was one of the earliest signs, or results, of this admittedly gradual process. Between 1550 and 1600, one begins to note a general tendency for households to employ a greater percentage of women, whose roles could seldom have been more than wholly domestic. Women were considerably cheaper to employ and were equally competent at the performance of domestic and farm administration to which household service had been reduced. Once a stubborn enclave of men devoted to the furtherance of their master's political authority, the group of household members had become by the late seventeenth century an almost entirely female and largely privately employed staff of servants. The household was as politically impotent as were the women who staffed it.

Certainly by the early seventeenth century, servants such as William Basse (of minor gentry stock, who served as page and later footman to Lord Wenman of Thame Park, Moreton (Oxfordshire) from 1602 to 1633) were complaining about the loss of status and influence once theirs by virtue of their service.[7] Basse states quite specifically that whereas serving men were once regarded as gentlemen by virtue of their position of service, now that position rendered them no better than knaves, and service no longer was valued. By the later seventeenth century, the fostering of noble children within the household had largely ceased;[8] and by the eighteenth century, even stewards (when not completely replaced by female housekeepers) and ushers ceased to be drawn from gentle landholding families.[9] Households also became much smaller; after the restoration, households numbering more than forty were very rare. With the household's role restricted, large numbers

---

[7]William Basse, *The Poetical Works of William Basse* (Ellis and Elvey, London, 1893), especially pp. 1–18.

[8]Philippe Ariès, *Centuries of Childhood* (Macmillan, London, 1968), pp. 113–18.

[9]See, for instance, Merlin Waterson, *The Servants' Hall: A Domestic History of Erddig* (Routledge and Kegan Paul, London, 1980), pp. 35–6, 76–7, 168–87.

of servants were neither viable nor desirable, and only those needed to provide a comfortable standard of living were employed.

The process by which the servant class lost its gentility is a complicated one, due in part to what Lawrence Stone has called 'the crisis of the aristocracy' and their own loss of prestige, to the growing division between gentry and nobility, and to changing moral attitudes and assumptions which viewed lords and hence their servant as decadent. But at least part of the decline of the servant classes must be due to changes in the household environment in which they lived, and in particular to the gradual withdrawal from the household of an active part in the political career of its master. With less chance of prestige, vicarious power, influence, or advancement through the household, gentle families and more ambitious if less wealthy people must have been understandably reluctant to put their younger sons to work under a noble master. The common people and the women who necessarily filled their positions were unlikely to be trusted generally by noble masters for some of the delicate negotiations formerly undertaken by household members; and hence the cycle continued. It is perhaps significant that, by the late seventeenth century, there had appeared the phenomenon of rapid turnover among servants, which was to continue to be a serious problem through the rest of householding history.[10]

Throughout the seventeenth and early eighteenth centuries, one notes the increasing numbers of female servants, virtually reaching the majority by the 1690s;[11] the steady withdrawal of political power from the realm of servants; and the household's loss of major treasury roles including any part in estate receipts, and in some cases the entrusting of only minor sums to cover specific payments to the steward or housekeeper, rather than a regular household income.[12] The household continued to be a domestic centre, contributing to the working of local economy, and became if anything more than ever a showpiece exhibiting its master's status. But the breakdown of old systems of self-support and self-perpetuation in the early modern period, occasioned by the altered needs of the nobility, ultimately transformed the secular noble household into a radically different body from its medieval predecessor.

The gradual domestication of the English nobility by the crown eventually changed the character of the secular noble household; but

[10]Ibid., pp. 187–206.

[11]Cheshire RO, DC H/K/2/8, 10; seventeenth and eighteenth century local household and estate accounts.

[12]Waterson, *Servant's Hall*, pp. 56, 79, 124.

until the sixteenth century at least, the medieval noble establishment operated as an institution which helped those within and without the household to structure and control their lives. Besides functioning as its master's machine for exerting political authority, as a religious community, as a controller of cash flows, as a substitute kin group and as a means for servants to better their circumstances, the household interacted with other concepts and institutions. For instance, it worked within the balance of the local economic community, provided for legitimate forms of retaining, acted as a platform for the use of pageantry, coped with seasonal and generational changes, and assisted in the complex duties of estate administration. Ultimately, of course, the household acts as a guide to and illustration of the role of the nobility in society. Between 1250 and 1600, the secular noble household in England, by its omnipresence in the concerns of individuals and groups of all kinds, sheds a new light on the extent of noble influence and involvement, while demonstrating an important structure through which medieval society controlled existence.

Appendix A
A List of Household Records
*ca.*1250–1600

This list includes all the manuscripts used as source material in this work. There are undoubtedly other accounts still in existence; and particularly, more bishops' accounts probably survive. This list, however, is the most comprehensive now available. Peers are listed by surname, not title (with the exception of kings' sons); bishops, however, are listed by see, and monastic establishments by the name of the house. Those monastic accounts are listed which contain information concerning the abbot's household. The numbers in brackets are estimates of total numbers of household members, and are based upon either chequerrolls or average amounts of food consumed regularly, or on amounts of cloth bought for livery. References in brackets refer to printed copies, extracts and summaries available.

Abingdon Abbey		
obedientiaries' accounts	15th century	(20)
(pr. *Camden Soc.*, new series 51, 1892)		
Anonymous		
household payments list	12th century	(—)
Bodleian Lyell MS 1/102v		
Anonymous		
day-roll (fragment)	*tempus* Henry II	(—)
PRO E 101/631/1	or Richard I	
Anonymous		
Countess's household chequerroll	*tempus* Edward I	(20)
PRO E 101/370/28/8		
Anonymous		
non-royal household ordinance (fragment)	1283	(15)
PRO C47/3/33		
Anonymous		
fees of a chaplain and steward	1284–9	(—)
Bodleian MS 35/97v		

Anonymous
   day-roll (fragment)   1302   (—)
   PRO E 101/505/30

Anonymous
   day-roll   *tempus* Edward   (—)
   PRO E 101/510/13   III

Anonymous
   day-roll (in French)   *tempus* Edward   (—)
   PRO E 101/510/14   III

Anonymous
   day-roll   *tempus* Edward   (13)
   PRO E 101/510/17   III

Anonymous
   household expenses   15th century   (—)
   Bodleian MS 540

Anonymous
   monastic cellarer's roll   1483–4   (—)
   Essex RO D/DRG/2/13

Anonymous, near Standish, Lancs.
   Easter offerings of household   1500   (40)
   Bodleian Lyell MS 12/88–89

Anonymous
   list of payments   16th century   (80)
   Bodleian MS 361/i–vi

Anonymous
   day-book   *tempus* Henry   (25)
   PRO E 101/519/21   VIII

Anonymous
   brewing account   1544   (—)
   Bodeian MS Dugdale 43/1

Anonymous
   servant's expenses   1567   (—)
   PRO E 101/632/3

Anonymous
   ordinance   1605   (—)
   (pr. *Archaeologia* 13, 1800)

Arches, Lady Joan, of Dorset
   day-roll (fragment)   1419   (—)
   Nott. U. Lib. Mi I/26

Bath and Wells, Ralph Shrewsbury, Bishop of
   year-rolls   1337–8   (150)
   (pr. *Somerset Record Society* 39, 1924)

Beauchamp, Thomas, 3rd Earl of Warwick
   book of war payments   1372–4   (—)
   BL Add. MS 37, 494/3

Beauchamp, Richard, 5th Earl of Warwick
   year-roll summary   1414–15   (100)
   BL Add. MS 24,513/185
   household expense account
   BL Add. MS 32,091/32–38   1427–8   (—)
   daily kitchen account, travelling household
                                                1431–2   (100)
   Warks. RO CR 1618/W19/6 (pr. *U. Birmingham Hist. Jour.* 2, 1950)

Beauchamp, Elizabeth (nee Berkeley) 5th Countess of Warwick
   day-book
                                                1420–1   (80)
   (pr. *Trans. Bristol and Gloucester Arch. Soc.* 70, 1951)

Berkeley family
   day-book   early 16th century (—)
   Berkeley Castle muniments general series no. 33
   kitchen day-book   *c.*1584–5   (—)
   Berkeley Castle Muniments general series no. 32

Berkeley, Henry, lord   *c.*1613   (—)
   ordinance
   City of Gloucester Library, Smyth of Nibley papers, vol. iii

Bertie, Robert, Earl of Linsdey
   ordinance   1601   (—)
   Lincon RO Ancaster MSS 2 Anc 14/17
   day-books
                                                1560–2   (50)
   (pr. *HMC*, Grimsthorpe House Papers, 1907)

Blois, John and Guy, Sons of Charles de (wards of the crown)
   expenses
   PRO E 101/29/15   1364–8   (—)

Bohun, Humphrey de, and Roger Mortimer, sons of (wards of the crown)
   day-roll
   PRO E 101/624/22   1341–2   (25)
   see also Mortimer

Bourchier, William, 4th Earl of Bath
    day-book   1566–80   (70)
    BL Harleian MS 7,390

Bozoun, Thomas, of Woodford, Beds.
    day-roll   1328   (17)
    Beds. RO Bozoun (pr. *English Historical Review*, 55,1940)

Brabant, John of, and Thomas and Henry of Lancaster
3 day-rolls with household rules attached   1292–3   (30)
    PRO C47/3/15/2; C47/3/21/12; C47/3/46/31
    see also Lancaster

Braithwait, Richard
    ordinance for an earl   *c*.1590   (—)
    (pr. Braithwait, *Some Rules and Orders*, 1821)

Brown, Sir Anthony (ambassador to France)
    day-book   1527–32   (—)
    Soc. Ant. MS 624
Brown, Anthony, 1st Viscount Montague of Cowdray
    day-book
                                            1568–70   (60)
    BL Add. MS 33,508 (pr. *Sussex Arch. Coll.*, 71,854)

Bryene, Alice de, of Acton Hall, Suffolk
    2 day-books
    PRO C47/8/A   1411–12 and   (35)
                                            1412–13
    2 year-rolls
    PRO C47/8/B   1412 and 1419   (40)

Camoys, Lord
    see Strange, Hamon Le

Canterbury Cathedral Priory
    treasurer's accounts   1206–1384   (—)
    Canterbury MSS Fii and Fiii
    accounts of prior's chaplain
    Canterbury MSS XYZ/v   1360–1424   (40)
    priors' accounts
    Canterbury MSS XYZ/xvii   1396–1473   (40)
    chequerroll
    Canterbury MSS D.E.29   15th century   (50)

Canterbury, John Stratford, Archbishop of
    year-rolls
    WAM 9222, 9223   *c*.1342–4   (400)

Canterbury, William Wareham, Archbishop of
   year-roll
   PRO E 101/518/33   1521–2   (300)

Capel, Arthur
   day-book   1596–7   (70)
   BL Add. MS 40,632c

Carlisle, Richard Bell, Bishop of
   year-roll   1485–6   (100)
   Carlisle RO DRC/2/7–30

Carlisle, John Penny, Bishop of
   day-books   1515–17   (100)
   Carlisle RO DRC/2/7–30

Catesby, John de, of Asheby (Northants)
   counter-rolls for household and building   1379–80 and   (28)
     accounts   1391–2
   PRO E 101/510/21 and PRO E 101/511/15

Cecil, William, 1st Lord Burghley
   day-book   1575–7   (130)
   Hatfield House Cecil Papers vol. 226 (pr. *Econ. Hist. Rev.* 9, series 2, 1956)

Clare, Bogo de, treasurer of York Minster
   day-rolls   1284–6   (40)
   PRO E 101/91/1–7,31
(pr. *Archaeologia* 70, 1918–1920)

Clare, Gilbert de, Earl of Gloucester and Hereford
   expenses of horses   1300–1   (—)
   PRO E 101/91/8
   household expenses   1305   (—)
   PRO E 101/91/9
   chequerroll   *tempus* Edward I   (50)
   PRO E 101/91/10
   wardrobe account, daily   1307–8   (—)
   Staffs RO D 641/1/3/1
   day-roll   1309   (50)
   (pr. *Abbotsford Club* 3, 1836)

Clare, Elizabeth de Burgh, Lady of
   chamber accounts   1325–56   (—)
   PRO E 101/91/12,22
   PRO E 101/93/5,8,12,19
   wardrobe and household accounts   1327–59   (100)
   PRO E 101/91/17,24,26,27
   PRO E 101/92,3,4,7,9,11,13,27
   PRO E 101/93/6,8,19

PRO E 101/94/2,15,18
day-journals   1330–61   (80–120)
PRO E 101/91/14,25
PRO E 101/92/2,12,22,24,30
PRO E 101/93/2,4,9,13,17,18,20
PRO E 101/94,4,11
yearly counter-rolls   1336–53   (—)
PRO E 101/92/5,8,14,18,25,28
PRO E 101/93/3,10,11,14
PRO E 101/94,13,17
views   1325–43   (—)
PRO E 101/91/11
PRO E 101/92/6,16,20,21
PRO E 101/94/3
household indentures   1329–50   (—)
PRO E 101/91/23,28,29
PRO E 101/92/19,29
PRO E 101/93/1,7
chapel accounts at Clare   1327–8   (—)
PRO E 101/91/15
accounts for the Earl of Ulster   1328–9, 1360   (30)
PRO E 101/91/18 and PRO E 101/510/19
goldsmiths's accounts   1332   (—)
PRO E 101/91/30
brewer's account   1333–4   (—)
PRO E 101/92/1
travelling expenses   1327–9   (50)
PRO E 101/91/16,19,20
PRO E 101/507/8
private accounts   328–53   (—)
PRO E 101/91/21
PRO E 101/92/23,26,30,16
kitchen accounts   1340–1   (—)
PRO E 101/92/15,17

Clarence, George Duke of
ordinance   1469   (—)
(pr. Soc. Ant., *Collection of Ordinances*, 1790)

Clifford, Henry, 1st Earl of Cumberland
chequerroll   1510–11   (90)
Chatsworth MSS Clifford accts 1
chapel stock account   1515–16   (—)
Chatsworth MSS Clifford accts 2
chapel chequerroll   1516–17   (6, chapel)
Chatsworth MSS Clifford accts 3
year-roll   1522–3   (100)

Chatsworth MSS Clifford accts 6
wardrobe account   *tempus* Henry   (95)
                                           VIII
Chatsworth MSS Clifford accts 7
travelling household account   1535   (50)
Chatsworth MSS Clifford accts 9
legal expenses   1541   (—)
Chatsworth MSS Clifford accts 11
travelling household account   *tempus* Henry   (55)
                                           VIII

Chatsworth MSS Clifford accts 12
expenses for entertaining the justices of 1555   (—)
  York
Chatsworth MSS Clifford accts 12A
year-roll   1575–6   (90)
Chatsworth MSS Clifford accts 13
year-roll   1594   (88)
Chatsworth MSS Clifford accts 13A

Cobham, Sir John of Bradley, Hants.
year-roll   1408   (45)
(pr. *Antiquaries Journal* 2, 1922)

Coldingham, Priory of
inventories and year-rolls   1311–1446   (?25)
Durham Cathedral MSS (pr. *Surtees Society* 12, 1841)

Courtenay, Philip, Admiral of the Western
  Fleet   1372–4   (—)
war payments
BL Add. MS Latin 37,494/10

Courtenay, Edward, 3rd Earl
year-roll   1383   (80)
DEVON RO CR 538
year-roll   1384–5   (80)
DEVON RO CR 491
chequerroll   1384–5   (85)
BL Add. Roll 64,320
steward's personal accts   1381–1402   (—)
DEVON RO CR 488
day-roll   1395–1400   (90)
DEVON RO CR 1466

Courtenay, Henry, *Armiger*
London register of household expenses   1463–4   (50)
WAM 9215

London register of household expenses   1464–5   (50)
    with auditor's view
WAM 3527

Courtenay, Edward, 11th Earl of Devon
    day-book of Earl's household at court   1518   (28)
PRO E 36/218
    day-roll, with Henry Pole, for expenses in   1542   (—)
        tower
BL STOWE MS 554/23b and 43b

Courtenay, Katherine, 9th Dowager Countess of Devon
    stock account   1523–4   (—)
PRO E 36/223

Courtenay, Henry, Marquis of Exeter
    personal account   1525   (—)
PRO E 36/225

Courtenay, Henry and Gertrude
    personal expenses   1531–2   (—)
BL Add. MS 33,376/11
see also Norwich

Coventry and Lichfield, John Hals, Bishop of
    day-book   1461   (150)
Staffs RO D(W) 1734/3/3/264

Cromwell, Ralph, 2nd Lord, of Tattershall, Lincs.
    appointment of servants   1415 or 1416   (—)
Sheffield City Lib. CD 412

Cromwell, Sir William, and Margaret of Tydd, Lincs.
    year-roll   1417–18   (40)
Kent RO CAT Mk U1475 A82

    year-roll   1419–20   (50)
Kent RO CAT Mk U1475 A83

Cromwell, Ralph, 3rd lord
    note of expenses   ?1440   (—)
Sheffield City Lib. CD 434
    appointment of wardrober   1440   (—)
Sheffield City Lib. CD 392
    kitchen year-roll   1444–6   (—)
Kent RO U1475 A90
    day-book   1447   (70)
Kent RO u1475 A93
    year-roll   1450–1   (70)
Kent RO U1475 A91

Cromwell, Thomas
   personal privy-coffer accts   1536–9   (—)
   PRO E 36/256

Dacre, Leonard, Lord
   kitchen acct   1541–2   (60)
   Bodleian MS Eng. Hist. c.267

Don, Sir Edward, of Saunderton, Warks.
   personal day-book   1510–51   (—)
   Warks RO CR 895/106

Dudley, Robert, Earl of Leicester
   inventory   1588   (—)
   (pr. *Archaeologia* 15, 1834)

Durham College
   annual rolls and bursars' account-books   1400–50   (—)
   Durham Cathedral Muniments

Durham Priory
   nearly complete run of annual rolls   1400–50   (30)
   Durham Cathedral Muniments: Account rolls (pr. *Surtees Society* 99, 100,
      103, 1898–1901)
   Bursar's private account book   1530–4   (50–60)
   Durham Cathedral Muniments (pr. *Surtees Society* 18, 1844)

Ely, Thomas Arundel, Bishop of
   2 year-rolls   1381–4   (300)
   PRO E 101/510/27 and E101/400/28
   9 monthly rolls   1380–4   (300)
   Camb. U. Lib. Ely diocesan records D5(2)

Fairfax, Sir William, of Gilling Castle, Yorks.
   day-books   1571–82   (40)
   (pr. *HMC* ii,1903)
   inventory   *tempus* Elizabeth I   (—)
   (pr. *Archaeologia* 48, 1884)

Fairfax, Sir Thomas
   inventory   *tempus* James I   (—)
   (pr. *Archaeologia* 48, 1884)   and II

Farne, Monastery of
   annual rolls   1400–50   (20)
   Durham Cathedral Muniments

Fastolf, Sir John, of Caister, Norfolk
   building accounts   1432–59   (—)
   BL Add. Chs. 17,229–17,231 (pr. *Norfolk Archaeology* 30, 1952)

inventories   1459   (—)
Magdalene College, Oxford MSS (pr. *Archaeologia* 21, 1827)

Ferrers family, of Badesley Clinton, Warks.
day-book   1533–4   (20)
Shakespeare Birthplace Trust RO DR 3/731a,b

Finchale Priory, Co. Durham
year-rolls   1303–1536   (—)
Durham Cathedral Muniments (pr. *Surtees Society* 6,1837)

Fitzroy, Henry, Duke of Richmond
inventory   1526   (—)
(pr. *Camden Misc.* III, 1855)

Fitzwilliam, Sir William (Treasurer of the King's Household)
year-roll for Fitzwilliam's household   1528   (—)
PRO E 101/518/46

Freyville, Sir Baldwin de
day-roll   1355   (—)
Nott. U. Lib. Mil/40

Gaunt, John of
register   1379–82   (—)
PRO DL misc 13,14 (pr. *Camden Soc.* 56,57,1937)
indentures of retinue   1367–99   (—)
PRO Patent Rolls 280–352 (pr. *Camden Misc.* 22,1964)
household account (fragment)   c.1383–4   (200)
Peterhouse MS 42 (pr. *Bull. Inst. Hist. Research* 13,1936)

Gawdy, Bassingbourne, of Norfolk
2 week-books   1570–86   (35)
BL Add. MS 27,398 and 27,399

Gawdy, Framlingham
week-book   1626–39   (30)
BL Add. MS 27,399

Gloucester, Thomas, Duke of
inventories   1397   (—)
Staffs RO D 641/1/3/2

Godsalve, Dame
year-roll   *tempus* Edward   (10)
PRO E 101/510/4   III

Gray, Lord de, of Codnor, Derbys.
day-roll   1304–5   (—)
Notts. U. Lib. Mi A/1 (pr. *HMC* Middleton MSS, 1904)

Gressham, Paul, of Little Walsingham, Norfolk
   household and farm accts (fragments)   1542–9   (25)
   PRO E 36/255

Hastings, Hugh and Katherine (payments made by Thomas Le Strange)
   travel expenses, Hugh   1531–2   (—)
   Norfolk and Norwich RO NH/15/1,8
   receipts and expenses   1536–40   (—)
   Norfolk and Norwich RO NH/15/2,3,4,5,6,7,10
   see also Strange, Thomas Le

Henry IV (when Earl of Derby)
   day-book   1381–2   (150)
   PRO DL 28/1
   day-book and wardrobe acct   1387–8   (150)
   PRO DL 28/2
   4 wardrobe accounts   1390–7   (120)
   PRO DL 28/3,4,5,6
   travelling household accts   1390–3   (80)
   PRO DL 28/7,8 (pr. *Camden Soc.* 52,1894)
   day-book   1396–7   (150)
   PRO DL 28/9
   year-roll   1397–8   (150)
   PRO DL 28/10

Herbert, Henry, 21st Earl of Pembroke
   day-book and chequeroll   1575–1613   (80)
   BL Harleian MS 7,186

Hereford, Bishop de Swinfield, Bishop of
   year-roll   1289–90   (50)
   Hereford Cathedral MSS (pr. *Camden Soc.* 59 and 62,1853 and 1855)

Hillary, Thomas
   personal day-book   1548   (—)
   PRO E 101/520/5

Holm, Roger de, of Holm, Norfolk
   day-roll   1328–9   (18)
   NORFOLK/NORWICH RO NH/1 (pr. *Archaeologia* 25, 1834)

Holy Island, Priory of
   annual rolls   1400–50   (15)
   Durham Cathedral Muniments

'Holy Trinity Priory', Abbot of (? location uncertain)
   day-roll   *tempus* Edward I   (—)
   PRO E 36/108

Howard, John, 1st Duke of Norfolk
    day-books   1481–90   (200)
    (pr. *Roxburghe Club* 61, 1844)

Howard, Thomas, 2nd Duke of Norfolk
    day-book   1525   (—)
    (pr. *Norfolk Archaeology* 15, 1904)

Howard, Sir William, of Naworth Castle, Co. Durham
    year-books   1612–40   (50)
    Carlisle RO (pr. *Surtees Society* 68, 1877)

Huntingdon, the Earls of
    accounts and inventories (fragments)   1564–1744   (—)
    (pr. *HMC* Hastings MSS I, 1928)

Hussey, John
    2 day-books   *tempus* Henry VII   (25)
    PRO E 36/282,283   or VIII

Jarrow, Monastery of
    annual rolls   1400–1450   (18)
    Durham Cathedral Muniments

Kempe, Sir Robert
    wages and expenses of household   1584–96   (40)
    BL Add. MS 19,208/42–57

Kytson, Elizabeth, Lady
    year-book   1596   (35)
    BL Add.MS 19,191/66
    stable book   1602   (—)
    BL Add. MS 19,191/77

Kytson, Thomas
    see Long

Lacy, Henry de, Earl of Lincoln
    purchases at Corbridge fair   1282   (—)
    PRO DL 28/11
    day-roll, travelling household   1299   (20)
    Notts RO Foljambe VIII B/i/iii/5

Lancaster, Thomas, Earl of
    bill of household expenses   1318   (40)
    Notts RO Foljambe VIII B/2/v/33
    wardrobe account   1318–19   (50)
    PRO DL 29/1/3
    day-roll   1319–20   (—)
    PRO DL 29/1/4
    see also Brabant

Langley, Hugh
   day-book   1473   (40)
   PRO E 101/516/9

Long, Lady Margaret, of Hengrave Hall,
   Hants.
   day-book   1541–5   (30)
   Cambridge University Library Hengrave Hall MS 82(1)
   day-book   1563–4   (30)
   Cambridge University Library Hengrave Hall MS 82(2)
   day-book   1571–2   (20)
   Cambridge University Library Hengrave Hall MS 82(3)
   includes the accounts of Thomas Kytson, her ward

Lovell, Sir Thomas
   year-roll   1522–3   (60)
   Duke of Rutland MSS (pr. *HMC* IV)

Luttrell, Sir Hugh, of Dunster Castle, Somerset
   day-roll   1405–6   (28)
   Somerset RO DD/L P37/7
   year-roll   1421–2   (35)
   Somerset RO DD/L P37/9
   year-roll   1422–3   (40)
   Somerset RO DD/L P37/10A
   year-roll   1423–4   (40)
   Somerset RO DD/L P37/10B
   year-roll   1425–6   (40)
   Somerset RO DD/L P37/10C

Luttrell, Sir John
   year-roll   1428–9   (30)
   Somerset RO DD/L P37/11
   year-roll   1430–1   (30)
   Somerset RO DD/L P37/12

Lytham, Priory of
   annuals rolls   1400–50   (20)
   Durham Cathedral Muniments

Manners, Thomas, 1st Earl of Rutland
   day-book   1524–5   (80)
   Duke of Rutland MSS (pr. *HMC* IV)
   year-rolls   1525–37   (80)
   Duke of Rutland MSS (pr. *HMC* IV)

Manners family, Earls of Rutland
   various accounts (fragments)   1551–1700   (60)
   Duke of Rutland MSS (pr. *HMC* IV)

Mauduyt, John de
   day-roll   1312   (15)
   PRO E 101/506/19

Mauley, Peter, Baron de
   day-roll   *tempus* Edward   (25)
   PRO E 101/509/29   III

Melton, Robert of Suffolk
   commonplace book of accounts   1499–1508   (17)
   (pr. Kerrison and Smith, *Commonplace Book*, 1886)

Monk Wearmouth, Monastery of
   annual rolls   1400–50   (?30)
   Durham Cathedral Muniments (pr. *Surtees Society* 29,1854)

More, Sir William, of Loseley, Surrey
   private account book   c.1552–76   (50)
   (pr. *Archaeologia* 18,1817 and 36,1855)

Mortimer, Roger
   day-roll   *tempus* Edward I   (—)
   PRO E 101/370/19
   see also Bohun and Warrenne, John de

Mountford, Eleanor, 6th dowager Countess of Leicester
   day-roll   1265   (25–30)
   BL Add. MS 8877 (pr. *Roxburghe Club* 57, 1841)

Mowbray, John, Earl Marshall
   war payments   1416–17   (—)
   Berkeley Castle Muniments Box no. 9

Munden's Chantry, Bridport, Dorset
   week-book   1453–60   (4–5)
   Bridport Corporation Archives, Munden muniments
   (pr. Wood-Legh, *A Small Household*, 1956)

Neville, Hugh de, of Essex
   3 day-rolls   *tempus* John or   (20)
   PRO C 47/3/1,9   Henry I
   PRO E 101/350/9

Neville, Richard, Earl of Warwick
   year-rolls   1450–60   (200)
   Warwick Castle Muniments (pr. *Journal of Brit Arch Assn.* 75,1919)

Nevyll, Sir Thomas
   see Talbot, Richard

North, Roger, Lord
    2 day-books   1575–80   (?60)
    BL Stowe MS 774 (pr. *Archaeologia* 19, 1821)

Norwich, Richard Courtenay, Bishop of
    household travelling expenses   1414–15   (90)
    BL Add. MS 24, 513/68
    see also Courtenay

Nowell, Robert, of Read Hall, Lancs.
    expenses   1568–80   (30)
    Towneley Hall MSS (pr. Grossart, *Spending*, 1877)

Nyete, Madame La
    day-roll   *tempus* Edward I   (10)
    PRO E 101/371/8/972

Paget, Sir William
    kitchen account   1547–8   (60)
    Middlesex RO Acc 446/H/12
    kitchen day-book   1550–2   (60)
    Middlesex RO Acc 446/H/13
    2 inventories   1552 and 1556   (60)
    Middlesex RO Acc 446/H/1,2

Parr, William, Marquis of Northampton
    2 day-books   1553   (80)
    PRO E 101/631/43 and PRO E 101/1520/9

Paulet, William, Earl of Wiltshire and 1st Marquis of Winchester
    day-book   1549 or 1550   (70)
    PRO E 101/520/7

Percy, Henry Algernon, 5th Earl of Northumberland
    ordinance   *c.*1510   (500)
    Alnwick Castle MS (pr. *NHB*)
    ceremonial ordinance   *c.*1512   (500)
    Bodleian MS Eng. Hist. b.208
    day-book (fragments)
    PRO E 36/226   1524–5   (500)
    wardrobe account   1525–6   (500)
    Alnwick Castle MS (pr. *Archaeologia* 26,1836)

Percy, Henry, 9th Earl of Northumberland
    ordinance for son   *c.*1572   (—)
    Petworth House, Sussex, Leconfield MSS 24/1 and 24/2 (pr. *Archaeologia*
    27,1838)
    summary year-accounts of the household,   1585–1632   (200)
        kitchen and privy coffers
    Alnwick and Syon House MSS (pr. *Camden Soc.* 93,3rd series, 1962)

Petre, Sir William
   8 day-books   1539–71   (55)
   Essex RO D/DPR 1–4,10,12,13,16

Pole, Henry
   see Courtenay, Edward

Pusey, John de
   day-roll   1171   (7–8)
   Berks RO W/Z-H/1

Radcliffe, Sir Robert, and Joan, of Tattershall and Tydd, Lincs.
   quarter-year-roll   1473   (40–60)
   Kent RO U 1475 A88
   day-book   1475   (40–60)
   Kent RO U1475 A92

Ramsey, Robert of Reading, Abbot of
   day-roll   *tempus* John   (20)
   PRO E 36/107

Ross, William, Earl of (Scottish Peer in service to Edward I)
   household ordinance and catering account   1306   (50)
   PRO E 101/10/11

St Leonard, Priory of, Stamford
   annual rolls   1400–1500   (15)
   Durham Cathedral Muniments

St Swithun's Priory, Winchester
   annual rolls   14th–15th   (30)
                                            centuries
   (pr. Kitchin, *Winchester*, Hampshire Record Society, 1892)

Selby Abbey, Yorks,
   kitchen day-book   1335–42   (—)
   Westminster Diocesan Archives Sec. Ac. 6
   kitchen year-roll   1413–14   (—)
   Hull U. Lib. DDLO/20/54 (pr. *Yorks. Arch. Jour.* 48,1976)
   kitchen year-roll   1416–17   (—)
   Westminster Diocesan Archives Sec. Ac. 10
   kitchen year-roll   1438–9   (?30)
   Hull U. Lib. DDLO/20/50
   kitchen year-roll   1475–6   (—)
   Hull U. Lib. DDLO/20/51

Seymour, Sir John (Queen Jane (Seymour)'s father)
   day-book   *tempus* Edward   (60)
   PRO E 101/520/11   VI

Shuttleworth familly of Gawthorpe Hall, Lancs.
    household and farm accounts   1582–162   (40)
    Lancs. RO Shuttleworth MSS (pr. *Chetham Society*, 35,41,43,46,1856–1858)

Stafford, Humphrey, 1st Duke of Buckingham
    year roll   1438–9   (200)
    BL Add. MS Egerton roll 2208
    list of household creditors   1445–6   (—)
    Staffs RO D 641/1/3/3
    year-roll   1444–5   (—)
    BL Add. MS roll 5962
    year-roll
    Staffs RO D 641/1/3/4   1452–3   (300)
    year-roll   1454–5   (300)
    BL Add. MS Egerton Roll 2209

Stafford, Anne (nee Neville) Dowager Duchess of Buckingham)
    day-book   1463–4   (150)
    BL Lat. Egerton roll 2822 (pr. *Abbotsford Club* 3, 1836)
    day-book   1465–6   (150)
    BL Add. MS 34,213

Stafford, Margaret (nee Beaufort) and Henry Lord Stafford
    14 day-books   1466–71   (150)
    WAM 5472, 5472*, 12181–12190, 22911, 31795
    expense account   *tempus* Edward   (150)
    WAM 5479**   IV

Stafford, Edward, 3rd Duke of Buckingham
    secretary's accounts   1502–7   (—)
    Staffs RO D641/1/3/6
    year-roll, privy coffers   1503–4   (—)
    Staffs RO D 641/1/3/7
    year-roll   1503–4   (500)
    Staffs RO D 641/1/3/8
    day-book   1507–8   (500)
    Staffs RO D 1721/1/5 (pr. *Archaeologia* 25,1834)
    year-roll, wardrobe   1513–14   (500)
    PRO E 101/631/20
    year-roll, wardrobe   1516–17   (400)
    Staffs RO D 641/1/3/9
    chequerroll   1517   (450)
    PRO E 101/518/5
    day-book   1520   (500)
    PRO E 36/220
    inventory   1520–1   (—)
    Staffs RO D 641/1/3/10

Stafford, Henry, Baron
    year-roll   1532–3   (20)
    Staffs RO D 641/1/3/11
    year-roll   1554–5   (50)
    Staffs RO D 641/1/3/12
    letter-book   1547–53   (—)
    Staffs RO D 1721/1/10
    year-book   1556–7   (60)
    Staffs RO D 1721/1/2

Stanhope, Edward, for Anne, Lady Stanhope
    day-book   1569–70   (—)
    BL Add. MS 34,785

Stanley, Edward, 3rd Earl of Derby
    household expenses   1561   (120)
    (pr. *Chetham Society* 31,1853)
    household ordinances   1568   (—)
    (pr. *Chetham Society* 31,1853)

Stanley, Henry, 4th Earl of Derby
    week-book   1586–90   (100)
    (pr. *Chetham Society* 31,1853)

Stonor, Sir Ralph, of Stonor, Oxon.
    day-roll   1378   (17)
    PRO C 47/37/1/25

Stonor, Thomas II
    day-book   1432–3   (20)
    PRO C 47/37/2
    expense accounts   1466–70   (—)
    PRO C47/37/3/21,23; PRO C47/37/4/5; PRO C47/37/9/41
    chequerroll   1468–72   (25–30)
    PRO C47/37/3/24
    3 day-rolls   1468–72   (25–30)
    PRO C47/37/3/26–33,37–43 and PRO C47/37/18/25
    year-roll   1470   (25–30)
    PRO C47/37/4/2

Stonor, Sir William
    expense accounts   1474–82   (—)
    PRO C47/37/4/12,13,14,26,35
    PRO C47/37/5/1–4,6–9,17
    PRO C47/37/18/21,30,32
    household bills   1475–82   (—)
    PRO C47/37/4/16,17,57
    6 day-books   1476–82   (25–30)

PRO C47/37/4/24,33,34,47–56,59; PRO C47/37/5/22; PRO C47/37/7
list of creditors   1479   (—)
PRO C47/37/4/36
(many documents pr. *Camden Soc.* 29,30, misc. 13, 1919 and 1923)

Strange, Hamon Le, of Hunstanton, Norfolk
day-rolls   1341–52   (33)
Norfolk and Norwich RO NH/2–8, 10-12 (pr. *Archaeologia* 69,1920)
day-rolls including the expenses of Lord Camoys, 1347–1349, NH/7,8

Strange, Thomas Le
day-book   1530–1   (60)
Norfolk and Norwich RO NH/13
private accounts (fragments)   1531   (—)
Norfolk and Norwich RO NH/15/9
see also Hastings

Strange, Nicholas Le
private accounts of Nicholas   1578   (—)
Norfolk and Norwich RO NH/14 (pr. *Archaeologia* 25,1834)
day-book (fragments)   1578–9   (35)
Norfolk and Norwich RO BOX 23 misc.

Talbot, Richard, of Blakemere and Longford, Salop.
year-roll   1393–4   (40)
Salop RO Box 85 Bridgewater Collection SR 0212/1
travelling household account   1401–2   (40)
Salop RO BOX 85 Bridgewater Collection SR 0212/2; includes expenses
of Sir Thomas de Nevyll, Lord Furnivall (husband of Ankaretta, below)

Talbot, Ankaretta, Dowager Lady (Richard's daughter)
ale account   1410–11   (60)
Salop RO Box 85 Bridgewater Collection SR 0212/7
year-roll   1411-12   (60)
Salop RO Box 85 Bridgewater Collection SR 0212/3
year-roll   1419–20   (60)
Salop RO Box 85 Bridgewater Collection SR 0212/5

Talbot, Gilbert, Lord
year-roll   1417–18   (68)
Salop RO Box 85 Bridgewater Collection SR 0212/4
year-roll   1424–5   (70)
Salop RO Box 85 Bridgewater Collection SR 0212/6

Talbot family of Longford, Salop. (cadet branch)
day-book   *tempus* Elizabeth I   (35)
Salop RO Box 86 (pr. *Trans. Shrops. Arch. and Nat. Hist. Soc.* 1,1878)

Talbot, George, 6th Earl of Shrewsbury
kitchen accounts   1588–90   (60)
BL Harleian MS 4,782

Tresham, Sir Thomas
4 weekly account-books   1593–1602   (30)
BL Add. MS 39,832–39,835

Tyrrell, John and Ann, of Heron Hall, Essex
day-book   1531–40   (22)
Essex RO D/DP/A/16

Valence, Joan de, dowager of William de Valence, styled Countess of Pembroke
3 day-rolls   1294–6   (26)
PRO 3 101/505/25–27

Valence, Aymar, Earl of Pembroke
day-roll   1320   (34)
PRO E 101/372/4

Vere, Hugh de, 4th Earl of Oxford, or Robert de, 5th Earl of Oxford
day-roll   c.1250–90   (35)
Essex RO D/DPR 136

Vere, John de, 12th Earl of Oxford
year-roll   1431–2   (120)
Essex RO D/DPR 137
expense account   1437–8   (—)
BL Add. MS 40,009a,b

Vere, John de, 13th Earl of Oxford
day-book   1490–1   (300)
Soc. Ant. MS 77/126–128
day-book   1506–7   (300)
MS Longleat BPA 5949

Vere, John de, 14th Earl of Oxford
4 ordinances   1524   (100)
BL Add. MSS 34,324/1 and 38,632/113; BL Hargrave MSS 22,712 and
24,943

Vernon, George, of Haddon Hall
year-roll   1549   (65)
Derbyshire RO (pr. *Journal Derbys. Arch. and Nat. Hist. Soc.* 16,1894)

Vernon, John, of Haddon Hall
year-roll   1564   (65)
Derbyshire RO (pr. *Journal Derbys. Arch. and Nat. Hist. Soc.* 16,1894)

Vredale, William, of Wickham, Hants
    personal day-book   1478–9   (35)
    Bodelian MS Lyell 35/35–38

Warrenne, William and Isabell de, 6th Earl and Countess of Surrey
    day-roll   1230   (35)
    PRO E 101/505/17

Warrenne, John de, 7th Earl of Surrey
    day-roll   *tempus* Edward I   (35–8)
    PRO E 101/371/8/97
    with Roger Mortimer
    household ordinance   *tempus* Edward I   (—)
    PRO E 101/370/19
    with Roger Mortimer
    see also Mortimer

Waterton, Robert, of Mexborough, Yorks.
    year-roll   1419–20   (40)
    Leeds RO Mexborough Collection, Methley accts 9
    monthly expense book   1427–8   (40)
    Leeds RO Mexborough Collection, Thorner 14

Wharton, Philip, 3rd lord
    household expenses   1585–6   (60)
    BL Add. MS 22,289 (pr. Trevelyan, *Household Expenses*, 1829)

Willougby, Sir John, of Wollaton, Notts.
    day-books   1541–50   (60)
    Nott. U. Lib. MiA/23,25,27,29
    personal accounts   1541–52   (—)
    Nott. U. Lib MiA/23–1,24

Willougby, family of Wollaton, Notts.
    fragmentary accounts   1556–1640   (30)
    Nott. U. Lib. MiA/42,44,47,51,52,55,62,64,66,69,70,71,74,75,76,90a,91,95,
        128,129,137–1. (pr. *HMC* Middleton MSS, 1911)
    inventories   *tempus* James I   (—)
                                  and Charles I
    Nott. U. Lib. MiI/3–25,27–31,34

Willoughby, Sir Henry, of Wollaton, Notts.
    valet's accounts (personal servant to Sir   1509–27   (—)
      Henry)
    Nott. U. Lib. MiA/2,6,7,10,12,16,19
    Alice's account (wife to Sir Henry)   1521   (—)
    Nott. U. Lib. MiA/3
    Middleton Hall day-books   1520–7   (55)
    Nott. U. Lib. MiA/4,9,14,15,18,20

Wollaton day-books	1522–6	(60)
Nott. U. Lib. Mia/8,11,13,17		

Worcester, Priory of
annual rolls	13th–15th centuries	(30–60)

(pr. *Worcester Historical Society*, 1908 and 1910)

York, Princess Cecil, Duchess of
ordinance	*c*.1460–70	(—)

(pr. Soc. Ant., *Collection of Oridinances*, 1790)

York Minster, Vicars Choral of
about 400 rolls of college officials	1312–1707	(20–40)

York Minster muniments (pr. Harrison, *Life Med. Col.*, 1952)
year-book	1563–88	(30)

York Minster muniments (pr. Harrison, *Life. Med. Col.*, 1952)

York, Richard, Duke of
day-book	1450–1	(90)

Hampshire RO 23M 58/57b

York, Thomas Wolsey, Cardinal Archbishop of
year-roll	1528–9	(500)

PRO E 101/518/14 (compiled by Thomas Cromwell)

Appendix B
Income and Expenditure Averages, 1350–1530

The averages of income and expenditure shown on this chart are derived from the accounts used throughout this work dating from post-1350. Earlier accounts are not complete enough to allow for such statistics. Certain of the post-1350 acounts, as well, do not adapt themselves readily to this kind of statistical presentation, and therefore the sums and percentages given are only approximations which must be used carefully. Accounts dating from after 1530 are also difficult to quantify in this manner, because of inflation, and also because they frequently fail to break down expenditure by item sufficiently. Ninety-two documents representing thirty-five families, individuals or monasteries with households of over fifty were used, and seventy-one documents representing twenty households under fifty.

	Households numbering over 50		Housholds numbering under 50	
Lord's average yearly income	2462 li		1108 li	
Average income of the household in: (% of household income)				
arrears	91 li	(5.2%)	36 li	(5.9%)
cash from estates	379 li	(21.2%)	329 li	(54.1%)
sales	62 li	(3.6%)	12 li	(1.9%)
cash from private coffers	932 li	(52.2%)	200 li	(32.9%)
goods received	81 li	(4.5%)	26 li	(4.2%)
credit	238 li	(13.3%)	5 li	(1.0%)

	Households numbering over 50		*Housholds numbering under 50*	
Average household income total: (% of lord's income)	1783 li	(72.4%)	608 li	(54.9%)
Average yearly expenditure				
Non-food items: (% of non-food expenditure)				
cloth and clothing	210 li	(43.2%)	23 li	(30.0%)
other goods	74 li	(15.3%)	12 li	(16.0%)
carting expenses	32 li	(6.5%)	1 li	(1.5%)
craftsmen's wages	24 li	(4.9%)	2 li	(2.8%)
building material	31 li	(6.4%)	1 li	(1.5%)
agricultural expenses	18 li	(3.7%)	4 li	(5.5%)
servants' wages	97 li	(20.0%)	32 li	(42.7%)
Total expenditure, non-food items: (% of total expenditure)	486 li	(44.1%)	75 li	(14.9%)
Food items: (% of food expenditure)				
red meat	118 li	(19.2%)	87 li	(20.3%)
poultry	45 li	(7.4%)	34 li	(7.9%)
fish	92 li	(14.9%)	91 li	(21.4%)
dairy products, eggs	97 li	(15.7%)	50 li	(11.6%)
grain	55 li	(8.9%)	47 li	(11.0%)
ale and wine	142 li	(23.0%)	83 li	(19.4%)
fruit, vegetables, spices	67 li	(10.9%)	36 li	(8.4%)
Total expenditure, food items: (% of total expenditure)	616 li	(55.9%)	428 li	(85.1%)
Average yearly expenditure, total: (% of household income)	1102 li	(61.8%)	503 li	(82.7%)

Appendix C
Average Household Size, 1250–1600

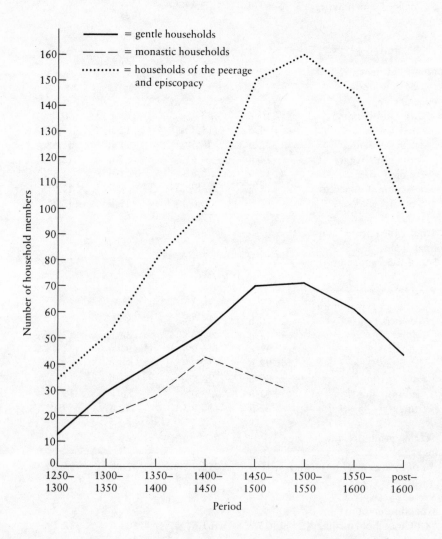

Select Bibliography

Introduction: Methods, Materials and Early History

There are very few works dealing with the medieval noble household in general, but a number of books consider individual households and are most useful. Information about very early aristocratic establishments can be found, as well as a study of the king's household, which also gives helpful clues to the state of early noble *familae*.

Altschul, Michael, *A Baronial Family in Medieval England: The Clares, 1217–1314*, Johns Hopkins Press, Baltimore, 1965

Aston, Margaret, *Thomas Arundel: A Study of Church Life in the Reign of Richard II*, Oxford University Press, Oxford, 1967

Baldwin, James Fosdick, 'The Household Administration of Henry Lacy and Thomas of Lancaster', *English Historical Review* 42, 1927, pp. 180–200

Byrne, Murial St Clare, ed., *The Lisle Letters*, 6 vols, University of Chicago Press, Chicago, 1981

Calmette, Joseph, *The Golden Age of Burgundy*, Weidenfeld and Nicolson, London, 1962

Collier, J. Payne, ed., *Household Books of John Duke of Norfolk and Thomas Earl of Surrey, 1481–90*, Roxburghe Club, London, vol. 61, 1844

Coward, Barry, *The Stanleys, Lords Stanley and Earls of Derby 1385–1672*, Chetham Society, Manchester, 1983

Dale, Marion K., and Vincent B. Redstone, eds, *The Household Book of Dame Alice de Bryene*, Suffolk Institute of Archaeology and Natural History, Ipswich, 1931

Davis, Norman, ed., *Paston Letters and Papers of the Fifteenth Century*, 2 vols, Clarendon Press, Oxford, 1971 and 1976

Duby, Georges, *The Chivalrous Society*, trans. Cynthia Postan, Edward Arnold, London, 1977

Duby, Georges, 'The Diffusion of Cultural Patterns in Feudal Society', *Past and Present* 39, 1968, pp. 3–11

Dunning, R.W., 'The Households of the Bishops of Bath and Wells in the Early Fifteenth Century', *Proceedings of the Somerset Archaeological and Natural History Society* 110, 1966, pp. 24–39

Emmison, F.G., *Tudor Secretary*, Longman, London, 1963

Hanham, Alison, *The Celys and Their World*, Cambridge University Press, Cambridge, 1985

Hanham, Alison, ed., *The Cely Letters*, Early English Texts Society, Oxford, vol. 273, 1975

Heers, Jaques, *Family Clans in the Middle Ages*, trans. Berry Herbert, North Holland Publ. Co., Amsterdam, 1977

Herlihy, David, *Medieval Households*, Harvard University Press, Cambridge, Mass., 1985

Jones, Paul V.B., *The Household of a Tudor Nobleman*, University of Illinois, Chicago, 1917

Kerrison, Lady Caroline, and Lucy Toulmin Smith, eds, *A Commonplace Book of the Fifteenth Century*, Trubner, London, 1886

Kingsford, Charles Lethbridge, ed., *The Stonor Letters and Papers, 1290–1483*, Camden Society, London, vols 29, 30 and miscellany 13, 1919 and 1923

Kirby, J.L., 'The Hungerford Family in the Later Middle Ages', an unpublished PhD thesis of the University of London, 1941

Knowles, David, *Religious Orders in England*, 2 vols, Cambridge University Press, Cambridge, 1950

Labarge, Margaret Wade, *A Baronial Household of the Thirteenth Century*, Eyre and Spottiswoode, London, 1965

Lawson, Laurence Marcellus, *The King's Household in England Before the Norman Conquest*, University of Wisconsin Press, Madison, 1904

Lodge, Eleanor C., ed., *John of Gaunt's Register, 1379–82*, Camden Society, London, vols 56 and 57, 1937

Maddicott, J.R., *Thomas of Lancaster, 1307–22: A Study in the Reign of Edward II*, Oxford University Press, Oxford, 1970

Maxwell-Lyte, H.C., *Dunster and its Lords, 1066–1811*, privately printed, 1882

Miller, Edward, *The Abbey and Bishopric of Ely*, Cambridge University Press, Cambridge, 1969

Musgrave, Clare Aemilia, 'Household Administration in the Fourteenth Century; with Special Reference to the Household of Elizabeth de Burgh, Lady of Clare', an unpublished MA thesis of the University of London, 1923

Platt, Colin, *The Abbeys and Priories of Medieval England*, Secker and Warburg, London, 1984

Rawcliffe, Carol, *The Staffords, Earls of Stafford and Dukes of Buckingham*, Cambridge University Press, Cambridge, 1979

Ross, Barbara, 'The Accounts of the Talbot Household', an unpublished MA thesis of the Univerity of Canberra, Australia, 1970

Smith, Lucy Toulmin, ed., *Expeditions to Prussia and the Holy Land by Henry Earl of Derby*, Camden Society, London, vol. 52, 1894

Steel, Anthony, 'The Place of the King's Household in English Constitutional History to 1272', *History* 15, 1930–1, pp. 289–95

Stone, Lawrence, *An Elizabethan: Sir Horatio Palavicino*, Oxford University Press, Oxford, 1956

Stonor, R.J., *Stonor*, R.H. Johns, Newport, 1952

Storey, R.L., *Thomas Langley and the Bishopric of Durham*, SPCK, London, 1961

Tacitus, Publius Cornelius, *On Britain and Germany*, trans. H. Mattingley, Penguin, Harmondsworth, 1948

Tucker, Melvin J., *The Life of Thomas Howard*, Mouton and Co., London, 1964

Webb, John, ed., *Household Roll of Bishop Swinfield*, Camden Society, London, vols 59 and 62, 1855

Williams, Ethel Carleton, *My Lord of Bedford: 1389–1435*, Longman, London, 1963

Wood, Susan, *English Monasteries and their Patrons in the Thirteenth Century*, Oxford University Press, Oxford, 1955

Chapter 1   Household Organization

Readily available primary sources illustrating household organization are included in this list. Royal household ordinances frequently take account of noble structural arrangements for purposes of economy and example; the royal material included herein gives such useful information. Some of the following secondary works also discuss household structure, mainly in the course of estate administration.

Cavendish, George, *The Life and Death of Cardinal Wolsey*, ed. Richard Sylvester, Early English Texts Society, London, vol. 243, 1959

Denholm-Young, N., *Seignorial Administration in England*, Frank Cass, London, 1963

Dobson, Richard Barry, *Durham Priory, 1400–50*, Cambridge University Press, Cambridge, 1973

Fitznigel, Richard, *The Course of the Exchequer and Constitutio Domus Regis*, ed. Charles Johnson, Thomas Nelson, London, 1950

Given-Wilson, Chris, *The Royal Household and the King's Affinity*, Yale University Press, New Haven, Conn., 1986

Griffiths, R.A., 'Public and Private Bureaucracies in England and Wales in the Fifteenth Century', *Transactions of the Royal Historical Society* 30, 1980, pp. 109–30

Hay, Denys, *Europe in the Fourteenth and Fifteenth Centuries*, Longmans, London, 1975

Holmes, G.A., *Estates of the Higher Nobility*, Cambridge University Press, Cambridge, 1957

Lawrence, C.H., *Medieval Monasticism*, Longman, London, 1984

Markland, James Heywood, ed., 'Instructions by Henry Percy, Ninth Earl of Northumberland, to his Son Algernon', *Archaeologia* 27, 1838, pp. 306–58

Myers, A.R., *Crown, Household and Parliament in Fifteenth Century England*, Hambledon Press, London, 1985

Myers, A.R., ed., *The Household of Edward IV*, Manchester University Press, Manchester, 1959

Nicholas, Nicholas Harris, *Privy Purse Expenses of Elizabeth of York and*

Wardrobe Accounts of Edward IV, Frederick Muller, London, 1872

Oschinsky, Dorothea, ed., *Walter of Henley and Other Treatises on Estate Management and Accounting*, Clarendon Press, Oxford, 1971

Percy, Thomas, ed., *The Regulations and Establishments of the Household of Henry Algernon Percy, Fifth Earl of Northumberland*, privately printed, 1770, 1827 and 1905; also in Francis Grosse and Thomas Anstle, eds, *The Antiquarian Repetory*, vol. 4, Edward Jefferey, London, 1809 (also known as *The Northumberland Household Book*, or *NHB*)

Petrus Blesensis, *Opera Omnia*, 4 vols, ed. J.A. Giles, I.H. Parker, Oxford, 1847

Society of Antiquaries, eds, *A Collection of Ordinances and Regulations*, John Nichols, London, 1790

Storey, R.L., *Diocesan Administration in the Fifteenth Century*, St Anthony's Hall Publications, York, no. 16, 1959

Stretton, Grace, 'The Travelling Household in the Middle Ages', *Journal of the British Archaeological Association*, 90, 1935, pp. 75–103

Tout, T.F., *Chapters in Medieval Administrative History*, 6 vols, Manchester University Press, Manchester, 1930

Wood, Margaret, *The English Medieval House*, Phoenix, London, 1965

Chapter 2 Household Members

There are very few scholarly considerations of medieval servants and service, and much work remains to be done. These books include some preliminary surveys. See also works under chapter 6, 'Family and *Familia*', for material about the noble family itself, and on servants as family. The bibliography for the conclusion, 'The Demise of the Household', also contains material on early modern servants, who have attracted more critical attention.

Harte, N.B., 'State Control of Dress and Social Change in Pre-Industrial England', in D.C. Coleman and A.H. John, *Trade, Government and Economy in Pre-Industrial England*, Weidenfeld and Nicolson, London, 1976

Kempe, Margery, *The Book of Margery Kempe*, eds S.B. Meech and H.E. Allen, Early English Texts Society, Oxford, vol. 212, 1940

Laslett, P., *The World We Have Lost – Further Explored*, Methuen, London, 1983

Power, Eileen, *Medieval Women*, Cambridge University Press, Cambridge, 1975

Power, Eileen, ed. and trans., *The Goodman of Paris*, George Routledge and Sons, London, 1928

Reaney, P.H., *A Dictionary of British Surnames*, Routledge and Kegan Paul, London, 1958

Richardson, H.G., 'An Oxford Teacher of the Fifteenth Century', *Bulletin of the John Rylands Library* 23, 1939, pp. 436–57

Richardson, H.G., 'Business Teaching in Medieval Oxford', *American Historical Review* 46, 1940–1, pp. 259–68

Turberville, A.S., 'The "Protection" of Servants of MPs', *English Historical Review* 32, 1927, pp. 89–106

Chapter 3   *The Household and the Economy*

Medieval accounting methods are discussed in the following sources. The income of medieval households often forms part of studies in seignorial estate administration and can be located in such works, mentioned in chapter 1's bibliography. The books below also contain useful information about household income. Expenditure, particularly as regards food, is a favourite topic of many authors, and some of the works included on this list should be helpful as further reading. General studies of agricultural history are also of assistance in understanding household economy, as are works on town development, particularly as they relate to markets.

Baxter, W.T., ed., *Town Origins* D.C. Heath, Boston, 1968

Cantor, Leonard, *The English Medieval Landscape*, Croom Helm, London, 1982

Chartres, J.A., *Internal Trade in England, 1500–1700*, Macmillan, London, 1977

Corran, H.S., *A History of Brewing*, David and Charles, Newton Abbot, 1975

Davenport, F.G., *The Economic Development of a Norfolk Manor, 1086–1565*, Frank Cass, London, 1957

Davies, Robert Rees, 'Baronial Accounts, Incomes and Arrears in the Late Middle Ages', *Economic History Review* 21, 1968, pp. 211–29

Gordon, Cosmo, 'Books of Accountancy, 1494–1600', *Bibliographical Society Transactions* 13, 1945

Harvey, Barbara, *Westminster Abbey and its Estates in the Middle Ages*, Clarendon Press, Oxford, 1977

Jeaffreson, John Cordy, *A Book About the Table*, 2 vols, Hurst and Blackett, London, 1875

Littleton, A.C., and B.S. Yamey, *Studies in the History of Accounting*, Sweet and Maxwell, London, 1956

Platt, Colin, *The English Medieval Town*, Granada, London, 1979

Pugh, T.B., and Charles Ross, 'Materials for the Study of Baronial Incomes in Fifteenth Century England', *Economic History Review* 6, 1953–4, pp. 185–94

Rogers, James Edward Thorold, *A History of Agriculture and Prices in England*, 8 vols, Clarendon Press, Oxford, 1876

Sass, Lorna, ed., *To the King's Taste – Richard II's Book of Feasts and Recipes*, John Murray, London, 1975

Snape, R.H., *English Monastic Finances*, Cambridge University Press, Cambridge, 1926

Thirsk, Joan, *The Rural Economy of England*, Hambledon Press, London, 1984

Thirsk, Joan, ed., *The Agrarian History of England and Wales*, 8 vols, Cambridge University Press, Cambridge, 1981

Wilson, C. Anne, *Food and Drink in Britain*, Penguin, Harmondsworth, 1973

Yamey, B.S., 'Scientific Book-keeping and the Rise of Capitalism', *Economic History Review* 1, 1949, pp. 99–113

Chapter 4   In Negociis Domini: *Politics and the Household*

The following are all relevant studies of noble life and noble power in the middle ages, discussing the decline of feudalism, problems of indenture and retaining, baronial councils and the role of household staff in noble life.

Anglo, Sidney, *Spectacle, Pageantry and Tudor Policy*, Oxford University Press, Oxford, 1969

Bennett, Michael J., *Community, Class and Careerism*, Cambridge University Press, Cambridge, 1983

Campbell, J.K., *Honour, Family and Patronage*, Clarendon Press, Oxford, 1964

Denholm-Young, N., *Country Gentry in the Fourteenth Century*, Oxford University Press, Oxford, 1969

Dobson, Richard Barry, ed., *The Church, Politics and Patronage in the Sixteenth Century*, Allan Sutton, New York, 1984

Dunham, W.H., Jr, *Lord Hastings' Indentured Retainers, 1461–83*, Transactions of the Connecticut Academy of Arts and Sciences, Hartford, Conn., vol. 39, 1955

Griffiths, Ralph, A., ed., *Patronage, the Crown and the Provinces*, Allan Sutton, Gloucester, 1981

Griffiths, Ralph A., and James Sherborne, *Kings and Nobles in the Later Middle Ages*, Allan Sutton, Gloucester, 1986

Hilton, Rodney Howard, *Class Conflict and the Crisis of Feudalism*, Hambledon Press, London, 1985

Jones, Michael, ed., *The Gentry and Lesser Nobility in Later Medieval England*, Allan Sutton, Gloucester, 1986

Lander, Jack Robert, *Crown and Nobility, 1450–1509*, Edward Arnold, London, 1976

Levett, Ada Elizabeth, *Studies in Manorial History*, Clarendon Press, Oxford, 1938

McFarlane, K.B., *England in the Fifteenth Century*, Hambledon Press, London, 1981

McFarlane, K.B., *The Nobility of Later Medieval England*, Clarendon Press, Oxford, 1973

Moers, Stephanie L., ' "Backers and Stabbers": Problems of Loyalty in Robert Curthose's Entourage', *Journal of British Studies* 21, 1981, pp. 1-17

Pugh, T.B., *The Marcher Lordships of South Wales 1415–56: Select Documents*, University of Wales Press, Cardiff, 1963

Rosenthal, Joel T., *Nobles and the Noble Life, 1295–1500*, Allen and Unwin, London, 1976

Tuck, Anthony, *Crown and Nobility, 1272–1461*, Blackwell, Oxford, 1986

Virgoe, R., 'The Composition of the King's Council, 1437–61', *Bulletin of the Institute of Historical Research*, 43, 1970, pp. 134–60

Chapter 5   The Household as a Religious Community

These books give relevant information on personal piety in general, and noble Christian practice in particular, between 1250 and 1600. Some deal with specific topics; others are more general.

Baker, Derek, ed., *Religious Motivation: Biographical and Sociological Problems for the Church Historian*, Studies in Church History, Blackwell, Oxford, vol. 15, 1978

Barratt, D.M., 'A Second Northumberland Household Book', *Bodleian Library Record* 8, 1967–72, pp. 93–8

Bentley, James, *Restless Bones: The Story of Relics*, Constable, London, 1985

Boase, T.S.R., *Death in the Middle Ages*, Thames and Hudson, London, 1972

Bossy, John, *Christianity in the West, 1400–1700*, Oxford University Press, Oxford, 1985

Brooke, Rosalind and Christopher, *Popular Religion in the Middle Ages*, Thames and Hudson, London, 1984

Evans, John, 'The Wedding of Richard Posted and Elizabeth, Daughter of William More of Loseley, Surrey', *Archaeologia* 36, 1855, pp. 35–52

Harrison, Frank, *Music in Medieval Britain*, Routledge and Kegan Paul, London, 1958

Harthan, John, *Books of Hours and Their Owners*, Thames and Hudson, London, 1982

Hope, Sir William St John, ed., 'The Last Treatment and Inventory of John de Vere, Thirteenth Earl of Oxford', *Archaeologia* 66, 1915, pp. 275–348

Huizinga, Jan, *The Waning of the Middle Ages*, Edward Arnold, London, 1924.

Lovell-Cocks, H.F., *The Religious Life of Oliver Cromwell*, Independent Press, London, 1960

Pantin, W.A., *The English Church in the Fourteenth Century*, Notre Dame Press, Notre Dame, Indiana, 1963

Rosenthal, Joel T., *The Purchase of Paradise*, Routledge and Kegan Paul, London, 1972

Scarisbrick, J.J., *The Reformation and the English People*, Blackwell, Oxford, 1984

Sheils, W.J., and Diana Wood, *Voluntary Religion*, Studies in Church History, Blackwell, Oxford, vol. 23, 1986

Wood-Legh, K., *Perpetual Chantries in Britain*, Cambridge University Press, Cambridge, 1965

Chapter 6   Family and Familia

Considerable literature on families and households has been published in the last twenty years, and though much of it deals with peasant rather than gentle families, it is nevertheless of invaluable assistance in understanding the familial nature of noble families and their wider households. Books on childhood, education and anthropology which are relevant to the subject have also been included in this list.

Ariès, Phillippe, *Centuries of Childhood*, Macmillan, London, 1968

Duby, Georges, *The Knight, the Lady and the Priest: The Making of Modern Marriage in Medieval France*, trans. Barbara Bray, Allen Lane, London, 1983

Duby, Georges, *The Three Orders: Feudal Society Imagined*, trans. Arthur Goldhammer, University of Chicago Press, Chicago, 1980

Furnivall, F.J., ed., *The Babees Book*, Early English Texts Society, Oxford, vol. 32, 1868

Goody, Jack, *The Development of the Family and Marriage in Europe*, Cambridge University Press, Cambridge, 1983

Goody, Jack, ed., *The Developmental Cycle in Domestic Groups*, Cambridge University Press, Cambridge, 1971

Goody, Jack, Joan Thirsk and E.P. Thompson, eds, *Family and Inheritance: Rural Society in Western Europe, 1200–1800*, Cambridge University Press, Cambridge, 1976

James, Mervyn, *Family, Lineage and Civil Society: A Study of Society, Politics and Mentality in the Durham Region, 1500–1640*, Oxford University Press, Oxford, 1974

James, Mervyn, *Society, Politics and Culture: Studies in Early Modern England*, Cambridge University Press, Cambridge, 1986

Kent, Francis William, *Household and Lineage in Renaissance Florence*, Princeton University Press, Princeton, N.J., 1977

Krause, J., 'The Medieval Household: Large or Small?', *Economic History Review* 9, 1956–7, pp. 420–32

Laslett, P., and Richard Wall, *Household and Family in Past Time*, Cambridge University Press, Cambridge, 1972

Macfarlane, A., *Marriage and Love in England, 1300–1840*, Blackwell, Oxford, 1986

Macfarlane, A., *The Origins of English Individualism*, Blackwell, Oxford, 1978

Mitteraurer, Michael, and Richard Sieder, *The European Family*, Blackwell, Oxford, 1982

Moran, Jo Ann Hoeppner, *The Growth of English Schooling, 1340–1548*, Princeton University Press, Princeton, N.J., 1985

Orme, Nicholas, *English Schools in the Middle Ages*, Methuen, London, 1973

Ross, J.B., 'The Rise and Fall of a Seventeenth Century Clan', *Speculum* 34, 1959, pp. 340–90

Stone, Lawrence, *Sex, Marriage and the Family*, Oxford University Press, Oxford, 1978

Wall, Richard, et al., *Family Forms in Historic Europe*, Cambridge University Press, Cambridge, 1983

Zaniewicki, W., *La Noblesse 'Populaire' en Espagne et en Pologne*, Lyons, 1967 (no publisher)

Conclusion: The Demise of the Household

These works are chiefly books on the Tudor nobility, and document numerous scholarly debates about the nature and rate of change in noble life between 1500 and 1600. A number of contemporary works containing mention of noble household practice and servant life are included, as well as a recent work on women and housework which discusses women and service in particular.

Basse, William, *The Poetical Works of William Basse*, Ellis and Elvey, London, 1893

Bean, J.M.W., *The Decline of English Feudalism, 1215–1540*, Manchester University Press, Manchester, 1968

Bernard, G.W., *The Power of the Early Tudor Nobility*, Harvester, Brighton, 1985

Castiglione, Baldesar, *The Book of the Courtier*, trans. George Bull, Penguin, Harmondsworth, 1980

Davidson, Caroline, *A Woman's Work is Never Done: A History of Housework in the British Isles, 1650–1950*, Chatto and Windus, London, 1986

Elton, G.R., *The Tudor Revolution in Government*, Cambridge University Press, Cambridge, 1969

Fitzherbert, Master, *The Book of Husbandry*, ed. Walter W. Skeat, English Dialect Society, London, 1882

Fortesque, Sir John, *De Laudibus Legum Angliae*, ed. S.B. Chrimes, Cambridge University Press, Cambridge, 1942

Fortesque, Sir John, *The Governaunce of England*, ed. Charles Plummer, Clarendon Press, Oxford, 1885

Hazlitt, W.C., ed., *A Health to the Gentlemanly Profession of Servingmen (1598)*, Roxburghe Library inedited tracts, London, 1868

Holme, Jane, 'A Comparison Between Hedingham Castle, 1432–3, and Audley End, 1765–6', an unpublished thesis submitted for the Emmison Competition, Essex Record Office, 1972

Loades, David, *The Tudor Court*, B.T. Batsford, London, 1986

MacDonald, John, *Memoirs of an Eighteenth Century Footman*, Century Publishing, London, 1985

Miller, Helen, *Henry VIII and the English Nobility*, Blackwell, Oxford, 1986

Stone, Lawrence, *The Crisis of the Aristocracy, 1558–1641*, Oxford University Press, Oxford, 1974

Stone, Lawrence, *Social Change and Revolution in England, 1540–1640*, Longmans, London, 1966

Waterson, Merlin, *The Servants' Hall: A Domestic History of Erddig*, Routledge and Kegan Paul, London, 1980

Wrightson, Keith, *English Society, 1580–1680*, Hutchinson, London, 1982

Index

A

I